MICHAEL APICHELLA

Foreword by
DENNIS WRIGLEY

**kevin
mayhew**

First published in 2003 by

KEVIN MAYHEW LTD
Buxhall, Stowmarket, Suffolk, IP14 3BW
E-mail: info@kevinmayhewltd.com

KINGSGATE PUBLISHING INC
1000 Pannell Street, Suite G, Columbia, MO 65201
E-mail: sales@kingsgatepublishing.com

9 8 7 6 5 4 3 2 1 0

ISBN 1 84417 075 6
Catalogue No 1500590

The cover painting is by artist Daniel Watts, who works out of his studio
in Tamaqua, Pennsylvania. Cover design by Angela Selfe
Edited by Elisabeth Bates. Typeset by Fiona Connell Finch

Printed and bound in Great Britain

Contents

Dedicated to David and Jane Harrison, whose loving support has made the writing of this book possible.

About the author

Michael Apichella grew up in the coal region of Pennsylvania. After earning an MA at Wheaton College in 1984, he moved to England where he is an Associate Professor of Communications with the University of Maryland University College (Europe). An award-winning journalist, Michael spends his working week teaching, writing, and speaking at conferences and retreats in the United Kingdom and the United States.

Most people would rather see a sermon than hear one.
An old Alabama saying

Foreword

In a world bursting with sorrow, Christians are called to be hope-filled. This is a book full of hope. The Gospel is good news and this book is filled with good news.

In the early church Christians were known as people of 'the Way'. In the face of the huge spiritual and social problems facing our nation today, this book is a new and exciting exploration of the way of life offered by Christ.

Church influence and attendance has hugely declined. The influence of the media committed to secular humanism is enormous. Yet there are increasing signs of rediscovery of Christian faith in its purity and simplicity.

The invitations of Jesus are simple. Come! Go! Follow! Ask! Seek! Knock! In a complicated and confused culture, Christians are discovering the refreshing simplicity of an encounter with Jesus.

In spite of our imperfections, we are called to be the Body of Christ – visible and recognisable as the healing, tangible and real presence of God.

In this book we discover how God reveals himself through his pilgrim people. As pilgrims we need to discard much of our heavy baggage and constraints. We need to travel light. When we do this we discover that the Body of Christ is living and moving. Jesus is always on the move. He strides across the pages of history. He calls us to run with him. His pace may be fast.

He demands radical changes in our lifestyle and in society

as a whole. He comes to change individual men and women and entire cultures. The Gospel is about change. If we refuse change, God cannot use us.

This book helps us to focus on the real nature of Christ present with his people.

Michael Apichella reasserts that God is real, not imaginary, that he is present, not absent and that he is speaking, not silent.

DENNIS WRIGLEY
Maranatha Community Leader

It is better to light one little candle than to curse the darkness.
Motto of the Christophers

Introduction

Jesus bids us shine

Many Christians know the words from the children's hymn that tells us to shine like a little candle burning in a small, dark corner. Simple as this hymn is, it contains a profound truth people often miss. Jesus doesn't bid us to blaze like a bonfire on a mountain peak! He just wants us to be a bright spark wherever we happen to be.

Put another way, we are to be light right where we do our living, working, playing, and even our dying. So forget smuggling Bibles into Iraq. Don't worry about single-handedly rescuing the street children of Brazil. Forget about being asked to present 'Thought for the Day' on the radio. (In fact, just forget about 'Thought for the Day'. *Please!*)

Seriously, God will show you if he wants you to do something special in his service. Meantime, whether he calls you to become a Christian martyr, or whether he asks you to live in quiet suburban comfort, you may be sure of one thing. When lived simply and sincerely, the Christian lifestyle will affect people for good.

When preparation and opportunity intersect

In the pages ahead, I'd like to show you how you may enrich your own life as well as the lives of people around you by being prepared to live a fully committed Christian life. You don't even need any special talent. The Holy Spirit does the hard work when the opportunity presents itself. And make no mistake, when the right opportunities arise – at home, at work, or anywhere we happen to be – God's power is released through our example. As St Peter tells us: 'His divine power has given us everything we need for life and godliness through our knowledge of him who called us by his own glory and goodness' (2 Peter 1:3, NIV).

I'm not an evangelist

It's true that not all of us are called to be evangelists; nevertheless, the Christian faith is evangelistic. St Francis of Assisi put it like this: 'Preach the Gospel by any means possible. Use words if necessary.' Francis meant we're here to show people Jesus. This is the essence of the Christian faith, and it happens naturally when our lifestyle conforms to biblical models. All that's required is a sincere desire to do God's will.

Our faith should affect every aspect of our lives – from how we spend our money, to how we entertain ourselves and our friends, to how we worship God – 24 hours a day, seven days a week. What does this mean in practical terms? If you want to know more, then read on, and get ready to live the Christian lifestyle 24/7.

I thank my God through Jesus Christ for all of you, because your faith is proclaimed in all the world.
Romans 1:8

CHAPTER 1

Christianity is powerful

Power is the Christian's birthright. In Acts 1:8, Jesus promised, 'But you shall receive power when the Holy Spirit comes upon you; and you shall be my witness in Jerusalem, and in all of Judea and Samaria and to the end of the earth.' The Greek word for this power is related to the English word *dynamite.* If you've ever seen what high explosives can do, you'll know that Jesus meant it when he said to his followers, 'I tell you the truth, anyone who has faith in me will do what I have been doing. He will do even greater things than these, because I am going to the Father' (John 14:12, NIV).

Ordinary people – extraordinary lives

History shows us that when people do try to live a Christian lifestyle, great things happen – even in hopeless circumstances. That is the power to be had by living a Christian lifestyle. Here are three examples of what I mean.

Raul Gustav Wallenberg, a Swedish businessman, saved countless Jewish lives in Hungary during World War II. Before the war, Wallenberg lived a selfish life. A bright but unambitious son of a wealthy Swedish businessman, he travelled the world, seeking pleasure and adventure. Eventually, his family connections led to his being made a diplomat at the Swedish Embassy in the Hungarian capital in 1944. At the time he arrived in Hungary, nearly half a million Hungarian Jews had been deported to death camps around Europe. This callow young man had had a dramatic reawakening of his inactive Christian faith when he saw first-hand the extraordinary evil of the Jewish Holocaust. Now he was about to discover the power of the Christian lifestyle.

Knowing that his life was at risk if he assisted the Jews, he boldly used his status as a diplomat to help hundreds of Jews out of Hungary, finding them safe homes in Sweden and elsewhere. Wallenberg became a deliverer to people with no hope. Placing his trust in Jesus, he ignored the threats – at first veiled, and later overt – of the irate Nazi supremo Adolph Eichmann, who suspected what Wallenberg was up to. More than once he escaped arrest by Eichmann, who had a personal vendetta against Wallenberg. Indeed, it was as if it was impossible for Eichmann to stop Wallenberg.

Ironically, after the Russian Army crushed the Nazis, instead of rewarding Wallenberg as a hero, the Soviets accused him of being a spy and sent him to the Gulag with half-a-million other anonymous political prisoners. He was last reported alive as late as the 1960s. Following *Glasnost*, it was confirmed that Wallenberg died in a stark Soviet prison camp.

Was his life and death in vain? I don't think so. Thousands of Jews in Europe and America today are indebted to this brave man who, following the example of Jesus, gave his life for the benefit of others. It's impossible to say how many people he influenced by his supremely selfless actions. Thanks to the openness in the former Soviet Union, reliable biographies are being written about this remarkable young man. Doubtless, they will provide evidence that miracles still occur in the lives of people who live 100 per cent for Christ.

In the closing days of 2002, the world received the tragic news of the four American medical missionaries who were shot by an Islamic extremist in Yemen. The hospital was popular with the local people and operated under tightly regulated restrictions that prohibited any form of Christian proselytising. Although Christian witnessing was against the rules, the killer stated that he attacked the hospital because Christians ran it.

The gunman tricked security guards into allowing him into the Jiba Baptist hospital, and, bursting into a meeting, he opened fire, killing hospital director William Koehn, Dr Martha Myers and Kathleen Gariety, and wounding Donald Caswell. That attack underscored the danger faced by Christians in the Middle East, a fact the Baptists knew before they asked to be sent there as medical missionaries. To the astonishment and delight of many in Yemen and elsewhere, the surviving missionaries asked to remain in Yemen, offering their much-needed services to the people. This determination to stay touched the Yemeni people, and prompted local and national Yemeni leaders to condemn the attacks and to express sympathy for the families of the dead and wounded.[1]

Commitment to the Christian lifestyle doesn't automatically mean you are going to live a dramatic life like Raul Wallenberg and the Baptist missionaries. Rosemary Attlee tells about the tragic death of her son William at age 17.

Admitting that none of her family was particularly interested in their Christian faith, when William contracted

1. 'Missionaries vow to stay in Yemen', Alan Philps, Middle East Correspondent, *Daily Telegraph*, Tuesday, 31 December 2002, pp. 1-2.

leukaemia and doctors gave him less than a month to live, she asked a cousin, a man near to her son's age who was a Christian minister, to come and see William. A relationship was established, and the two cousins saw each other frequently. Rosemary tells of standing outside the sick room of her emaciated son, hearing them chatting and laughing. One evening, William announced to the rest of his family that he had given his life to Jesus. After this, William received communion in his room regularly. During one visit, the cousin prayed over William, rebuking the sickness in Jesus' name – a prayer neither William nor his mother had ever heard before.

Later, the medical consultant pronounced the cancer to be miraculously in remission, though he held firmly to the original diagnosis that William was living on borrowed time.

At the end of his young life, despite being skeletal and covered in purple blotches where capillary blood vessels were leaking, William spoke of a profound peace that defies human understanding. Rosemary admits that not only did William's faith help him die peacefully, but the effect on the rest of the family was to open their eyes to the joys and the power of the Christian lifestyle.[1]

As I have tried briefly to show here, the Christian lifestyle empowers us to do great things with God's help; yet it is not a lifestyle free from persecution, pain, and death. Nevertheless, because of the sacrifice made on our behalf by Jesus on the cross, and the mysterious work of the Holy Spirit, we have the power to conquer all circumstances (Romans 8:37-40).

1. Rosemary Attlee, 'A Mother's Story', *Readers' Digest*, April 1984.

Jesus Christ is for life, not just for Christmas

Each Christmas, parents of very young children are flabbergasted when their little ones prefer the bright, crinkly wrapping paper to the expensive gifts they wrapped. It's a bit like that for God. He has given his church gifts to do great things, yet often we get distracted by the outer wrappings of Christianity, and we miss out on the power to rise above – not sink below – our circumstances.

The Apostle Paul puts it like this: 'I know how to be abased, and I know how to abound; in any and all circumstances I have learned the secret of facing plenty and hunger, abundance and want. I can do all things in him who strengthens me' (Philippians 4:12-13). Paul was not putting on a brave face and hoping for the best. The historic record shows that in his life and in his death, Paul demonstrated the *power* of the Christian lifestyle.

All or nothing

Living the Christian lifestyle means we have help in this life and the promise of eternal peace in the next. 'But thanks be to God, who gives us the victory through our Lord Jesus Christ. Therefore my beloved brethren, be steadfast, immovable, always abounding in the work of the Lord, knowing that in the Lord, your labour is not in vain' (1 Corinthians 15:57-58). This promise becomes null and void, however, if we compromise our faith, or try to blend in with our culture to the extent that there's no way to tell us apart from our unbelieving neighbours and friends. This is what God meant when he said of his children, 'You are a people holy to the Lord your God, and the Lord has chosen you to be a people of his own possession' (Deuteronomy 14:2). I prefer the language of the Authorised Version, which says we are to be a *peculiar* people. Peculiar means unusual, exceptional and extraordinary.

If we want see power in our lives, if we want to stand out from the rest of the world, then we must try to live like Raul Wallenberg, the Baptist medical missionaries, William Attlee, and millions of others over the last 2000 years who have lived in hope though Jesus Christ.

For many people today, Christianity is seen as having been tried and found lacking, but according to G. K. Chesterton, the problem is that Christianity has never really been tried this century. When tried, Christianity is relevant. And what makes it all the more relevant is *us* – we who are called to live our lives so others may see Jesus through us. Living the Christian lifestyle each day – and not just when it suits us – will improve our ability to serve others in love. It will lead us into new adventures of faith, hope, and charity. Moreover, it will put the *dynamite* into our lives that Jesus constantly spoke of. That is a guarantee.

Time to act

The genuine Christian lifestyle always yields a bumper crop of produce. That's why Jesus said of his followers: 'You will know them by their fruits' (Matthew 7:16). To paraphrase the psalmist, if the heavens are demonstrating the glory of God, and the earth proclaims his handiwork (Psalm 19:1), then how much more should our lifestyles be enlightening the unbelieving world around us day and night?

No one in Britain will forget the anguish caused by the murders of schoolgirls Holly Wells and Jessica Chapman in August 2002. The entire community looked to the Rev Tim Alban Jones, vicar of St Andrew's Church, Soham – himself a father of three young children – to speak on its behalf. Daily he faced the news media, speaking words of courage, faith and comfort.

During this national tragedy, the people of Soham turned to the church. There people of faith, and many with none, found a credible forum to express sympathy for the families and friends of the dead girls as well as to come to terms with their own grief. Clearly, it is in the midst of hard circumstances that we see the relevancy – indeed the fruit – of the Christian faith.

Not surprisingly, the vicar received an MBE in the New Year Honours List for services to the community.

Real world application

Author Elizabeth Elliot wrote: 'A man is no fool to give up the things he can't keep in order to gain the things he can't lose.' She is talking about giving up anything that gets between God and us so we may gain eternal life with God though Jesus Christ. This is the basis of living the Christian lifestyle.

To the church of God . . . with all the saints . . . Grace to
you and peace from God our Father and the Lord Jesus Christ.
2 Corinthians 1:1-2

CHAPTER 2

Selecting a church

A wag once said when it comes to successful property development, there are only three factors – location, location, and location. What makes people want to come to a church? John Wimber of the Vineyard Fellowship once said people come to church for a lot of reasons, but they stay there for only one – relationships. So when it comes to church, the three factors surely must be relationships, relationships, and relationships.

What does it take to be a successful church?

What is meant by the word relationship? Relationship is a highly complex word. Most people, however, would agree that relationship embodies three main ingredients: loyalty, friendship, and shared values. I want to shed some light on these three things as we think about choosing a church.

Loyalty

Let's begin with the first point: loyalty. Few people fully appreciate the meaning of this word until their friends disappoint them. The mercurial apostle Peter let Jesus down many times, including his betrayal of the Lord on the Thursday night that Jesus was paraded before a sham trial (Luke 22:54-71). 'I never knew the man!' squealed the agitated apostle when a woman accused him of being a follower of Jesus. The pained look on Jesus' face told Peter that his words lacerated Jesus' heart (Luke 22:61). Nevertheless, Peter could be loyal when the chips were down.

Jesus was wonderfully pleased when Peter demonstrated loyalty in John 6. By referring to himself as food for the spirit (48) which all people must eat (51), Jesus made it clear to his Jewish followers that he considered himself to be the bread of life – that is the living Son of God – and not merely a highly gifted rabbi (58) as many supposed. This was something the disciples simply could not accept – and they said so.

Imagine Jesus' face as he took in their reaction – the reaction of people who had followed him week by week for most of his ministry in the Holy Land. The stunned silence, the raised eyebrows, and the murmuring of the doubters spoke volumes about their disloyalty. Jesus' warm, brown eyes and broad, open face must have exposed his crushed spirit as his friends showed their true colours. Only Peter had the sense to offer words of encouragement. They were just what Jesus needed to hear. Here is what John records:

> From this time many of his disciples turned back and no longer followed him. 'You do not want to leave too, do you?' Jesus asked the Twelve. Simon Peter answered him, 'Lord, to whom shall we go? You have the words of eternal life. We believe and know that you are the Holy One of God.' (John 6:66-69, NIV)

Despite one or two other errors in judgement, Peter remained among the most loyal of Jesus' apostles, right up to the time of his own death on an inverted cross sometime between AD 64 and 67. That's loyalty.

We see a similar inspiring act of allegiance in the Old Testament Book of Ruth. There Naomi, a woman who has lost her husband and her sons and has nothing left to live for, dismisses her two daughters-in-law, freeing them to seek new husbands and new lives. One daughter-in-law, Orpah, leaves, albeit regretfully, but the other one, Ruth, remains loyal to her dead husband's mother. She cries out: 'Entreat me not to leave you or to return from following you; for where you go I will go, and where you lodge I will lodge; your people shall be my people, and your God my God; where you die, I will die, and there I will be buried' (Ruth 1:16-17). Devotion, allegiance, and fidelity – that, too, is loyalty.[1]

First and foremost, when seeking a church to join, look for a church filled with loyal people. They must be loyal to the leadership. This loyalty, however, should not amount to what author Mary Cullinan calls 'Groupthink'. According to Professor Cullinan, Groupthink happens when members of any organisation blindly follow, refusing to disagree with their leaders because to do so would invite rejection from the group or the leaders.[2] Groupthink drains the life out of any congregation, and when it is allowed to run its course unopposed, it could destroy a church.

The leadership of any church must be loyal to the congregation – loyal in the way that Jesus was loyal to the least of his disciples. Here is where most modern churches get it wrong

1. It is worth noting that Ruth's loyalty had far-reaching ramifications. Ruth's decision to remain with Naomi led to her meeting and marrying a man called Boaz. By giving birth to a boy called Obed, Ruth and Boaz became the great-grandparents of King David and the ancestors of Jesus Christ. What might have happened if Ruth had been disloyal?

2. Dr Mary Cullinan (PhD, University of Wisconsin) *Business Communication – Principles and Processes,* 2nd edition (Harcourt Brace College Publishers: London, 1993), p. 650.

big time. Many people will recall the beautiful song 'Servant King' by Graham Kendrick. The lyrics make it abundantly clear that Jesus came to earth to serve, and not to be served.

Consider this man Jesus. Clearly he was a leader, for wherever he went, men and women followed. When he spoke, people responded – many up to the point of martyrdom for his sake. Now look at Jesus' leadership style. When his disciples were hungry, he fed them. When they were thirsty, he gave them a drink. When they were scared, he encouraged them. Up to his last few days as a man, he served his congregation. The Lord's final object lesson on leadership is best illustrated by his taking a towel and a basin of water and washing the filthy feet of the twelve apostles. His message to church leaders? If you want your congregation to remain loyal to you, then you must make yourself the least of all by serving others. Paul warns: 'Do nothing from selfishness or conceit, but in humility count others better than yourselves. Let each of you look not only to his own interests, but also to the interests of others.' Of course, this is a message to all members of a church. But I think the rest is specifically for the leadership: 'Have this mind among yourselves, which is yours in Christ Jesus, which, though he was in the form of God, did not count equality with God a thing to be grasped, but emptied himself, taking the form of a servant (the Greek word is *slave*), being born in the likeness of men. And being found in human form he humbled himself and became obedient unto death, even death on a cross' (Philippians 2:3-8).

The following are two case studies of leadership. You decide which one of these examples of leadership comes closer to the example Jesus gave us.

A couple of years ago, I was asked to speak at a church in

Suffolk. As is my habit, I turned up early to have a look around. Upon arriving, I met a busy man who was hauling a large container of water. He greeted me and continued to scurry about. Following him into a hall I watched him set up a table where tea and coffee were to be served after the service. Assuming he was the caretaker, I introduced myself. He shook my hand and astounded me by saying, 'Hi, I'm Jim.' I was taken aback, because this was the leader of the church.

Here is another style of leadership. I went to a church fête at the invitation of a friend who ran a stand. As scores of people poured into the church grounds, the women (and a few men) scurried about, serving food, drinks, and keeping the guests happy. Throughout the morning and into the early afternoon, the minister walked to and fro, greeting guests and looking on benignly. Eventually, volunteers began to leave the various stands, but the guests continued to turn up. At last, my friend pleaded with the minister, 'Won't you please come and help us?' Without a trace of irony, he dryly replied, 'My dear, *you* are helping *me*.' With that, he turned and walked off.

Two types of leadership; two types of church: You decide which you'd prefer to join.

Loyalty breeds excellence

Loyalty may be defined as devotion, homage, and faithfulness. If you turn to the gospels, you see that loyalty breeds excellence. Although scripture doesn't record it, it is clear that Peter's words, 'Lord, to whom shall we go?' greatly pleased Jesus when the other disciples abandoned him because they could not accept his claim to be God. In this case, loyalty encouraged a broken-hearted Jesus. In some cases, however, such loyalty can lead to miracles.

It's clear that Jesus enjoyed a close relationship with his mother. In fact, Mary's prompting at the wedding at Cana produced Jesus' first recorded miracle when he was about age 30. Mary realised that their host had run out of wine, so she confidently suggested that Jesus change several gallons of water into wine.

Jesus demurred, saying, 'Woman, it is not my time!' Knowing the power her son possessed, Mary blithely ordered the jars of water to be brought by the servants. Jesus produced a wine with an exquisite bouquet, and the rest, as they say, is history (John 2:1-11). The centurion in Matthew 8:9 so impressed Jesus that the Lord's physical presence wasn't even required to heal the man's servant. Look at what happened as the result of this devotion to Jesus: 'And to the centurion Jesus said, "Go; be it done for you as you have believed." And the servant was healed at that very moment' (Matthew 8:13).

Conversely, the absence of such loyalty may prevent the miraculous from happening in a church. In Mark's gospel, Jesus returns to his hometown of Nazareth. There, he teaches in the synagogue (Mark 6:1-6). This well-known young rabbi frankly astonished the members of the congregation by his authoritative words and his wisdom. But instead of giving Jesus even a shred of credit (never mind allegiance!), they turned on Jesus, questioning even his right to speak. The net result of this lack of faithfulness led Mark (and other chroniclers) to record that Jesus '. . . could do no mighty work there . . .' (Mark 6:5).

Friendship

There are many theological explanations for why Jesus chose key companions to be his disciples. Primarily, Jesus selected these men to train in order to carry out his ministry after his resurrection and departure from earth. Moreover, each was selected for a particular role to play based on some gift or attribute he possessed. Finally, each apostle was selected because Jesus wanted his close followers to be witnesses to his miracles and his death and resurrection. But quite apart from that, I am convinced that Jesus aligned himself with these people because he wanted friends.

Someone once wrote that no man is poor who has friends. Motivation experts point out that people are more stimulated when they have friends. Among workers, isolation leads to less risk-taking, less productivity, and fewer innovations. But work executed in collaboration with trusted colleagues has this plus more.

If a spiritual community is a brick wall, then friendship is the mortar that holds the bricks together. That's why you should look for a church that offers friendship. I have a friend who pastors a Vineyard church in Suffolk. He once said he is excited about the prospect of growing old together with his congregation. I recall thinking, 'Wow! That is commitment in a pastor!' Remember that loyalty and friendship are the ingredients needed for making church work.

Friendship is another term for familiarity. Cynics point out that familiarity breeds contempt. Certainly it may, but it needn't. If we look to the apostles, we see a life that included shared meals, mutual goals, intimacy, and good old-fashioned companionship. Anyone who has ever taken time to consider the apostles will know that the defining characteristic of that band of men was not similarity but diversity. Old Peter, bold, outspoken, and rough and ready, was so different from quiet, contemplative, somewhat refined young John. Luke was a Gentile. Phillip was an encourager. Thomas was a profound sceptic. Nathaniel was illogical.[1] Paul was an intellectual. My point is our friends don't have to be clones of us to be true friends. What makes people friends is the intersection of their lives at the place called shared values.

Shared values

Shared values equal strength. Powerful as Britain's army was during the Second World War, it never would have been able to serve the nation if it attempted to combine its ground-based expertise with, for example, sea-based duties. For defence on the sea, King George VI looked to his navy which was every bit as committed to defending Britain as the army. Likewise, the navy hadn't the skills or the aptitude to protect the skies as well as the sea. For the air war, a band of brave young pilots were called up to engage the *Luftwaffe* over southern England in the Battle of Britain, and later, over enemy territory in the later years of the war. Diversity and shared values. This is a vision of what church life should be all about.

Far from being a so-called militant Christian, I see the church in these very same military terms. Instead of Nazis, however, the church is engaged in war with sin and satanic forces. Like the various branches of the military forces, certain denominations and churches have specialised. For example, some focus on social action. Others have made evangelism their forté. Still others stress signs and wonders, and so on.

Over the centuries, Christian denominations sprouted out of controversy, disagreement, and in some cases, for the

---

1. See John 1:46. Here we see that not only is his logic faulty, but he is a borderline racist: 'Can anything good come out of Nazareth?'

sake of purity. Clearly, this has been to our disadvantage. Because we have been fiercely divided, Satan has won many battles over the centuries. However, God is sovereign. Far from desiring his church to be fragmented into a mitosis of denominations, God is still able to use his churches if we will look past our differences and focus on similarities. Paul, who may have anticipated the rise of denominations, writes:

> Only let your manner of life be worthy of the gospel of Christ, so that whether I come and see you or am absent, I may hear of you that you *stand firm in one spirit, with one mind striving side by side for the faith of the gospel*, and not frightened in anything by your opponents (Philippians 1:27-28; italics mine).

Not mere ecumenism, this is a vision of a diverse church army that can unify under the orthodoxy of the creeds (see Appendix A for a discussion of creeds). Instead of bullets and bombs, the church's weapons are praise, prayer, social action, and people. Instead of shooting other Christians, through unity, we may now shoot the enemy.

Which church shall I join?

Avoid one-man churches. Within the churches individual people – like the individual apostles – have special interests and gifts. This is the meaning of the curious phrase 'living stones' found in Peter: '. . . like living stones be yourselves built into a spiritual house, to be a holy priesthood, to offer spiritual sacrifices acceptable to God through Jesus Christ' (1 Peter 2:5).

So if you are looking for a church to join, first find your own gifting and then look for a church or a denomination that offers loyalty, friendship, and shared values. Make sure it is a church that will encourage you to make your unique contribution towards its mission to the wider community.

Avoid a sleepy church

Many critics are saying that the Church is dead. I disagree. Far from being moribund, it is merely sleeping when it ought to be awake. This is something all of us do from time to time. Do you recall when Peter, James and John fell asleep on the Mount of Transfiguration (Mark 9:2-13)? The three apostles and Jesus were climbing a high mountain. Suddenly, Jesus began to glow with a white-hot intensity and Moses and Elijah appeared from the dead to confer with Jesus. Incredibly, precisely when God was doing a powerful thing for the early Church, Peter, James and John somehow fell asleep.[1]

Consider Peter in the garden on the night before Jesus' trial and execution (Matthew 26:36-56). 'Will you not watch and pray with me for just one hour?' asked Jesus. But Peter fell asleep instead of praying. To be sure, many churches are very like the disciples who fell asleep at inopportune times. That is, no sooner than God begins a wonderful work in their midst, they fall asleep as it were. This is what is behind Paul's admonition: 'Awake, O sleeper, and arise from the dead, and Christ shall give you light' (Ephesians 5:14).

---

1. Eventually, the apostles awoke, but now seeing Jesus speaking earnestly with two of Judaism's greatest saints the event overawed them, and the writers of the gospel tactfully say that the men 'did not know what to say for they were exceeding afraid' (Mark 6). Instead of upbraiding the men for their behaviour, Jesus gently lets the matter drop until later on, when he asks that they keep quiet about what they saw 'until the Son of Man should have risen from the dead' (Mark 9:9).

Find a spirit-led church

When it comes to the mission of the church, nothing happens without a move of the Holy Spirit (Romans 8:26; John 4:24). When God means to do a thing, he sends his Spirit in quiet power to do it. Someone once made an analogy that drives home this point. The church is like a glove and the Holy Spirit is like the hand. Without the hand, the glove is powerless.

Groucho Marx once quipped, 'I would never join a club that would allow a person like me to become a member.' His point is well taken, but when it comes to joining a church, most of us actually want to join one that would be glad to have someone like us.

Middle-class people want to join a middle-class church. Working-class people want a working-class church. Young people want a youthful church. Some people want a church that is identified by a special theological emphasis, say baptism. Here is a church with a free-and-easy family atmosphere, plenty of hand-clapping and dancing, some prophecies and some speaking in tongues; just around the corner there is a solemn and formal church where no one but the minister, the choir, and other delegated lay people speak out – all in keeping with the order of service.

All of the above is fine, but it is important to keep in mind how dangerous it is to become too introspective – that is, too fixed on our own likes and needs. After all, what about the likes and needs of people who don't go to our church? Many may feel that what non-members think is not important. But it's good to recall something that the late Bishop Leslie Newbegin often pointed out to Christians: the Church is the only organisation on earth that exists for the benefit of its non-members. He means the church is here not only to serve its members, but also to serve the communities outside its four walls.

Time to act

This chapter is titled 'Selecting a church'. I have tried to show that God values the various churches and denominations. Some of us have a clear calling on our lives to join one church over another, but owing to confusion about what constitutes the right church for us, we often choose to join the wrong one. Eventually, we lose all sense of commitment and drift away, perhaps never joining a church again. (Could this be why our church attendance rates are so low?)

Why not take time to think about your attitudes towards church. Do you agree that God has a special church for each of us? If yes, what type of church is for you? Do you stereotype other denominations without even having first-hand experience of them? Do you have any prejudices against any particular denomination? Do you have any expectations that you impose upon other churches, but you don't necessarily impose upon your own? How does your church use the gifts of the people in its congregation? Is your church making a difference for good in your community? If so, how? If not, why not?

Every Christian alive today has been selected by Jesus to be part of a church. If you aren't in one you need to be. Find a church that matches your spiritual profile and join it. Someone once said, if you find a perfect church, don't join it. You'll be the one to bring it down. Amusing as this may be, it is very misleading. There are no perfect churches. As the sign that stands outside of a small, white clapboard church in Tupelo, Mississippi, proclaims, 'Welcome liars, cheats, drunks, prostitutes and other of God's Children!'

Although there is no such thing as a perfect church, it is better to be in one than in none. Churches have the potential to be like a flock of migrating geese, which fly in a V formation. The aerodynamics of a flying V is such that the updraft caused by the lead geese's wings pulls the flanks along almost effortlessly. The geese will always position themselves so that the weaker ones may benefit from the combined efforts of the stronger, and they will do this for as long as is necessary, or until the weaker ones may take their place towards the front.

Moreover, when it becomes clear that a goose cannot go on, even with the aid of the strong, two geese will drop out of the flock and glide to the earth with the ailing goose where they will stay until that goose regains its strength or dies. After that, they will rejoin the original flock or join another flock for the rest of their migration.

Remember: As a Christian, you are uniquely called to tasks that are impossible to fulfil on your own. One man cannot move a piano. Ten men can do it effortlessly. This is especially true for church leaders. If you are a minister or priest, you should begin to create opportunities to include lay people in the life of the church, particularly once you have helped them to find out what their spiritual and natural gifts are.

Real world application

Gifts and talents are spread liberally throughout congregations, and they are without respect to age, ethnic group, gender, or education. In teaching about special spiritual gifts, St Paul points out, 'To each is given the manifestation of the Spirit for the common good' (1 Corinthians 12:7). This means that God equips every church with the necessary spiritual resources to sustain its life and spread its influence. Since this is so, when it comes to using special gifts and talents the church is in the best position to provide ways and means for people to exercise their gifts.

In many communities where the local authorities have had to cut back on social services, churches may use their own funds and members to offer alternative services. After all, the modern social state is the offspring of an earlier Christian era marked by sense of compassion. Non-Christians needn't worry that this is just a ploy used to make converts. There needn't be any mention of the name Jesus; a sincere desire to reach out and love others will do wonders for all concerned. Even Groucho Marx can't gripe about a church like that.

*Your problem is that you don't know the Scriptures, and you
don't know the power of God. For when the dead rise, they
won't be married. They will be like the angels in heaven.*
Matthew 22:29-30, NLT

CHAPTER 3

The gift of being single

Without wanting to seem flippant, Jesus may be said to
have been the Bible's most eligible bachelor. Think about
it. A decent, hard-working twenty-something, he was the
oldest son of a well-established businessman. A skilled
craftsman and a rabbi to boot, he was born into a culture
that put the highest premium on marriage and full sexual
expression through producing children. No doubt many a
Jewish mother had her eye on Jesus as a future son-in-law.
Yet he chose to be single. Why would anyone wish to
remain single?

On the whole, singles fare worse than married couples.
Singles often find they are shunted to undesirable seats in
restaurants, to the less desirable rooms in hotels, and frequently companies offer discounts for couples or families,
but never for singles.

Perceptions of single people are unflattering. Single
women cruelly are perceived as 'spinsters' or 'old maids'
who have been left on the shelf too long, and single men
are frequently regarded as selfish, too preoccupied with
career, or possibly confused about their sexuality.

Many singles resent the assumption that they are lonely.
Often well-meaning but misguided couples will invite a

single person to a meal, and then blithely announce that another single has been invited in order to approximate a twosome. I say approximate because often the two singles mix about as well as oil and water. I recall a time while I was single and a colleague invited me to join him and his partner for an outing followed by a meal. 'Our friend Olive [not her real name] will be joining us,' he said cryptically. When we all met, I don't know who was the more appalled – Olive or me. Clearly we were not meant for each other.

Many single people would like to tell their friends who are couples that they are secure, well adjusted, and happy as singles. What's more, they would be very happy to join couples for the theatre, the cinema, or a meal, making it a *threesome*. Still, couples continue to include singles, only to 'even things out' with another single. How would it be if singles invited their married friends out, but insisted that one of the partners remain home – just to 'even out' the evening?

Jesus made the most of being single. It's clear his singleness afforded him more time with God. Because of this, he was aware from a very early age that God had intended him to carry out important tasks, tasks which were better achieved if he remained single and celibate. Is God asking you to do the same? You could do worse. Jesus' life is evidence that singleness is an attractive alternative to matrimony. Certainly God has said he will bless those who feel the call to remain single and celibate. As Isaiah wrote: 'I will give in my house and within my walls a monument and a *name better than sons and daughters*; I will give them an everlasting name which shall not be cut off (Isaiah 55:5, italics mine).[1]

Single women and church

Research shows that there are more single women than single men in church. Moreover, this same research shows that more women than men have joined churches over the last few years. So the problem of singleness affects females more than it does males. The crux of the problem for these women is should they wait, hoping to marry a shrinking number of Christian men, or should they compromise and marry an unbeliever? Of course, this is for each woman to decide for herself. Moreover, some women rise above this problem, learning that their true identity may never be found through marriage. They are seeing their singleness in a positive light. Author Kristin Aune spoke to nearly 100 single women and reports that many feel that God is guiding them. They believe that singleness is in their best interest.[2] They have good reason to believe this. After all, with more and more marriages breaking up today, marriage has become a high-risk occupation, even for Christians.[3]

1. Isaiah is referring to eunuchs here. While I cannot be dogmatic about this term, we see from Jesus' words in Matthew 19:12, there are three types of eunuchs in scripture. Those born eunuchs, those made eunuchs by men, and those who have made themselves eunuchs. The IVP *New Bible Dictionary* clarifies this last category as 'spriritual eunuchs', that is people who give up natural desires for the sake of the Kingdom of God, as did Jesus and the apostle Paul and countless others. I believe that this is what the passage in Isaiah refers to. Some, including the early Church father Origen, have misinterpreted self-made eunuchs as having muti- lated themselves, which is not the case at all. *New Bible Dictionary*, 2nd edition (IVP: Leicester), s.v. 'Eunuch'.

2. Kristin Aune, 'Single Christian Women', *Christianity and Renewal*, March 2002, pp. 19-21.

3. The UK leads the EC in divorce rates.

Marriage is not for everyone

Scripture states that a man should have one wife and a woman one husband (Genesis 2:24; Mark 10:6-8). But it is equally scriptural to devote one's fullest energies to God through Christian service as a single person, thereby avoiding the many pitfalls and distractions associated with marriage. While marriage is a good thing, living as a single person is an equally good lifestyle with its own unique opportunities to draw people to God.

For the sake of argument, let's assume that some people are better off single. Have you ever wondered what kind of spouse the apostle Paul would have made? The mind boggles! Although Paul stands out from all the other New Testament saints because of his accomplishments, he is hardly the ideal marriage partner. The testimony of Paul's travelling companion, Luke, and the evidence found in Paul's letters are proof – if indeed such proof is needed – that Paul would have been a terrible spouse.

In Acts, we read of his travelling overland on foot, being shipwrecked, delivering fiery sermons, enduring beatings by wrathful city officials, being chased by irate rabbis and spending long hours fasting and praying. Paul would have been hard pressed to find time for romance, for repairing leaky plumbing, and, more importantly, for being around the house to help in raising his sons and daughters. Paul's letters show that he spent most of his time on the road planting churches, preaching, adjudicating spats between Christian factions, and when he wasn't preoccupied doing all this, he languished in prisons in the far-flung corners of the Roman Empire.

A typical Type-A personality (some would say an *extreme* Type A), Paul was a hard man to please, as faithful

Barnabas discovered when he and Paul had a falling out over the effectiveness of a missionary trainee called John Mark (Acts 15:36-41). St Peter also came in for a ticking-off from pugnacious Paul when Peter came to Antioch and withdrew from the company of Gentiles when certain Jewish friends of James turned up. Peter began to act as if only Jews could be saved, not Gentiles. Paul didn't wait for an opportunity to take Peter aside to correct him discreetly. No. Paul called Peter a hypocrite in front of everyone and demanded that he repent (Galatians 2:11-21). How might he have dealt with a wife or son who erred?

Paul's critics have represented him as being more Greek than Jewish in his attitude to women, representing him as a misogynist (woman hater) and a bully who belittled marriage. This, of course, is to completely misrepresent the man. Consider what Paul taught to the church in Corinth about matrimony and the Christian lifestyle:

> Are you married? Do not seek a divorce. Are you unmarried? Do not look for a wife. But if you do marry, you have not sinned; and if a virgin marries, she has not sinned. But those who marry will face many troubles in this life, and I want to spare you this. (1 Corinthians 7:27-28, NIV).

As you can plainly see, Paul was not against marriage as many people have supposed. In fact, he encouraged people to marry (see also Ephesians 5:22-33). Still, his attitude was that it is better to be single! (1 Corinthians 7:8) Why? Paul's conviction was based on two things – a desire for Christians to be free of anxiety; and the realistic assumption that married people always have two loyalties – one to their spouse and one to Christ. Hence he wrote:

> I want you to be free of anxieties. The unmarried man is anxious about the affairs of the Lord, how to please the

Lord; but the married man is anxious about worldly affairs, how to please his wife, and his interests are divided. And the unmarried woman or girl is anxious about the affairs of the Lord, how to be holy in body and spirit; but the married woman is anxious about worldly affairs, how to please her husband (1 Corinthians 7:32-34, NIV).

Whether or not Paul wanted to marry is a moot point, for he is a good example of a person who was better off unmarried. Paul isn't the only example that comes to mind.

John Wesley was very like the apostle Paul in that in his life it is estimated that he travelled over 5000 miles a year on horseback planting churches and preaching. His private journals show that he frequently preached up to five sermons a day. He wrote prodigiously, mass-producing books and tracts, many of which required long hours of research and study before they were written. Unlike Paul, however, Wesley was a married man. In 1751, at the age of 48, Wesley married Mary Vazeille, a widow with four children. The marriage was an unhappy and an unfulfilled union, producing no children of their own. Eventually, Mary Vazeille-Wesley deserted John. I would argue that Wesley should have remained single and celibate. Certainly, he would have been a happier man.

Many people will have heard of Corrie Ten Boom, author of *Tramp for the Lord* and other books and articles. No doubt as a younger woman Corrie hoped she would marry; however, she never met the right man. At the start of *The Hiding Place*, a memoir of World War Two, Corrie is in her forties and unmarried. She and her sister (also single) ran a highly successful family business. Both shared the not unpleasant responsibility of looking after their aged widowed father, and they used their free time to look after the spiritual needs of a group of mentally retarded children at their church. Because of their compassionate lifestyle, many people in Amsterdam knew the sisters to be godly and trustworthy women. If serving the community in this way were the only reason why they decided to remain single, by all estimations, these women would have faithfully served God and their community. As it happened, God had another plan for the Ten Boom sisters.

After the Nazis invaded Holland, all Jews were targeted as *persona non grata.* The fortunate ones escaped with the clothes on their backs and whatever they could carry in each hand, but the majority of Jews were trapped in the Netherlands with no place to hide and no one to help them. One day Corrie was approached by a leading member of the Dutch Resistance, an underground network of patriots who opposed the Nazis and who wanted to help the Dutch Jews escape to safety. The man came to Corrie precisely because as a single person she had stood out in her city as a strong woman of great character.

After consulting her sister and father, Corrie agreed to harbour some Jews in her home, and for the next year, she risked her life on a daily basis, helping Jews find a way out of the city. Corrie had no husband or children to worry about. Her father was a widower and her sister unmarried. Because they were free to act in a way that would affect only them and not others, their singleness was a part of God's plan for saving the lives of scores of innocent Jews who would have otherwise perished in the brutal Nazi concentration camps. One woman changed history because her will was focused on doing God's will – even though it meant she never would marry. That is a powerful testimony.

Societal pressure to marry?

Most people wish to be married. That is understandable. There are many pressures that make life tough for singles. Although more and more younger people are putting off getting married, recent studies show that they still expect to find a marriage partner for life. So the expectation to marry is there.

Families and friends also put pressure on single members to marry – often unintentionally. Nick (not his real name) recalls a time driving home from a wedding aware that he was the only unattached person left in his immediate circle of family and friends. Stopping for a meal, he noticed he was the only patron on his own in the restaurant. According to Nick, 'I can tell you, by the time the bill came, I was so depressed at the thought of going home to my empty little flat that I stayed away from it for a few days. Instead I stayed with my brother and his wife in another town.'

Families put pressure on singles to marry. Although nothing may be said about it, when a younger sister or brother marries before an older sibling, there is a very real sense of urgency for the older one find a mate. Family experts agree that an only child may sense an unspoken but nevertheless palpable pressure to marry and have children in order to maintain the family name.

The idea that people are incomplete unless they marry for love is a fabrication created by eighteenth-century romance novels, artificially inflated by nineteenth-century penny-press magazines, and perfected today by Hollywood films. The message is reinforced annually on 14 February. Valentine's Day concentrates everyone's minds on romance: the mushy cards, the chocolates and flowers, the candlelit dinners. Single people who are lonely can feel frustrated on so many levels, and in extreme cases, they may actually suffer from stress, insomnia, and loss of self-esteem.

The theology of singleness

Unfulfilled expectations, family pressure, our culture's fixation with 'living happily ever after' in unrealistic wedded bliss – all this contributes to the dilemma faced by single people. But perhaps the greatest contributing factor to the problems faced by singles comes from the Church. Many churches do an excellent job providing activities for singles. In fact, many people meet a marriage partner through a church connection when they are desperately lonely and seeking a spouse. But this is missing the point. More than providing opportunities for singles to meet, the Church needs to teach about the theological soundness of choosing to live as a single man or woman.

Our churches must present being single as an attractive alternative to marriage. Ministers must stress that no single Christian is alone. God is with us. His presence is a mystery; nevertheless, it is real. I have read the testimonies of many people who have found themselves cut off from family and marriage partners – through wars, acts of political intrigue, through death, or other circumstances. In each case, their testimony is that when they were alone before God, he showed himself to be real, loving, and most importantly, *there*. A single person is better placed, I think, to experience this phenomenon than a married one. Rather than causing them to become self-absorbed, this closeness with God enables willing single people to reach out in love to others in great need.

Consider Corrie Ten Boom again. Her singleness gave her the time to cultivate closeness with God. This closeness inspired her to risk her life to help others in need. Yet by her own admission, she felt completely unprepared for the next phase of God's plan for her life. After a year bravely working with the Resistance, a Dutch Nazi sympathiser betrayed her, and she was arrested for aiding fugitive Jews.

Corrie tells of the blackness that engulfed her when she and her sister were flung into a vermin-infested concentration camp run by brutal psychopaths. Things got worse for her when her sister, sick and alone, died in the so-called camp infirmary. Suddenly, not only was she an unmarried woman, she was cut off from the companionship of her sister whom she loved. One might have expected her to lose her mind at this point. Instead, she opened up herself even more to God, who proved to be eager to commune with his lover. To make a long story short, this intimacy with God, partially borne of her years of living as a single person, inspired Corrie to perform even greater acts of Christian charity within the confines of the death camp, and later, after the war, when Corrie was forced to learn to forgive the Nazis for their atrocities.

The point of this chapter is not to prove that being single is better than being married (although it may be); it is to show that singles may use their lifestyle as a 24/7 witness of God's goodness. Corrie Ten Boom did this. She is only one of scores of Christians who have used their singleness to bring glory to God. Consider this who's who of single Christians: Jesus, St Paul, Jerome (the Bible translator), St Columba (missionary to Scotland), St Patrick, St Boniface, Anselm (First Archbishop of Canterbury), Francis of Assisi, Thomas Aquinas, Teresa of Avila, Catherine of Siena, John Wycliffe,

John Hus, Michelangelo, John Knox, John Keble, Florence Nightingale, C. S. Lewis,[1] Dietrich Bonhoeffer, Mother Teresa, John Stott, Sir Cliff Richard, and many, many more. Because they were blessed with singleness, they discovered that God is our lover – body, mind, and soul.

If it's true that we are made in God's image, we are, therefore, made to express love. But according to the New Testament, our highest expression of love is the love of our fellow human beings. Jesus had this in mind when he said, 'Greater love has no man than this, that a man lay down his life for his friends' (John 15:13).[2] Friendship between men and men, women and women, women and men – indeed, the whole idea of community – is the highest expression of love. Jesus' life is a living example of a love that willingly lays life down for the good of others. In this sense, all people, whether married or single, may participate in this cardinal virtue.

Who will we marry in heaven?

I have already shown that the apostle Paul approved of the single lifestyle for Christians. We've also seen that God will abundantly bless any of his people who see fit to live single, celibate lives. So does God favour singles? No. But this frequently overlooked piece of eschatology sheds light on God's plans for all our futures. Jesus taught that in heaven, none of us will be married, humanly speaking.

---

1. Single for most of his life, he was married to American Joy Davidman Gresham from about 1956 to her death from cancer in 1960.
2. In fact, Jesus used the Greek word *Agape*, the special love that God has for his children, not *philia*, the affection of friends. By doing this, Jesus is actually talking about his love for us that led him to lay down his life on our behalf.

Jesus plainly said this when a group of Sadducees, who taught there was no resurrection, tried to trick Jesus into making a contradictory statement about the resurrection.

They asked Jesus who in the resurrection would be legally married to a woman that married seven brothers, each of whom died in succession. Jesus replied, 'Your problem is that you don't know the Scriptures, and you don't know the power of God. For when the dead rise, they won't be married. They will be like the angels in heaven' (Matthew 22:29-30, NTL). Jesus could not be clearer about our future as singles. Yet often at funerals I hear well-meaning but misguided ministers talking of married couples being reunited in heavenly matrimony. Although I believe there will be a reuniting of family and friends in heaven, I frankly doubt that people will be married there chiefly because the Bible is clear that we won't marry. So what's planned for us? [1] Let's go back to Paul. In his second letter to the Corinthians, Paul says that he knew a man who had been privileged to go into a place called the third heaven (2 Corinthians 12:2). This man went into Paradise where he heard things that Paul cannot reveal to his readers (3-4).

Clearly, Paul was privy to some knowledge that later may have prompted him to teach an astonishing truth about one aspect of heaven and marriage. In the new heaven and the new earth, we will all be in a marriage relationship not with another departed soul, and certainly

1. One of the best books I have ever come across regarding what the Bible actually teaches about the afterlife is *Heaven: it's not the end of the world* by David Lawrence (Scripture Union, 1995). I highly recommend it to anyone who wants to know what the Bible teaches on this and related subjects.

not with our former marriage partners. We will be in a nourishing marriage relationship with God himself. After all, Paul has called God's chosen people the bride and God the groom (2 Corinthians 11:2; Ephesians 5:25-27, 32). This theme is taken up elsewhere in the scriptures, including Revelation 19:7; 21:9, etc. Meanwhile, God is blessing people who marry, and God blesses those who hear and respond to a call to singleness and celibacy.

But I want to marry!

Finally, what if a person is currently unmarried, and God has clearly not called that person to be single, and the desire for intimacy is great. What then? In that case, we must believe that God cares about our feelings. I will develop this point in greater detail in Chapter 6.

Time to act

This chapter is titled 'The gift of being single'. I have tried to show that God values the single lifestyle as much as he values marriage. Many of us have a clear calling on our lives to remain single, but owing to cultural pressures, we choose to ignore the calling and marry. (Could this be why our divorce rates are so high?)

Why not take time to think about your attitudes towards singles. After reading this chapter, do you agree that God has a special role for single men and women in church, in society, in other people's lives? If yes, what are those roles? If not, why do you feel this way? Do you stereotype singles? Do you have any prejudices against them? Do you have any expectations that you impose upon them? How do you use the gifts of single people in your church or fellowship group?[1] Remember, whether it is a life-long calling or a temporary one, the single lifestyle provides ways for us to give God our undiluted love and devotion.

Real world application

Every Christian alive today has been commissioned by Jesus to present the Gospel. If you are single and content that, at least for the time being, God wants you to remain single and celibate, you have your work cut out for you. People will be drawn to Jesus when they see you living the Christian lifestyle. Remember: as a single person, you are uniquely called to tasks that it is impossible for a married person to fulfil. If you are married you should begin to create opportunities to include single people in your life, particularly at weekends, holidays, and in between times, too!

1. Single people deserve more respect than they get in our society. We observe Mother's Day and Father's Day; we honour parents and children. But what do we do to congratulate or encourage single people? Singles make up the majority of career missionaries, Sunday school teachers, youth workers, carers, and scores of other service-based ministries. I'd hate to think what might happen if singles called a moratorium on their service. Married couples' priorities are such that our culture would be the poorer because we would simply have to do without the important services provided by singles that many take for granted.

Do you see a man skilful in his work? He will stand before
kings; he will not stand before obscure men.
Proverbs 22:29

CHAPTER 4

Choosing a career that will honour God

'God is not dead. He is merely unemployed.' I smiled when
I saw that bit of homespun philosophy, but I knew it wasn't
true. God has a busy career. He's a creator, and he's been
working at his chosen profession for millennia. Indeed, the
first sentence of the Bible declares: 'In the beginning God
created the heavens and the earth' (Genesis 1:1). God is busy
today creating, and the evidence is all through the visible universe. The Psalmist repeatedly calls attention to the inventive
nature of our God. Take a concordance and look up the
words *creates, created, creator,* and you will see that God is
busy manufacturing, producing and fabricating. In this,
we are very like God – all of us have been created to work.

Most people who work do so for a number of reasons,
including obtaining long-term security, providing for their
needs and the needs of their dependants, and, ultimately,
to save up for when they may no longer work. In our grandparents' day, most people worked at the same occupation
for their whole lives. Today, this is rare. Most workers will
change careers at least once and more likely two or three
times in their life.[1] This is a departure from past working
patterns when a job for life was taken for granted.

1. The Top 10 Steps for Choosing a Career, http://topten.org

Even the idea of 'full-time' retirement has been challenged over the last 25 years. More and more retired people are working at part-time jobs in service industries in order to make ends meet. What's more, current contributions being made by an increasingly smaller workforce [1] means that state pensions are expected to be woefully inadequate for a majority of tomorrow's retired people who will have to work or go without many necessities.

An article in the 20 September 2002 *Telegraph* describes plans to make the current state retirement age 70. Business gurus predict that Americans and Europeans under 25 will work well into their 70s and even their 80s before they will think of retiring. This is because the cost of living, as well as life expectancy due to improved medicine, is expected to increase sharply. If this is so, some people reading this book will probably work until their eighty-fifth birthday! No wonder it's important to choose our career carefully.

Work is good and part of God's will for all of us. That's why after he created Adam, he placed him in the garden and told Adam to name the plants and animals, till the soil, and do many other tasks (Genesis 2:5). Far from being tiresome chores, Adam took to these tasks as an eagle takes to the sky. Of course, after Adam and Eve sinned (Genesis

---

1. There are many reasons why the workforce is significantly smaller than in the past. Thirty years ago, alarmist demographers warned that western nations were heading for a population explosion. The opposite is true today. The industrialised nations have approached a near-zero population growth rate. Women having fewer children, women having millions of abortions and other mitigating societal factors have achieved this level of population growth. Demographics expert Peter Schwartz states that by 2010, the population ages 0-24 will be less than half of the total population in each of the world's regions except Africa, where it will be over 60 per cent. (Statistics cited from *The Church's Hidden Asset – Empowering the Older Generation*, Kevin Mayhew, 2001.)

3:1-7) all work suddenly became difficult (Genesis 3:17-19). Yet Adam and Eve – and all that came after them – continued to have a keen appetite for work.

It's worth noting that in his lifetime, Jesus had a career. He was a skilled carpenter. Few ministers or priests refer to Jesus' work in their sermons. More's the pity, for I believe that Jesus greatly glorified his heavenly father though his labour. This point was made in the animated film *The Miracle Maker*. Screenwriter Murray Watts inserted a short but powerful scene depicting Jesus' last day on an important job prior to embarking on a career as an itinerant rabbi – a career move that frankly confuses his employer. As Jesus packs up his tools, the boss, far from deriding this pious labourer, asks his foreman how much money it would take to keep Jesus with their firm. The upshot of this scene is that Jesus the carpenter is less interested in making money than he is about being about his Father's business.

In his booklet *Ethics in the Workplace – A Guide for Catholics*, Mark Miller advises Christians not to privatise their faith. He argues that God puts each of us in our place of work so that we may be a witness to Christ. He adds that this is one of the reasons why Jesus left us the Holy Spirit. With the help of the Spirit, we may demonstrate integrity, obedience, and faith at work.[1] These three virtues are sadly missing from today's corporate world as evidenced by scandal after scandal in recent years.

Moreover, whether you are a neurosurgeon or a short-order cook at Burger King, God expects above all else that we will honour him through our labour (Ephesians 6:5-6).

---

1. Mark Miller, CSR, *Ethics in the Workplace – A Guide for Catholics* (Liguori Press: Liguori, Mo, USA, 2000), pp. 3-5.

That's why it's important to select the right career, so that we may maximise bringing glory to God through what we do for a living.

How to cook a hare

Mrs Beeton's plain-speaking cookbook states, 'In order to cook a hare, you first must catch it.' Her point is not lost here. Before you can start a career, you must get some experience and qualifications. Let's deal with experience first.

Someone once said, there is no substitute for experience. How true. If you are considering entering a particular career, try to meet people who already earn a living doing that job. Talk things over with them. Ask them questions. You may try working at a number of different jobs to see how they suit you. Once in a job, look for opportunities to learn other aspects of the work. Another way to gain experience is to do voluntary work. And remember, no job is too menial if it will teach you something about your chosen career. Radio presenter Simon Mayo began as a tea boy in hospital radio. Poet Pam Ayres began her illustrious career by sending bits of doggerel to BBC Radio Oxford. There are many biographies of well-known CEOs who began as clerks in the stockroom of the companies they now run. Now let's talk about qualifications.

More people go to university today than ever before. Clearly, having a degree is an advantage when choosing a professional career. However, a degree doesn't guarantee success in the world of work. Hundreds of graduates have secured a good degree only to find themselves unemployed and in debt following graduation. Many young men and women who go to university would be better off if they had chosen to learn a trade as alternatives to taking a degree. For one thing, the financial rewards are there. I used to employ a plumber who belonged to a golf club that I couldn't afford to join! Also, not everyone is cut out for academic work.

Suffice to say that whether one acquires a university education or learns a trade, a qualification of some sort is absolutely key to selecting a career. To that end, we may as well prepare for careers that we will enjoy. Once we have done that, we are ready to find the right job. That, of course, is easier said than done!

The danger of choosing a career for the wrong reason

Whether or not you are a Christian, before you choose a career know your skills and play to your strengths. The following are three case studies to help us to avoid some common pitfalls when it comes to choosing a career.

Don't chase status

After leaving university, Elizabeth[1] became a primary school teacher. This was a good choice. She was excellent at explaining complex issues in simple terms. Because she was an accomplished pianist, her musical abilities helped her in the classroom and during school assemblies, a thing that gave her great satisfaction. Elizabeth also demonstrated excellent people skills. That is, she is patient, kind, fair, and above all, consistent in her treatment of her pupils.

After a few years, however, she decided she'd like to become a headteacher, thinking that this would enhance her career and giver her higher job status. After making

1. Not her real name. Key details changed to protect the identity of the person.

many sacrifices, she qualified for a headship, which she eagerly accepted when one was offered.

Almost immediately, she regretted the decision. For one thing, she no longer worked in a classroom among the children. Instead, she spent the best part of her day carrying out what she considered to be dull administrative duties among adults.

To compensate, she assigned herself some classes to teach, including acting as a substitute to replace absent staff. Although she knew she had other important tasks to do, she considered her teaching to be 'good for the kids' who would respond better to a familiar face than to a stranger hired to teach for a day or two.

While her colleagues appreciated her effort, her supervisors did not. Her evaluations as a head were consistently unsatisfactory. Eventually, Elizabeth resigned her headship and only avoided the prospect of long-term unemployment when a headteacher who knew her real skills hired her to teach at her school. Although Elizabeth's ego was damaged, she once again is enjoying her job. As you can see, increased status won't necessarily bring fulfilment.

Money doesn't buy happiness

Thomas[1] works as a print journalist. He originally trained to be a radio producer/presenter. After ten years working in his field, he was offered a chance to head an entire news department in a bigger city. Thomas and his wife were overjoyed by this prospect. For one thing, it would allow him to influence for good the city in which he worked. For another, it could mean a large pay increase.

---

1. Not his real name. Key details changed to protect the identity of the person.

Because he was still a bit unsure about the new job, Thomas met with Ian, a counsellor who had an extensive background in mass media. He told Ian that he felt God was telling him to take the job, yet he was feeling ambivalent about it. For one thing, he loved his current job. Also, while he was confident of his skills as a producer/presenter, he was insecure about his ability to perform the management duties required of him. Ian pointed out that if you don't feel 100 per cent commitment to a task, you probably aren't the right person for the job. In the end, Thomas decided to settle the matter by 'setting out a fleece' as Gideon did in Judges 6:36-40.

Thomas' personal 'fleece' was the as-of-yet-undisclosed salary. If his new employer offered him a certain salary, 'Then I'll know it's a sign from God to take the job. If not, I won't take it.' As it turned out, the salary came close to his requirement, so he agreed to take the job subject to signing the contract. On the way home, he felt uneasy. Thomas supposed that his reservations came from fear of change rather than a conviction that the new job wasn't right for him. He waited as long as possible before he signed the contract and sent it in.

The new job required a long commute to the office by train on a very undependable line, so he was leaving home early and coming home later and later. Hidden costs cut deeply into his pay packet. The price of a season ticket for parking and the train were exorbitant, and his new salary put him into the highest tax band he'd ever been in. In real terms, he wasn't making that much more than what his old job had netted him.

The job wasn't as appealing as he'd hoped it would be either. He was spending a good bit of time producing programmes, but he was tasked with more and more administrative duties, with far too many meetings for his liking.

Within weeks, Thomas realised the fatter pay packet was poor compensation for the many headaches of his new job. In the end, he decided to find another job, and while he is making less money in a related media industry, he once again is enjoying his work. The moral? Money can't buy job satisfaction.

Without faith it is impossible to please God

But, you may say, didn't Thomas set out a fleece, proving God had called him to the new job? A brief word about setting out fleeces. Because Gideon defeated the Midianites, many Christians believe fleeces are a legitimate means to test God's will in a particular circumstance. Maybe. But I can't help but think that Gideon was being incredibly faithless. What is faith? The writer of Hebrews defines it like this:

Now faith is being sure of what we hope for and certain of what we do not see. This is what the ancients were commended for.

By faith we understand that the universe was formed at God's command, so that what is seen was not made out of what was visible. By faith Abel offered God a better sacrifice than Cain did. By faith he was commended as a righteous man, when God spoke well of his offerings. And by faith he still speaks, even though he is dead.

By faith Enoch was taken from this life, so that he did not experience death; he could not be found, because God had taken him away. For before he was taken, he was commended as one who pleased God. *And without faith it is impossible to please God, because anyone who comes to him must believe that he exists and that he rewards those who earnestly seek him* (Hebrews 11:1-6, NIV, italics mine).

He continues:

> By faith Abraham, when called to go to a place he would later receive as his inheritance, obeyed and went, even though he did not know where he was going. By faith he made his home in the promised land like a stranger in a foreign country; he lived in tents, as did Isaac and Jacob, who were heirs with him of the same promise. For he was looking forward to the city with foundations, whose architect and builder is God.
>
> By faith Abraham, even though he was past age – and Sarah herself was barren – was enabled to become a father because he considered him faithful who had made the promise. And so from this one man, and he as good as dead, came descendants as numerous as the stars in the sky and as countless as the sand on the seashore (Hebrews 11:8-12, NIV).

With all due respect to the practice of putting out a fleece, it's always better to be an Abraham than a Gideon. As St Paul wrote: 'Thus Abraham "believed God, and it was reckoned to him as righteousness". . . So then, those who are men of faith are blessed with Abraham who had faith' (Galatians 3:6, 9).

Jonah!

Margery[1] is a Christian who works as a freelance graphics designer. She felt that God had called her to freelance work, not full-time. After 15 years she had established a good track record, but she grew increasingly frustrated about having to live from contract to contract. She also resented the complete lack of benefits.

---

1. Not her real name. Key details changed to protect the identity of the person.

In 1997, she applied for a secure, full-time job working for a well-known Christian organisation. 'The pay wasn't great, but the benefits and job security seemed more than I could resist,' she admits. Creating a head-turning résumé and portfolio of her work, she threw all her efforts into landing that job because she wanted job security. Not surprisingly, she was offered the job.

Near the time she was to accept the job, she prayed about what she was about to do, and the word *Jonah* popped into her mind. Jonah was the prophet who was swallowed by a huge fish because he didn't do what God told him to do (Jonah 1:1-17). The thought of what happened to Jonah shook Margery. Not wanting to disobey God as Jonah did, Margery decided not to take the job, tempting as it was. During the tense telephone call, her new employer let her know he was very disappointed that she had changed her mind. It was a difficult phone call, but she was determined not to take the job.

Today, Margery still faces considerable job insecurity within her chosen field, but she has also seen a steady increase in her income and she is at peace about her circumstances.

You are the only Bible some people will ever read

A friend once asked me why I never put any Christian symbols on my car, such as the fish symbol, a cross, or any other such thing. I replied honestly, 'I don't because if I were to make a mistake on a roundabout or maybe cause a crash, I wouldn't want anyone to blame my bad driving on Jesus.'

Although it is a cliché to say it, we Christians are often the only Bible other people will read. This is especially true at work. For better or worse, if our colleagues know that we are Christians, they'll watch us closely and judge us and ultimately our faith by our performance. Since this is so, it's of the utmost importance that Christian workers consistently do their best work. Therefore, it's best to find out what you are good at, and then stick with it, even if it means turning down tempting promotions.

While there is nothing wrong with accepting a promotion and all that comes with it, including a higher salary, there is nothing worse than taking the promotion for the wrong reason. Research shows that all too frequently workers are offered senior positions whether they are competent to do the job or not. One of the best books I have ever seen on this subject is *The Peter Principle* by Dr Laurence J. Peter and Raymond Hull. In a nutshell, the Peter Principle hypothesises: 'All workers tend to rise to their own levels of *inefficiency*.' I suggest you try to read this book if you are interested in learning more about this phenomenon.[1]

The best way to avoid the Peter Principle is to stick to doing what you do well. When I was a football coach, I used to tell the boys, find out what you are good at and play to your strength. This is the same advice I would give to any Christian who is in the middle of making career decisions.

Round pegs function best in round holes

A good way to discover your own particular gifts and talents is to take a sheet of paper and make a career self-inventory that lists your likes and dislikes, your career strengths and weaknesses, and a summary of the type of work you think you'd enjoy doing. You may wish to show

1. *The Peter Principle* (William Morrow & Co. Inc, 1969).

this to a trusted friend or colleague. Ask for candid feed-back on your findings. Often, other people see strengths (and weaknesses) that we do not.

After this, take time to research different jobs. The research isn't difficult. Most public libraries have career sections for this purpose. Also, if you have access to the Internet, you may do this work from the comfort of your home. See which career fields match your particular talents. If your self-inventory strengths indicate that you are people orientated, and working closely with others motivates you, don't choose careers that require you to be cut off from co-workers as a self-motivated, independent agent.

Once you have narrowed your career prospects to one or two specifics, take it to a friend or minister and pray about it. I am of the opinion that God has a plan for our lives. Jeremiah 29:11 states, '"For I know the plans I have for you," says the Lord, "Plans for welfare and not evil, to give you a future and a hope."' And 'Many are the plans in the mind of a man, but it is the purpose of the Lord that will be established' (Proverbs 19:21).

Now take it to God in prayer. This is a principle that during his human life, Jesus modelled for his followers again and again. 'In the days of his flesh, Jesus offered up prayers and supplications, with loud cries and tears, to him who was able to save him from death, and he was heard for his godly fear' (Hebrews 5:7). If Jesus spent this much time in prayer during his earthly 'career', how much more time ought we to be spending praying for guidance in ours?

At the end of the day, you should have reliable indica-tors that will help you make a final career decision. Of course, the ultimate indicator is your gifts and talents. God has already endowed each of us with certain talents, talents that are meant to operate in concert with the Great Commission at home and at work. In this sense, our career may rightly be seen as our vocation.

Finally, Mark Miller points out that there is no rulebook to help Christians to do their jobs in a way that brings credit on them as well as on God. We do, however, have the Bible, which teaches us about God who considers our workplace to be holy ground.[1] Jesus commanded us to treat the needy in our midst with respect. To this end, be on the lookout for the poor, the marginalised, and the outré at your work. Are they your customers? Are they your co-workers? Are they some associates? Don't overlook them whoever they are. Each person deserves special care and attention.[2]

In the next chapter, I will continue with this theme as I discuss what I call the Theology of Work. Meantime, remember, God is not dead, nor is he unemployed. Far from it. He is as busy today as he has ever been. As the writer of Hebrews proclaims, he is the same yesterday, today, and forever (Hebrews13:8).

Time to act

This chapter is titled 'Choosing a career that will honour God'. I have tried to show that there is a correlation between what you do for a living, and maintaining a credible Christian lifestyle.

The apostle Paul talks about having confidence to dare to serve God in radical ways. Again and again, he reminds Christians that we have been adopted into God's kingdom

1. Mark Miller, CSR, *Ethics in the Workplace – A Guide for Catholics* (Liguori Press: Liguori, Mo, USA, 2000), p. 23.

2. Ibid. p. 13.

by faith, and are guaranteed eternal life in a resurrected body (1 Corinthians 15:42). We are promised that everything that happens to us – good or bad – is for our benefit (Romans 8:28). We are each endowed with blessings that will allow us to do the work God has called us to do (Ephesians 1:1). He has revealed his will to each of us through his Holy Spirit (Ephesians 1:9). And because of this, Paul admonishes us, 'Therefore, my beloved brethren, be steadfast, immovable, always abounding in the work of the Lord, knowing that in the Lord your labour is not in vain' (1 Corinthians 15:58). These we can all do every day at work, and by so doing, we can tell others about our faith in Jesus Christ, for most people would rather see a sermon than hear one.

Real world application

Author Mark Miller tells about the time the pacifist bishops in Texas suggested that Catholics shouldn't be employed in the production of nuclear weapons.[1] According to Miller, many men and women quit their jobs even though it was done at great cost to themselves and their families. I have a lot of respect for these people who demonstrated their faith to the wider community by having the courage of their convictions to make this personal sacrifice.

On the other hand, is the military industrial complex any more (or less) unchristian than other industries? Many military leaders and soldiers (activists) heard Jesus preach about living peaceful lives, and some consequently became his disciples, yet they continued to be soldiers with Jesus' tacit blessing. An example of what I mean can be seen when

1. Mark Miller, CSR, *Ethics in the Workplace – A Guide for Catholics* (Liguori Press: Liguori, MO, USA, 2000), p. 13.

Jesus commended the faith of a Roman centurion by saying; 'Truly, I say to you, not even in Israel have I found such faith' (Matthew 8:11). One may have expected Jesus to tell the soldier to leave the army, much the way he once told the rich young ruler who clearly loved God to give all his riches to the poor and 'follow me' (Luke 18:22). Additionally, Jesus forgave the woman caught in adultery, but he warned her to turn away from prostitution and 'sin no more' (John 8:11). However, Jesus did not tell the man to give up being a soldier.

It seems to me that when it comes to choosing professions, Christians must follow their conscience. In the following passage Jesus' use of opposites 'east' and 'west' demonstrates the eclectic nature of the Christian faith, a faith which includes people from many contradictory traditions: 'I tell you, many will come from east and west and sit at table with Abraham, Isaac and Jacob in the kingdom of heaven . . .' (Matthew 8:11). So, it is not paradoxical that the Christian tradition allows for both pacifists and activists.

God is busy today, working out his will in the universe. Each one of us is called to partner with him. To that end, every Christian alive today has been commissioned by Jesus to present the Gospel (Matthew 28:18-20), particularly at their place of work. I believe that a good worker is the best advertisement for Christianity. We draw people to Jesus when they see us doing an honest day's work with a cheerful demeanour.

Finally, some people may be frustrated by the work they now do. Perhaps they are looking for work in a Christian field. If so, why not look into UK Christian Web Recruitment Services? UK Christian Web Recruitment Services enables employers to post recruitment adverts on the web and allows job seekers to search for vacancies which meet their criteria. If you are hooked up to the Internet, click on to http://jobs.churchuk.org.uk/jobhunters/and take a look at the featured adverts.

North American readers may wish to log on to:

ChristiaNet – web page:
   http://www.christianet.com

Christian Jobs Online – web page:
   http://www.christianjobs.com
   or
   http://www.ministryemployment.com

She seeks wool and flax and works with willing hands.
Proverbs 31:13

CHAPTER 5

A theology of work

Birds are great people watchers. When a gardener turns rich soil with a spade, every bird within 100 metres is watching, hoping the gardener will turn up fat grubs and larvae. Non-Christian people are a bit like birds, in that they, too, watch us when we work. They are looking to see if we are any different from them when it comes to earning a day's wage for a day's work. I think they are entitled to do this, for Christians really ought to stand out from their colleagues in every honourable way possible. This shouldn't be done to call attention to themselves, or as a means of suggesting that they are somehow better than others. On the contrary, Christians should try harder because they serve a great God. Thus, we must strive to bring out our faith by all that we do, especially at work. (See Appendix C to read how the late astronaut Rick Husband, the team leader of the space shuttle Columbia, shared his faith at work.)

One of the best ways we demonstrate our faith at work is by honouring our bosses. St Paul reminds workers to be 'submissive to rulers and authorities, to be obedient, to be ready for any honest work, to speak evil of no one, to avoid quarrelling, to be gentle, and to show perfect courtesy toward all men' (Titus 3:1). Even if we think our employers don't deserve our respect, we are commanded to esteem others as better than ourselves: 'Do nothing from selfishness or conceit, but in humility count others as better than your-selves. Let each of you look not only to his own interests, but also to the interests of others' (Philippians 2:3-4).

Another truly important way to express our faith at work is to be scrupulously honest in all of our dealings: 'But as for you, man of God, shun [what is evil]; aim at righteousness, godliness, faith, love, steadfastness, gentle-ness (1 Timothy 6:11). I have heard of some workers who waste time surfing the Internet for pleasure. Others come in late and leave work early, stretch coffee breaks beyond 15 minutes, and use paid sick days like they were holidays. Most Christians' infractions are not likely to be so blatant. Nevertheless, I recall hearing about a man who after he became a Christian was determined to see his entire office converted. He took 2 Timothy 4:2 literally: 'Preach the word, be urgent in season and out of season . . .' Noble as this aim is, he frankly went about it all wrong. For one thing, he constantly used company time to preach. If we are in a salaried job, then we are expected to earn a day's wage for putting in a full day's work. If you must preach, do so on your own time, not the company's. However, while on company time, if you offer your labour up to God and work diligently, he will cause you to earn the respect of your colleagues, so when you do speak about your faith, you will make a favourable impression on them. This may be what the writer of Proverbs had in mind when he advised: 'Commit your work to the Lord, and your plans will be established' (Proverbs 16:3).

Another workplace vice is gossip. James warns Chris-tians of the dangers of the unbridled tongue. 'If anyone thinks he is religious, and does not bridle his tongue but deceives his heart, this man's religion is in vain (James

1:26). Also, 'So the tongue is a little member and boasts many things. How great a forest is set ablaze by a small fire. And the tongue is a fire' (James 3:5-6). I saw a great skit at church. Two friends are discussing a co-worker who isn't there. The first person says to the second, 'Have you heard about Bill?' He then dishes up details of Bill's personal life in great detail, ending it all by saying, 'Of course, I'm just sharing this with you so you can pray for dear old Bill.' This hits the nail on the head, and most people who have seen this skit, are changed for good – I know I was.

What about Christians who are bosses? The advice is the same. Managers must lead by example. Therefore, they must work hard. They must respect their employees. Also, they must never order an employee to do something that they themselves would not do. As a church planter, Paul was like a CEO of a large, multinational corporation; and as such, he was well aware that, among his other pressing duties, his was to lead by example, not mere dictation. In his letter to the Church in Thessalonica, he encourages the Thessalonians to follow his example, as well as the examples of his assistants Silvanus and Timothy not to be idle. 'For you yourselves know that you ought to imitate us; we were not idle when we were with you. It was not because we have that right, but to give to you in our conduct an example to imitate' (2 Thessalonians 7:9).

Towards a theology of work

Jesus once faced a crowd of men and women who worried about how they would earn money for decent housing, food and clothing. Here's what he told his followers:

> Don't be like the unbelievers who make their salary their god. You can't please my Father and be a lover of money.

Therefore, don't worry about your financial needs. Honour God, and he will give you what you require for this life (Matthew 6:24-33).

This means that, of all people on earth, Christians should be different from non-believers. But how different are we? Surveys show that we are obsessed with creating wealth. To put our obsession into theological terms, for many of us, our livelihood has become like a jealous god whom we serve, often to the exclusion of everything else in our lives. Our proof text declares: 'Blessed are the workaholics, for they will own bigger homes and drive fancier cars.'

How different are Christians in the workplace? An American survey conducted by the Princeton (University) Religion Research Centre and the *Wall Street Journal* concluded that there was no 'significant difference' between people who called themselves Christians and those who did not in terms of work ethics, practices, and values.[1]

Jesus is speaking to Christian workers today. He says, *work honestly. Honour your employer and your co-workers, and my Father in heaven will meet all of your needs. Go, therefore, into the office or factory, and in the name of the Father, the Son, and the Holy Ghost, be my hands, my feet, and my face!* This means that our ultimate career objective isn't making a fat profit; it's helping people.

Entrepreneur Rory Clark agrees. After becoming a Christian in his 30s, he wanted his career to be an extension of his faith. 'For me, this is an attitude that must affect all a person does whether in private or in the workplace. My faith affects all that I do.'

1. Source: Christianity in the Workplace,
   http://www.biblecenter.com/sermons/christianity

Your walk must match your talk

After studying estate management at the Royal Agricultural College, Rory went on to work as a land agent at the Badminton Estate and then on the Althorp Estate in Northamptonshire, childhood home of the late Princess Diana. Today he runs a business and helps manage a successful Suffolk land development agency. He understands that people are watching him to see if he is any different from non-Christians when it comes to putting his money where his mouth is. Rory has this advice for all businessmen and women. 'The purpose of running a business is to make a profit, but what you do with your profits afterwards is a personal decision. Whether that goes 100 per cent to shareholders or back to you as the owner of the business, or if some of it goes into a charity – this is a personal decision. We use some of our profits to support a number of Christian charities.'

Rory thinks the idea of sharing one's profits is a healthy attitude for anyone or any business. 'From my point of view, running a business ethically means that you should run your business with and for people. This means that you need to put people first by acting in their best interest. If I really do believe in Christ, then I should confirm that belief.'

Rory Clark considers Suffolk to be his mission field. Yet I have met many doctors, lawyers, teachers, accountants, engineers, and labourers who feel that to serve God properly, they must leave their careers in order to retrain as clergy or missionaries. They see this as their way of responding to the Great Commission. Some indeed may have to drop their normal routine and train before going overseas to preach, teach, or translate the Bible. But for the vast majority of Christians, simply putting God first in our careers – here and now – creates wonderful opportunities for us to say something to others about our faith.

Working in full-time ministry

If you feel, however, that God may be calling you to full-time ministry, but you are working in some other career, consider the late Alan Goddard.

Alan saw all that he did as ministry. He was a man with many years' experience in business and industry, and, following his conversion later in life, he became very committed to bringing Christian principles to the marketplace. In 1989, Alan put his whole life – including his professional life – in God's hands. I interviewed him in 1997 at the height of his ministry.

According to Alan, 'Even though business was all I knew at the time, I thought the Lord may be calling me into some full-time ministry. So in 1991, I gave up work and attended Moorlands Bible College as a mature student.' Returning to the classroom in his 50s was hard for Alan and his family, but it led to an enriching of his faith in a most unexpected manner. 'As part of my course, I was assigned to assist at a small Pentecostal church near the college,' Alan recalled with a broad grin. 'As I was not Pentecostal, I wasn't sure what I'd let myself in for. In this church, people knew their Bibles, and they expected God to speak to them through signs and wonders – which he did. I suppose it was what some people would call a 'happy clappy' church. But that's where I came into a deeper understanding of the working of the Holy Spirit. Through the ministry of this church, I matured, and was refreshed spiritually, mentally and physically.'

His tutors at Moorlands felt that God was preparing Alan

for a special ministry. 'The feeling was that God wasn't about to discount my 35 years in commerce,' Alan said. 'But at the time, having an outreach to the business world was the farthest thing from my mind.'

After leaving college in 1993, Alan began ministering in and around Bury St Edmunds – first at a Free Evangelical church, and until 1996 as an itinerant preacher. 'I really was learning more about the basics of preaching, teaching and, most importantly, counselling,' Alan said. 'And that's when the church leaders in Bury St Edmunds approached me and asked me to be their Chaplain in the Workplace.'

Alan began the salaried job in October of 1997, and from the start, his combined business acumen and understanding of the special spiritual needs of managers and employees made him a much sought-after commodity. A few weeks into the job, a young woman suddenly collapsed at work. Shortly afterwards, the staff learned that their vibrant, otherwise healthy co-worker was dead. 'No one knew how to react,' said Alan. 'So I was called in to help the staff to cope with their grief and the stress caused by this tragedy.' It was decided to hold a memorial service for the woman, and Alan was asked to take the service. 'It was a very moving experience for me,' Alan admitted. 'And later the management expressed their sincere appreciation for what I was able to do for them.'

Bury St Edmunds is a special town, combining the best of urban with the best of rural living. Twice a week farmers and small businessmen and women converge on the town square for the historic open market. And where there were people, there was Alan offering an informal, confidential, and caring service for those under stress at work.

Alan Goddard had his work cut out for him: 'It's not

just a case of the business community being ignorant of the church community; often, the churches are completely ignorant of the needs facing people involved in commerce and industry. I make it a point to help ministers to be aware of the problems faced by those in their congregations who are in business.'

The Christian ghetto?

As I said, not everyone is called to do what Alan Goddard did. In fact, leaving secular work to work in some sort of Christian career may be contributing to a Christian sub-culture.

We are in danger of pulling away from the world by establishing a comfy Christian buffer zone between here and Paradise. Author John Fischer warns that the Christian tendency to withdraw from the media, the commercial world, the universities and schools, the factories, and the High Streets is a mistake. 'This has done nothing but marginalise our influence in culture . . . in the end has made us, and the Gospel we carry, far too easy to dismiss.' He reminds us that Jesus taught us to engage the world with the good news, and he gave us the Holy Spirit for that very purpose. Rather than retreat into a Christian ghetto, John says go into the secular markets. 'It is through a Christian's presence and participation in the world, in every sector of society, that Christ will be known. The world does not need a Christian version of itself; it needs the love of Jesus.'[1]

All Christians are called to work without worrying about getting richer. Rather, our purpose in working is to make a useful contribution to our fellow human beings. If

1. John Fischer, as quoted in *Wheaton,* Spring 2002, p. 48.

we do this, God will meet all of our needs (Matthew 6:33). That is food for thought.

Our workforce is a needy mission field, and Jesus is still looking for missionaries to reach the lost. The upshot is that we must set aside worldly values in our careers and get on with serving others. Let's not worry about our job security. Don't love money. Earn profits, but give liberally to the poor. And remember, by being faithful in our business affairs, we can bring honour to the name of Jesus in the workplace.

Faith at work has a price

If you take God seriously at work, be prepared to suffer persecution in your job. Within a month of going to work for a large firm as head of accounts, my friend Tom[1] was repeatedly asked by his boss to make dubious adjustments to the company books. Tom, a committed Christian, quietly refused this order, doing his job honestly and effectively. When Tom returned from holiday recently, his boss called him into the head office and told him because he wouldn't follow orders, he must resign or be fired. Tom said he would resign, even though this would cause immediate financial hardships for him and his wife and three children.

Jesus once told his disciples that to be a Christian means that we will have to pick up our cross and carry it – that is to suffer persecution from time to time. In fact, persecution has the potential of driving us closer to God, allowing us to receive more of the Father's blessings. Ironically, then, persecution – at home, at work, or elsewhere – is good for Christians. St Paul knew this well. He writes:

---

1. Not his real name. Key details changed to protect the identity of the person.

We do not want you to be uninformed, brothers, about the hardships we suffered in the province of Asia. We were under great pressure, far beyond our ability to endure, so that we despaired even of life. Indeed, in our hearts we felt the sentence of death. But this happened that we might not rely on ourselves but on God, who raises the dead. He has delivered us from such a deadly peril, and he will deliver us. On him we have set our hope that he will continue to deliver us, as you help us by your prayers. Then many will give thanks on our behalf for the gracious favour granted us in answer to the prayers of many (2 Corinthians 1:8-11, NIV).

My friend Tom went several weeks without work, but at the time of this writing, he has found a new job with a former employer who was only too happy to offer Tom a job that is closer to his home and which was suited to his particular talents.

The salary is considerably less, but Tom has decided to trust God for the shortfall. Not long after Tom left his old firm, his assistant who is not a Christian rang him and confided that he himself would soon be looking for a new job. When Tom asked why, his colleague admitted he no longer wanted to be involved with the shady dealings at work. He concluded by saying, 'I want you to know how impressed I am. Until now I never saw anyone stand up for what's right like you did.' As I said at the start of this chapter, it isn't just the birds who are watching us at work! At the start of this book I wrote that people are more apt to respond to actions than mere words.

In January of 2003, the UK was shocked by the barbarous death of DC Stephen Oake, the 40-year-old Special Branch officer who was murdered during a police raid on a suspected terrorist cell in Manchester. In the days that followed, many officers spoke to reporters about the character of their fallen colleague, a husband, a father of three, and a much loved and respected officer.

Later DC Oake's father, the former chief constable of the Isle of Man, Robin Oake, joined his son's widow Lesley in telling the world they were praying for God to forgive the killer, as they were sure Steve would. He added that they were praying for the murderer.

What will the nation know about this born-again Christian who was also a leader in his Baptist church? Detective Chief Superintendent Bernard Postles praised DC Oake as a model officer who always gave 110 per cent. Many officers said that Stephen was a thoroughly reliable workmate. One of them said he could always rely on Steve to get the job done properly. Truly, DC Oake's example will affect the many who knew him, and the many who had only heard of him. Truly, his work was an expression of his faith.

Time to act

Our theology of work must be informed by this piece of scripture. 'Now may the God of peace, who brought again from the dead our Lord Jesus Christ, the great shepherd of the sheep, by the blood of the eternal covenant, equip you with everything good that you may do his will, working in you that which is pleasing in his sight, through Jesus Christ; to whom be the glory for ever and ever, Amen' (Hebrews 13:20-21).

Real world application

God reminds workers, bosses and stockholders: 'I own the cattle on a thousand hills' (Psalm 50:10). This means that it is God that generates wealth, not man-made political or economic systems. Therefore, all wealth is God's wealth. God also says, 'Many are the plans in the mind of a man, but it is the purpose of the Lord that is established' (Proverbs 19:21). Remember, no matter what career we enter, our theology of work must not turn into a form of legalism. The fact is, without God's help, our attempts to please him will fail. Therefore, God sustains and blesses us as we conform to his will. If we believe this, we may confidently view our career field as a way to earn a living while telling others about the love of God.

Wives, be subject to your husbands, as to the Lord . . .
Husbands, love your wives, as Christ loved the Church
and gave himself up for her.
Ephesians 5:22, 25

CHAPTER 6

Choosing a spouse

Any marketing executive will tell you that the best advertisement for a product is evidence that the merchandise delivers what it says it will deliver. Despite all of the bad publicity marriage receives in the media, and despite the obvious problems sinful people have within marriages, it still works. For this reason, marriage is, in fact, one of the best ways Christians may proclaim to the world that God is good.

In C. S. Lewis' *The Screwtape Letters*, senior devil Screwtape is all bluster and vinegar in a letter to his infernal nephew Wormwood. This is because Wormwood allowed the human he was minding to fall in love with another Christian. Of course, matrimony is the last thing that the devils want for the pair because Satan knows that Christian couples build upon each other's strengths. This is what the writer of Ecclesiastes meant when he proclaims, 'Two are better than one, because they have a good reward for their toil. For if they fall, one will lift up his fellow; but woe to him who is alone when he falls and has not another to lift him up' (Ecclesiastes 4:9).

To be sure, this promise isn't meant exclusively for Christian couples; it's for *all* married couples regardless of their religious faith or lack of it. But clearly, if a person hopes to lead a credible Christian lifestyle, then it's better to marry a fellow believer. St Paul warns Christians: 'Do not be mismated with unbelievers. For what partnership have unrighteousness and inequity? Or what fellowship has light with darkness? What accord has Christ with Belial?[1] Or what has a believer in common with an unbeliever?' (2 Corinthians 6:12-15).

Of course, a Christian is free to marry anyone he or she likes, as such a thing is permissible. But while it is permissible, it may not be wise. Consider Samson. Samson took a Nazarene vow (Judges 13:5), and from his birth, he was specially anointed by God to live an exemplary life (Judges 13:24-25).

A sort of Old Testament James Dean, Samson made the first of many critical blunders in his short life when he demanded that his parents arrange for a marriage between himself and a Philistine virgin from Timmah. The Philistines, it should be noted, were the archenemies of the Jews. Being weak parents, this they did, albeit, reluctantly.[2] Immediately, Samson's new wife plotted against him to give the Philistines the advantage over the Jews (14:15-20). After his wife is killed (Judges 15:6), Samson seems to be back in a right relationship with God (Judges 15:14).

Yet soon he seeks to slate his voracious sexual appetite with a Philistine prostitute (Judges 16:1). Later, he takes up with another non-Jewish woman called Delilah. Samson's choice of partner impedes his ability to serve God. In

1. The name suggests death, hell and worthlessness according to most commentaries.
2. The *Harper Study Bible* notes suggest that although Samson was acting sinfully when he took this wife, God, who is omnipotent, used this action to aid Israel. See Judges 14:4.

the end, Delilah is Samson's downfall (Judges 16:15-17). Samson's anointing is withdrawn, and his life literally comes tumbling down around him (16:23-31).

It may be argued that Samson's demise was not because he decided to marry out of the faith. Rather, it was the result of his breaking his Nazarene vow combined with his own sinfulness. I have a lot of time for that argument, but I want to suggest that had Samson actually married a fellow believer, he may have had just the help he needed to stay close to God. (Remember that spouses are helpmates! Genesis 2:20.) Moreover, by marrying a Philistine woman, not only did he become 'mismated with unbelievers', but Samson foolishly made a vow before the gods of Dagon, Ashtoreth, and Beelzebub, and by so doing, he made null and void his own Nazarene vow.[1] Whether or not we have made a similar vow, it is wise not to marry an unbeliever. The Psalmist reminds us that to do so invariably leads to our compromising what we say we believe, much like the Israelis did when they 'mingled with the nations and learned to do as they did. They served their idols, which became a snare to them. . . . Thus they became unclean by their acts, and played the harlot in their doings' (Psalm 106:35-36, 39).

What's so special about vows?

Let's be certain about one thing. God takes vows seriously. First of all, it is because it is impossible for God to break

1. Samson was required to obey the Jewish covenant (including his Nazarene vow) or suffer the dire consequences. The First Commandment of the Mosaic law is: You shall honour no other God but me (Deuteronomy 5:6-7). This and the nine other commands are to be obeyed or else the covenant between Israel and God is null and void and will lead to a curse (Deuteronomy 11:26-28).

his word. Paul states categorically that God never goes back on his word (Titus 1:2). St Peter declares that God always honours his promises (2 Peter 3:9). Therefore, he expects us to be prudent about making vows. That way we won't end up like Samson, who evidently thought little of making vows. For this reason, God warns: 'When you make a vow to the Lord your God, you shall not be slack to pay it; for the Lord your God will surely require it of you, and it would be sin in you' (Deuteronomy 23:21). (See also Deuteronomy 23:23 and Proverbs 20:25.)

Wedding vows

Matrimony is the exchanging of vows between a man and a woman; as such, it is a binding contract (Matthew 19:6). Briefly, when two people take their marriage vows something mystical occurs. Somehow, they cease to be two separate people and become one: '"This at last is bone of my bones and flesh of my flesh . . ." Therefore a man leaves his father and his mother and cleaves to his wife, and they become one flesh' (Genesis 2:23-24). Many films culminate in two attractive young people deciding to get married after a series of often hilarious or heart-wrenching disasters. Invariably, the final scene sees the minister reciting the words, 'I now pronounce you husband and wife. You may now kiss the bride.' Next, the film's theme music plays and the credits roll, and as we shuffle out of the cinema, we assume the pair will live happily ever after. And I hope they will. But many people who make these vows have no idea what they mean. I often find myself wishing some screenwriter would spend more than a few seconds on the wedding service. Let's consider the Christian wedding vows briefly.

When the minister introduces the vows in the wedding service, the bride and bridegroom face each other. The groom takes the bride's right hand and they make promises before many witnesses. In this, the ritual is all very straightforward. However, the words I *take* you to be my wife/husband can be misleading. When a man marries a woman, he isn't 'taking on' a wife. Just so, when a woman marries a man, she isn't 'taking on' a husband. Taking another person is like carrying him or her. A cargo ship takes on a load of pig iron. If a person takes on a spouse, before long, he or she becomes tired and unable to go on.

When God gave Adam and Eve to each other, they were called *helpmates*. A person trying to move a heavy trunk welcomes a helper! So for a marriage to work, it must begin from the basic presupposition that each is there to help the other.

I will love you always

Did you know that marriage is a wonderful metaphor for our relationship with God? According to Ephesians 5:25 and Revelation 21:2, we are the very bride of Christ, and he is our groom.[1] In fact, in his letter to the Corinthian church, St Paul goes so far as to describe himself as a matchmaker, a bit like Yente, the Yiddish matchmaker in the wonderful musical *Fiddler on the Roof* (2 Corinthians 11:2). What does this curious marriage metaphor mean?

Here's what I think. God loves you so much that he wants a deep and meaningful relationship with you alone.

---

1. One reason why I worry about Bible translations that tamper with gender-specific language is that it is very easy to confuse what God has said about us. This means that men must get used to the fact that we are God's bride; likewise, women must learn to be God's sons.

By creating marriage, God has given us an earthly example of what our eternal relationship with Jesus will be like. Through making wedding vows, we are promising to have and to hold our spouse from this day forward; for better, for worse, for richer, for poorer, in sickness and in health, to love and to cherish, till death us do part. That is what God says to us when we become Christians. Very like a married couple, we become one with God in a permanent relationship which begins now but lasts throughout eternity. Consider these passages:

- For the Lord will not reject his people; he will never forsake his inheritance (Psalm 94:14, NIV).

- '. . . Never will I leave you; never will I forsake you.' So we say with confidence, 'The Lord is my helper; I will not be afraid. What can man do to me?' (Hebrews 13:4-5, NIV).

- John 3:16, Psalm 9:10 and John 6:39 also attest to the permanency of God's relationship with us through his son Jesus Christ.

On a purely human level, many people are afraid to make this sort of promise to another person. And I can understand why. This is a vow to enter into a binding relationship before God and according to his holy law. It helps, however, if you don't think of this solely in terms of your responsibility to your spouse. Think of yourself as the recipient of this pledge. Seen in this light, you can take great comfort in the knowledge that you will have another person with whom to share this life's joys and sorrows, one who will stand by you in all circumstances. It is worth mentioning here, too, that when we enter into a covenant with God – by being born again (John 3:3) or through confirmation, we sometimes think that our relationship is all about serving God. Nothing could be further from the truth. Jesus is there to sustain us, to give us the power we need to effectively battle the wickedness and the wiles of the devil. Let's look at the rest of the wedding service.

The woman says: In the presence of God I make this vow. Taking you to be my husband, to have and to hold from this day forward; for better, for worse, for richer, for poorer, in sickness and in health, to love and to cherish, till death us do part; according to God's holy law. In the presence of God I make this vow.

The minister receives the rings and says a prayer that goes like this: Heavenly Father, by your blessing let these rings be a symbol of unending love and faithfulness, to remind this couple of the vow and covenant which they have made this day before these witnesses and through Jesus Christ our Lord.

The bridegroom places the ring on the fourth finger of the bride's left hand and says to the bride: I give you this ring as a sign of our marriage. With my body I honour you, all that I am I give to you, and all that I have I share with you, within the love of God, Father, Son and Holy Spirit. She makes the same promise. These are not cheap words.

It must be said that today's divorce laws give permission to marriage partners to leave one another for any number of reasons – many justifiable, some less so, many merely superficial. It isn't my aim here to attack divorce or divorced people. I merely wish to point out that God invented marriage to show the world something about the incredible relationship we may have with God through Jesus Christ.

Satan hates matrimony

A few years ago a wide-ranging report showed that people who believe in God and attend church regularly are healthier than those who do not. Many people don't realise that the same health benefits affect married couples. What's more, the children of married couples fare better than the children of single parents and people who merely live together.[1] The following was posted in October 2002 on LifeSite Daily News' Website and is reprinted in full with permission here:

> The health benefits of marriage are so large that single men suffer worse health effects than smokers, according to a new study.
>
> Professor Andrew Oswald of Warwick University . . . studied thousands of records from the British Household Panel Survey and the British Retirement Survey. He found that, even when the effects of smoking, drinking and other unhealthy activities were factored in, married men had a much lower risk of death. Over a seven-year period, the married male had a 9 per cent lower risk, and the married female 2.9 per cent lower, compared with the unmarried. But a male smoker had a 5.8 per cent greater risk, and a female smoker 5.1 per cent.
>
> The reasons for the positive marriage effect are hard to quantify, Oswald says. But the most likely factor is the 'social support' of having a wife or husband nearby. Another explanation is that both single men and women tend to have a less healthy lifestyle including sleep, diet and work habits, and to be more prone to loneliness and depression.[2]

Another study based on research carried out in Australia and published in the UK by Reuters shows that married women benefit as much as married men from marriage.

1. http://www.trinity.edu/mkearl/family.html
2. Published with permission of LifeSite Daily News, http://www.lifesite.net

Details of these findings may be read by logging on to: http://www.stuff.co.nz/stuff/0,2106,2069116a7144,00.html. Not only is marriage healthy, it could save your life. Many people will know Christopher Reeve, the actor who played superman in a series of films made in the 1970s and 80s. Reeve was the focal point of international media in May 1995 when he was thrown from a horse and severed the top of his spinal chord. The man who was once superman was suddenly a paraplegic unable to move even his little finger. The accounts of the events following his accident are poignant. But what stands out in my mind more than anything else is the way in which Reeve's wife Dana honoured her wedding vows.

In a frank memoir a year or so after his accident, Reeves admits that when he knew that he probably would never walk again, he had considered committing suicide. Eight years later, Christopher Reeve is not only alive and well, but he is writing, directing films, and speaking all around the world, despite his severe physical impairment. By his own admission, it was his wife's love that stopped him from throwing away his life. Dana's commitment to her vow to love him *unconditionally* so moved him that each day he finds courage to choose life in a wheelchair. Reeve considers himself to be a very blessed man, and I do, too.

Recently, the international media have carried reports of Reeve's remarkable progress towards recovering some of his body movement. This is mere speculation on my part, but I believe that part of the credit for his recovery is thanks to Dana who has given her husband hope and a reason to live. The more I read about Dana Reeve the spouse, the more I see why God invented marriage and why Satan would like to see it destroyed.

Let's return to *The Screwtape Letters* for a moment. I pointed out that the senior devil admonished the junior devil for allowing the human to fall in love with, and perhaps marry, a Christian. Lewis is at his satirical best when he describes the woman from the devil's point of view. Screwtape fulminates that although she seems harmless, she is dangerous beyond description because Christian marriage undoes Satan's work (1 John 4:18; 1 Peter 4:8, etc.). Take a Concordance and see how many entries there are for the word love and the far-reaching ramifications of marriage, and you will understand why matrimony is the devil's worst nightmare!

Marriage is proof that God loves us and wants us to be happy

Satan's ultimate desire is to see marriage ended. After all, as a God-ordained institution, it is an affront to Satan. In Chapter XIX of *The Screwtape Letters*, the devil lifts the curtain a bit to show how Satan, the master psychologist, plays on human weaknesses, tempting us to scoff at Christian virtues such as chastity, fidelity, modesty, and holiness. Satan tries his best to replace love with lust. Mostly, he goads men and women to choose marriage partners for mere physical gratification (which is destined to fade and, therefore, disappoint).

God invented marriage because it has the potential to make us happy. It offers us unrivalled opportunities to enjoy companionship, loyalty, fidelity. In a sex-crazed world, marriage alone offers us the fullest (and safest) sexual expression. This sexual gift leads to having children and thereby opens up ways to pass on the Christian faith from one generation to the next, and the next, and so on! Put simply, without marriage there would be no families. And without families, Christianity would die off in a generation or two. 'Posterity shall serve him; men shall tell of the Lord to the coming generation and proclaim his deliverance to a people yet unborn, that he has wrought it' (Psalm 22:30). No wonder Screwtape is apoplectic when two Christians fall in love and think of matrimony! I won't bother to say more about Lewis' brilliant book; suffice to say, if you've not read *The Screwtape Letters*, by all means do so. The sooner the better.

One final word about marriage. I am aware that many marriages face complex problems, and for many people, Christians included, divorce seems to be the only way to resolve these problems. Jesus himself said there were certain grounds for divorce (Matthew 5:31).

Having said that, Jesus' concession to divorce is an indictment of sinful human nature corrupting one of God's institutions, not an attack marriage itself.[1] Perhaps if Christians were taught to wait until God shows them the right time to marry, there would be fewer divorces among Christians.[2]

How to know you are ready for matrimony

Sooner or later, most people long to give themselves to someone completely – to have a deep soul relationship

---

1. According to the *Harper Study Bible*, Jesus' teachings on divorce are found in Matthew 5:31, 32; 19:3-9; Mark 10:2-12; Luke 16:18. Paul attributes his doctrines on divorce on the words of Jesus; see 1 Corinthians 7:10, 11. All of these scriptures suggest that divorce should be rare, or even non-existent except in the case of infidelity (Matthew 5:32; 19:9).

2. It's worth noting that psychologist Kary Tiffany wrote in *Psychology Today* (Dec 2002, Vol. 35, Issue 6, p. 26) about compelling research that found that two-thirds of unhappy marriages right themselves within five years, and depression and low self-esteem are rarely remedied by divorce.

with another, to be loved thoroughly and exclusively. In the following narrative, I want to suggest what God says to all men and women who want a life partner to have and to hold until death parts them.[1] He says: 'You cannot do this, not until you are satisfied, fulfilled, and content with being loved by me alone – with giving yourself totally and unreservedly to me.

'Only after having an intense, personal, and unique relationship with me alone, discovering that only in me is your satisfaction to be found, will you be capable of the perfect human relationship that I have planned for you. You will never be united with another until you are united with me – exclusive of anyone or everything else, exclusive of any other desires or longings.'

Let's examine this in the light of eternity. There we won't seek fulfilment through a physical or emotional relationship with another person, but rather with God (see Chapter 3). Since this is so, it makes perfect sense that our starting place for a nourishing and satisfying relationship with another person is by first being in a similar relationship with God. What's more, if we rush into marriage, we may end up missing the very person that God has selected for us (Jeremiah 29:11; Proverbs 19:21; Proverbs 19:14, etc.)

God says to all who may be frustrated by the thought of waiting for the right one to enter their lives, 'I want you to stop planning, stop wishing, and allow me to give you the most thrilling plan existing. It is one that you cannot imagine. I want you to have the best.

'Please allow me to bring it to you. You just keep watch-

1. This narrative showing God's point of view about finding and marrying the right person is based on a photocopy of a letter sent to me by a friend almost 25 years ago. I have no way of knowing its source.

ing me expecting the greatest things. Keep experiencing the satisfaction that I am. Keep listening and learning the things I tell you. You just wait. That is all. Don't be anxious. Don't worry. Don't look around at the things others have got or that I have given them. Don't look at the things you want. You just keep looking off and away up to me, or you'll miss what I want to show you.'

Of course, this principle is a hard one to grasp, and it takes time and practice before we can come to the place where we can trust God when we feel starved of human affection. Nevertheless, God may be trusted to provide us with a life partner if we trust him.

God adds, 'And then, when you are ready, I'll surprise you with love far more wonderful than any you could ever dream of. You see, until you are ready, and until the one I have for you is ready, until you are both satisfied exclusively with me, and the life I have prepared for you, you won't be able to experience the love that exemplifies your relationship with me, and thus the perfect love.

'And dear one, I want you to have this most wonderful love. I want you to see in the flesh a picture of your ever-lasting union of beauty, perfection, and love that I offer you with myself; know that I love you utterly. Believe it and be satisfied.'

Time to act

God loves love, human sexuality (he invented sex after all), and he loves marriage. To see evidence of this claim, take time to read the Old Testament book of *Song of Solomon*, a beautiful treatise that presents human sexuality as God intends it, within the context of marriage. Here, matrimony is used by the author to illustrate God's relationship to Israel in the Old Testament and of Jesus to the Church in the New Testament Church.[1]

Real world application

Every Christian alive today has been commissioned by Jesus to present the Gospel (Matthew 28:18-20). Being married won't guarantee that we'll become evangelists merely by the fact of our being married. But as we live out the Christian lifestyle within a loving relationship with our spouses, it's likely that we will find ample opportunities to share the love of Jesus with others.

1. *Harper Study Bible*, s.v. 'Introduction to Song of Solomon.'

*Fathers, do not provoke your children to anger, but bring
them up in the discipline and instruction of the Lord.*
Ephesians 6:4

CHAPTER 7

God invented families

Following a lecture by Mum and Dad, it was decided that
the three children would try to be more polite during
meals. At teatime, Tommy, aged six, sat at the table and
asked, 'Will someone please give me the ketchup?' Not
hearing the child, the rest of the family chatted away happily. Tommy politely asked two more times with no success.
Finally, Tommy stood on his chair and screamed, 'I want
the ketchup!' All eyes were on the small boy. The father
shook his finger and scolded, 'Just for that, young man, you
will go straight to your bedroom with no supper!'

Let's face it, being part of a family is difficult. Whether
they come to us through birth, adoption or fostering, children are on loan for a brief time from God. And as parents
or guardians, we can use all the help we can get when it
comes to raising kids God's way. This chapter attempts to
offer simple, godly advice that could make a difference in
the way people view the role of the family.

If you're a single parent or raising children alongside
your spouse, dealing with the realities of the twenty-first
century is tough. Sociologists have dubbed ours a 'Post-
Christian' society. And when it comes to parenting, the
social science crowd are right. The High Street shops are
bursting with magazines, videos and books offering tips on

family life. Despite this wealth of material, precious little reflects biblical principles. It wasn't always this way. Once upon a time elected officials, schools and health authorities fell in line with Christian teaching on family matters; today, however, all champion secular models which leave many Christian parents confused and frustrated.

Fathers – who needs them?

Children need fathers. This is the conclusion of a growing body of academic research here and abroad. Since this is so, it might be assumed that Government policy would reflect this fact. However, the opposite seems to be true.

In addition to dubious images seen in the media, American and British welfare benefits discriminate against couples with children in favour of single parents. Many single mothers are discouraged from marrying because they stand to lose more in welfare benefits than they would gain from their husbands' wages if they married.[1] Additionally, the married couples' tax allowance has long been eliminated, penalising couples who marry and have children.[2] Of course, it's not accurate entirely to blame the state for fostering a climate of absentee fathers. 'Successful parenting is funda-mental to achieving healthy families and communities,' says Home Secretary David Blunkett. Yet, many fathers are *choosing* to spend less time with their children each day.

Why do fathers shirk their parental responsibilities? Many simply take no pleasure in spending time with their children. Others claim they are too busy. The increasingly common 10-hour-a-day jobs leave almost no time for dads to participate in family life. Being busy is simply a poor

1. Welfare 'biased against families', *Daily Telegraph*, Tuesday, 3 January 1995.
2. Ibid.

excuse for an 'absentee dad'. In a moving letter written by the late singer-songwriter John Lennon during the height of his popularity, he regretted that his international acclaim as a superstar meant he couldn't recall the last time he played with his son, Julian. Perhaps this sad letter written alone in a hotel room in Manhattan inspired the words to one of the last songs he wrote before he was murdered in 1980: 'Life is what happens to us while we are busy planning the future.'

Many fathers claim it's quality not quantity of time that matters. But a growing number of psychologists point out quality is a by-product of *quantity*. Adrienne Burgess, author of *Fatherhood Reclaimed*, thinks 45 minutes a day is the ideal length of time for fathers to spend with their children. In fact, though, according to several recent reports, British fathers spend as little as 15 minutes a day with their children. In the United States, studies show a similar trend, with one study claiming that some men spend about a minute of daily quality time a day with their children.

Many fathers get home around children's bedtime. Weary from a day at work, these men often leave the tucking up to the mothers. This is a mistake. Bedtime is when most children open up about their fears, talk about their worries, or ask questions about important issues, including the Christian faith.

Sociologists say that children raised by single mothers suffer more than children from two-parent homes do. The children are more likely to be involved in crime; they are more likely to be disruptive, chronic underachievers at school; and they are likely to carry emotional scars into their adult lives. In the aftermath of the tragic shooting of

Charlene Ellis and Latisha Shakespeare outside a Birmingham nightclub at New Year 2003, Government ministers began trying to address the problem of gun crime in the inner cities. In a powerful article published in the *Sunday Telegraph* the actor David Oyelowo told of being bullied in school by fatherless black boys. Black himself, he says it will take more than new gun laws to change the reality of the inner city where men routinely abandon their children and an entire generation of fatherless boys have no idea of right from wrong. He credits his success as an actor to his loving parents and to his Christian faith.[1]

It may be argued that despite having two parents, children with absentee fathers suffer the same as children from fatherless homes. The message is clear: children need fathers. But many men don't know how to be fathers.

In *The Inheritance of Tools*, American essayist Scott Russell Sanders offers fathers this tip: Make time for your children. He recalls his busy father as having a work-ethic just short of a perfectionist's. Yet, his busy father always made time for young Scott. Sanders fondly recalls how as a boy he would frequently wander into his father's workshop. Amid the aroma of cherry, pine and oak wood, he would use adult tools to hammer away at wood scraps, banging together musical instruments, Aztec temples or whatever else took the boy's fancy.

Instead of ignoring the boy, the old man would stop what he was doing to admire the wooden gadget, and then he would lead the boy over to the workbench and hand him a plane or a saw. Taking Scott's little hand into his own, the father guided the son, offering tender encouragement as well as sound advice.

1. David Oyelowo, 'Why black boys turn to crime', *Sunday Telegraph*, [Review] 12 January 2002, p. 2

Often this would put paid to the senior Sanders' project, because these special moments were in the evening, ending only when it was time for the boy to go to bed. Sadly, in the light of the way our society undervalues the role played by fathers, fewer and fewer children today can claim or even expect this sort of fatherly attention.

Fatherless families are not the only thing undermining family life. Educator and author Gary Pritchard warns parents that teens are being specifically targeted by marketing agencies which use provocatively sexual images to sell everything from clothing to ice cream.[1] Sadly, the effects of this campaign have taken their toll, contributing to British teens' burgeoning sexually transmitted disease and pregnancy rates. The rise is so alarming that the Department of Health has set out a strategy to halve our teenage pregnancy rates – the highest in Europe and the second highest in the developed world. The plan? Use tax-payers' money to appoint confidential counsellors to give advice about sex as well as to hand out free pamphlets, condoms, and oral contraceptives to teens and preteens without parental knowledge or permission.[2] The thinking is that teens can't control their sexual activities, so we'd better allow them to have free birth control paraphernalia. This policy has been extended to many schools, as well.

A curious parallel to this permissive attitude is the tough (and equally well-funded) anti-smoking and anti-drug literature one finds in the same offices and schools. One pamphlet flatly advises teens to 'Just say no' to drugs. If the government thinks this hard line is effective for combating tobacco and drug abuse, it stands to reason that the same

1. 'Porn Again Britain', Compass, Autumn 2002, p. 10.
2. Ibid. p. 13.

approach could work with warning teens about the hazards of premarital sex. Spokesmen for the charity Life says that the Government's decades-long policy of promoting 'safe sex' has led to an increase in teen pregnancies, sexually transmitted diseases and abortions – what a recent Parliamentary report has called a 'crisis'.[1] One needn't be a Christian to be alarmed by this.

Mothers count, too

A report published in the USA in September 2002 proves that teenage girls who enjoy a close relationship with their mothers are more likely to remain virgins than those who are estranged from their mothers. The report states that it is not just about mothers talking to their daughters about sex. It is the result of mothers being deeply involved in their daughters' lives.

This report mirrors an earlier report that found when families eat together, when parents know their children's whereabouts and their friends, it's less likely that the children will engage in premarital sex. The findings were published in the *Journal of Adolescent Health.*[2]

Is the traditional family a thing of the past?

No, says our Prime Minister. 'Strong communities revolve around strong families,' so says father of three, Tony Blair.

Married parents, grandmothers, grandfathers, uncles, aunties, cousins, and lots of children – that is how I define the traditional family. I think that traditional families are

1. Safe-sex policy 'spreads disease among young', Lorraine Fraser, Medical Correspondent, *Sunday Telegraph*, 23 February 2003, p. 8.
2. 'Study: Mom has strong influence on teens' sex', *Stars and Stripes*, 8 September 2002, p. 14.

wonderful. I know this goes against the current views of society, but then so does much of our thinking as Christians, doesn't it?

Despite the bad news, there is hope. For example, some records suggest that nearly half of all couples in Britain are unmarried (49 per cent). But while statistics don't lie, they may be misleading. Consider the same statistic presented like this: Over half of all couples in Britain are married and live in *traditional* families. Presented this way, the traditional family is seen for what it really is – the more popular lifestyle choice. After all, 51 per cent is still a fairly hefty proportion of British couples.

In February 2003, when the above census figures were released, the media spin was such we were led to believe that marriage is on the decline. An unfortunate fact of life is that the majority of media pundits, publishers, educators, and lawmakers champion the belief that ours is a nation of non-traditional families. But with most families living in traditional two-parent households, it is quite misleading to suggest that the old-fashioned family is the exception to the rule. Sure, traditional families are under pressure from changing attitudes and pressures. But it is doubtful that they will ever die out.

In recent years a number of women have been making the case for reassessing traditional families, including Wendy Shalit, the philosopher and author of *A Return to Modesty* and Danielle Crittenden, author of *What Our Mothers Didn't Tell Us: Why Happiness Eludes the Modern Woman.* They are arguing that militant feminism and the sexual revolution has badly let women down. The upshot of these books is that women (and men) really do want to get married, settle down, and have families. The latest book to support this is *Stop Getting Dumped!* by Lisa Daily. Daily says a woman wanting to get married to a man and have a family isn't wrong, despite what they have been told by feminists. After all, she muses, love and family life aren't bad things. Moreover, anthropologists teach that the traditional family is the very building block of society.

To be sure, the state is struggling to keep families together, but it hasn't the moral imperative to cope. One needn't be a Christian to see that secular ideas regarding the family don't work. Indeed, in his book, *Faith in the Future*, Rabbi Dr Jonathan Sacks argues that the displacement of the family by the state – and hence the replacement of morality by transitory political values – has added to some of the problems addressed here. Moreover, Dr Sacks thinks individuals – not the state – must do something about the decline of the family in our society. In the light of this, perhaps it's time to try an *old* idea since the *new* one obviously doesn't seem to work.

Churches must lead the way

First, church leaders must teach congregations to take family life seriously. It is all well and good to put time and money into important issues such as evangelism, missions and roof repairs. But none of this matters if we neglect our children, for, after all, they are tomorrow's Church.

Of all people in Britain, Christians should not be looking to the state for help in family matters. In fact, this tendency is relative new, for until as recently as 100 years ago, the Church used its own resources to look after families in need in the same manner as the ancient Hebrews (Deuteronomy 15:4-6; 24:17; Psalm 82:2-4, etc.), and first-century Christians (James 2:1-7; Luke 12:13-34, etc.).

Eighteenth-century Mennonite Christians who left the civilised world of Europe for the dense forests and natural hazards of North America believed that God helps families that help other families. The Mennonites used church funds to assist the needy in their midst in practical ways, believing that if you *give* a family a fish they will eat for the day; but if you *teach* a family to fish, they will eat for the rest of their lives. So churches helped families in need to set up businesses which were run on Christian principles. Profits above a certain level were channelled back into the church and ultimately redistributed back into the local economy to meet the needs of more families. This is a picture of the Christian welfare state. Poverty was unheard of, but so, too, was excessive wealth – instead of only a few, all were blessed.

This sort of Christian stewardship helped Mennonite families find dignity and independence through work, eliminating any need for state help. Significantly, strong families are a fundamental part of Mennonite culture – even to this day.

A final word about these Mennonites. They inspired John Wesley whose Methodist Movement transformed the rotting social fabric of the eighteenth century. Indeed, many historians credit Wesley's work with saving the United Kingdom from a bloody revolution like that of France's. Modern Christian families could have an equally wholesome effect on our own society.

The power of *one*

The principle of one person having the potential to foster a social epidemic is hardly far fetched. This is the message of the international best-seller, *The Tipping Point – How Little*

Things Can Make a Big Difference.[1] In it, author Malcolm Gladwell argues that just as one sick man or woman may spark a world-wide epidemic, so may one person become an agent of change for good for a whole community and beyond. He is, of course, correct.

Consider the great social reformer William Wilberforce. His nanny was his surrogate mother. She converted him to the Christian faith when he was but a child in his nursery. As he grew from childhood into manhood, Wilberforce never forgot his conversion experience. The fruit of that conversion was seen in his far-reaching reforms in child-labour laws, housing and medical benefits for the needy, and his crowning glory, his work to chloroform the European slave trade.

What might have happened if Wilberforce's nanny had never shared the Gospel with the boy? In very many ways, it would have been an international disaster. The fact is Wilberforce's nanny was but one link in a long chain of people who have inspired others to attempt great things.

Since the younger generation is full of potential idealism and virtue, parents must appreciate the value of children reaching out to other children – an increasingly under-evangelised segment of our society.

Steve Chalke is known to many as the apostle to Generation X – that is the generation of young people between ages 12 and 24. Steve knows that to reach teens you need other teens, and so he trains and employs young Christians as evangelists. He knows that like sharpens like. Just so, the best way to reach pre-teens is to commission children of faith from the same age group. Unfortunately, when it

1. Malcolm Gladwell, *The Tipping Point – How Little Things Can Make a Big Difference* (Little, Brown and Company, London, 2000).

comes to outreach, most people leave the job to the professional youth workers; however, children reaching out to children is proving to be a less expensive and equally effective means of spreading faith to families that normally do not attend church.

The Rev Jonathan Ford, minister of Christ Church, Morton Hall, Bury St Edmunds, agrees. That's why each year his ecumenical church sponsors a popular holiday club designed to draw youngsters. It gives kids something fun to do while hearing the gospel in ways that are meaningful to them.

Caroline, aged 12, worked at the 2002 summer club. She told me, 'Over the five days the club ran, I saw kids go from being bored to being really excited about God. I think it was really brilliant the way entertainment and lessons were presented. It was clever to see the way they got Jesus into a lot of different topics – from gardening to TV shows.'

Jonathan says you don't have to have special gifts to reach children for Christ. 'Every person participating was an ordinary member of Christ Church . . . and we designed and used our own course material for the first time. It is a central part of the strategy of Christ Church to reach out to young people on the estate.'

Jonathan knows that it is through the children that churches may reach entire families who may have never heard the Gospel. 'I would like you to add that the best material available for developing young people as leaders, evangelists and disciples is the Delta course from Campaigner Ministries. This practical peer-led training has transformed the youth work of my church.'

No one can say what youngsters are capable of doing. One thing is sure, though. If children think they can do something for God, but there is no adult encouragement, then what they think doesn't matter. Therefore, it's up to the parents and guardians (and uncles and aunts, older siblings, and *grandparents*!) to create genuine opportunities for Christian boys and girls to tell others about Jesus.

Grandparents

It is a well-established fact that there is a special bond between children and grandparents. This point was made charmingly by American comedian Alan Sherman.

He tells of the time that his grandmother came to be with his family in Chicago. She had not been in America long, and she spoke with a broad Yiddish accent. One night she was to give a dinner party for the all the uncles, aunts, cousins, and in-laws. Young Alan overheard his grandmother say to his mother that all she needed for the party to be a success was a *football*. Wanting more than anything for his grandmother's party to be a big hit, he went out and at great cost to himself, traded his new sledge and all his marbles for an old football which he rubbed with shoe polish to make it look new.

Later that day, he crept into the dining room and placed the ball in the centre of the table thinking how impressed the company would be with Grandma's football. When Sherman's mother noticed the fat leather centrepiece, she scolded Alan for leaving a dirty ball on the table. The boy protested that it wasn't his. He asked his mother if she recalled that Grandma needed a *football* for the party. His mother creased up with the giggles, and corrected him, saying Grandma doesn't need a football, she needs a *fruit bowl* for the party.

Mortified at misunderstanding her thick accent, Alan ran out of the room and spent the afternoon sobbing up in his room. Later when the party had started, his mother called him to the dining room. Reluctantly, he came down. To his utter amazement, he beheld his grandmother regally walking around the room holding an exquisite cut-glass fruit bowl filled with figs, grapes, apples, tangerines – and Alan's big fat football. The old woman was beaming as she explained to the guests that her little Alan had given her the football as a gift.

A family affair

Christina and Malcolm Nichol live on a country estate in rural Aberdeenshire with their seven children plus two ducks, a hen and a cat. Malcolm is a farmer and an estate manager, so they have a peaceful and beautiful place to live.

The Nichols are committed Christians, taking their large family to church every Sunday. Christina says, 'My faith is an inner strength; it has been there as long as I can remember. I often forget to pray during the day, but as someone once said, "Your work is your prayer."'

In this day and age when family size is shrinking, why have the Nichols elected to have so large a family? Christina paused momentarily and said, 'I remember some advice given to me years ago by a mother of ten: *Just do as your heart tells you. Take the chance given to you in this life for sharing in God's creation and don't worry. He'll be there to help you every step of the way.* And that's how it's been. God has been with us every step of the way, in ways I never could have imagined.'

Rowena and Mike Turner have 11 children. The family live in a rambling bungalow with a pretty garden in a South Oxfordshire village. Committed Christians all, Mike is an accountant and Rowena exudes serenity and joy, as well as a passionate commitment to Jesus.

When the Turners go out as a family in their mini-van, people often stop and stare. But Rowena said, 'Mike and I are used to that.' Many people ask the Turners why they have so many children. 'Children are a blessing,' she says without hesitation. 'So why stop God from blessing us?'

Transportation is not as big a problem as it may seem. 'The boys can walk to and from the village school, and the older boys can cycle to the senior school three miles away. With four cars in the family, I can get wherever I need to go,' she added.

Like many Christian mothers of large families, this acceptance of their children as a blessing from God transforms their attitudes to the practical side of life. Rowena manages to look after her family without outside help. How does she cope? 'When they were younger, friends from church sometimes came to help, but now with older children in the home, I have plenty of practical help and baby-sitters laid on!'

Although the Turners eat together every night, Mike often works late, and their older children come home later than the younger ones. Because it is agreed that sharing meals is very important for catching up on each other's news, the whole clan meets around the table at weekends.

As hard as it may seem, Rowena can't think of any insurmountable problems associated with having a large family. 'It's fun. I love the busyness of it all.' She thought for a moment and then said, 'The children all love and appreciate each other, and the little ones get lots of attention from their older siblings. Yes, we are very happy to be a big family!'

Of course, large families aren't for everyone. Still, I would encourage all people thinking of starting a family, to consider having more than two or three children. As mentioned earlier, anthropologists teach that families are the building blocks of society. Sharing, caring and finding a way to get along with others is a normal part of living in a family with siblings. Families teach individuals how to get on with others in the wider community, and in this day and age of extreme antisocial behaviour, that can't be bad. But there is a very real economic incentive for having more children.

'Children are our future' is no mere cliché

Few realise that Britain's low birth rate is threatening National Insurance. Pensions Minister Baroness Hollis has pointed out that the current ratio of 3.4 working people for every retired person is set to fall to around 2.4 within the next 30 years. She added that the best remedy for this untoward situation would be for people to have larger families. She said 'an increase in the birth rate would help to reduce any future demographic pressure on the National Insurance Fund.'[1]

Paul Tully, general secretary of the Society for the Protection of Unborn Children (SPUC) told reporters, 'This is perhaps the first realisation by this government that the decline in births, which has been caused by the culture of abortion and population control, threatens the welfare state.' Tully added that according to the United Nations, if our current birth rate continues to decline, it will require around 1.2 million immigrants per year to prevent a decrease in the ratio between working people and the Old Age Pensioners.[2] Since this is so, large families are good for

1. '"Culture of abortion" threat to welfare state', *Woman Alive*, November 2002, p. 7.

2. Ibid.

society. Significantly, the situation in Britain mirrors that of the United States which is facing a crisis with its Social Security system. Too few children are being born to sustain a growing retired population.

Speaking to Italy's parliament in November 2002, Pope John Paul II brought a sobering message to that nation. With no reference to Catholic dogma, he urged politicians to make it clear to the nation that large families were key to economic prosperity. The pope repeated the message of the United Nations, which has warned Italy that its economic future is at risk because its shrinking population will not be able to support its ageing population without an influx of migrant workers. He called Italy's declining birth rate 'a crisis'.[1]

God's command to human beings, 'Be fruitful and multiply' (Genesis 1:28) makes sound economic sense. Moreover, the policies put forth by Planned Parenthood and all pro-abortion agencies, no matter how well intended, have backfired and may cause untold economic catastrophes throughout the industrialised world – unless Christians begin to lead by example.

History has shown that when times get tough – either because of war, natural disaster or economic hardship – people look to God for answers. This means that we of all people on earth are uniquely placed to lead the way. Words will not do, for post-modern men and women want action. The question remains will we have the courage and the insight to act?

1. 'Pope pays historic visit to Italian parliament', reported by Nicole Winfield, The Associated Press, Friday, 15 November 2002.

Time to act

One of the best ways to make family life attractive to a sceptical world is to raise happy, functional families. But how does one do this? I don't think there is any definitive way to accomplish this monumental task. However, the challenge does bear thinking about if we hope to make a difference for good in this world.

Steve Chalke penned *How to Succeed as a Parent: 10 Survival Tips for Busy Mums and Dads.*[1] In his introduction, Steve writes, 'One of my aims when I first thought of writing this book was simply to trigger thought and discussion, because I am convinced that what we come to believe about being parents makes a huge difference to the way we behave as parents.' As a father, I found myself challenged, encouraged, and inspired by Steve's Ten Tips. He managed to pack a good deal of common sense into ten slim chapters. I recommend you read it. There is something for all sincerely interested in improving their parenting skills.

Each chapter deals with one 'tip' – i.e. *Tip Five: Be Encouraging.* Nothing motivates youngsters more than parental encouragement. What happens when parents neglect their duty to encourage their children? The youngsters become discouraged, and many search outside of the family for the emotional nourishment they crave.

This thematic approach makes the book an easy read, keeping the topic focused, and making it simple to go back and reflect on a particular 'tip'. Here are my particular favourites.

1. To find out more about this book and others about family life, contact Steve at Oasis Trust, Tel: 020 7450 9000, Fax: 020 7450 9001, E-mail: enquiries@oasistrust.org, or write to: Oasis Trust, The Oasis Centre, 115 Southwark Bridge Road, London SE1 0AX.

Tip Seven: Be Clear. This is one of the most helpful chapters in the book with subheadings such as: Plan Ahead: Develop rules *before* you need them; Choose your battles carefully; and, best of all, Have fewer rules than lots of them.

Tip Nine: Be Flexible initiates a good train of thought. Parents must prepare children for the outside world early: 'Your children will soon leave home, so start getting ready now!' And parents must learn to trust their children: 'Children need to be trusted in order to become trustworthy'. This chapter merely broaches the issue of teaching about sex. Explaining human sexuality to children merits a whole book in itself, not just a subsection of an already slim chapter.[1] Meantime, the book is well worth reading if you are a parent or are planning to be one someday.

Real world application

This chapter is titled *God invented families*. I have tried to show that there is a correlation between how you raise your family, and maintaining a credible Christian lifestyle. I have argued that traditional family life is the oil that lubricates the engine we call society. For centuries, Christians have been encouraged to make their family their highest priority. Yet today, many Christian families are breaking down. Since this is so, why not take time this week to pray about your relationship with your family?

Here are some items to pray about:

- Most fathers spend as little as 15 minutes a day with their children. Pray that you will find ways and means to make more time for our children. Pray, too, that the

1. See *The Parent Talk Guide to Your Child and Sex*, Steve Chalke (Hodder & Stoughton).

hearts of the fathers in our nation would change and that they would put family life before work.

- Research suggests that even when fathers do have the time, they prefer not to spend it with their children. Pray that you will have the inclination and energy it takes to interact with your children at the end of a long day. Pray, too, that fathers would begin to prize the few short years they have before the children leave home.

- Investing time in young children pays dividends when your children become teens. Sooner or later they will have questions about sex. Pray that you and your church family – and not the state – would get involved in helping our teens find answers to their questions about sexual matters and unwanted pregnancies.

- The media influences our behaviour more than most people realise. Marshall McLuhan's *The Medium is the Message*[1] and Vance Packard's *The Hidden Persuaders*[2] show just how extensive the influence can be. Moreover, unlike in the USA, Britain's Christian media is woefully underdeveloped with almost no Christian media training centres set up to train believers for careers in radio, television, print media, and cinema. Pray, therefore, that more young Christians would go to secular universities to train to become tomorrow's writers, journalists, editors, and television, cinema, and radio producers. This way, Christians will be able to compete with secular media

1. For an excellent article on McLuhan from a Christian perspective written by Todd A. Kappelman, a field associate with Probe Ministries in the USA click on to:
   http://www.leaderu.com/orgs/probe/docs/mcluhan.html
2. These books may be found by logging on to Amazon.com or through another reputable bookseller.

producers for the mind and soul of this nation. For more on this, see Chapter 16.

- The secular 'remedies' affecting the family that grew out of the 1960s are now bankrupt. Christians must recognise that social work, education, and politics are legitimate mission fields. Pray that more Christians would choose careers in these influential institutions as a means of helping to solve the problems facing families through biblical principles, much the way the nineteenth-century reformers did.

- Contrary to popular belief, there is no population explosion in the West. Large families are actually necessary for a prosperous society. Pray that young Christian couples would buck the trend towards limiting family size and have larger families, thereby averting any future demographic pressure on the National Insurance Fund and Social Security.

- Finally, perhaps you can suggest that your church sponsor an annual family seminar dedicated to enriching family life in the light of the scriptures. Remember that families living out the Christian lifestyle are the best tools in spreading the Gospel in any community.

Christian family resources

Family and Youth Concern is one of the best known family advocacy groups in the United Kingdom. Family and Youth Concern (FYC) was founded in the early 1970s by Dr Stanley Ellison, a London GP, who became aware that many of the symptoms from which his patients were suffering were not unavoidable medical conditions, but from the consequences of the breakdown in family life. Among its founder members were people eminent in the fields of medicine, education and sociology.

The advent of divorce, abortions laws and the Pill were heralded as great social reforms which marked the dawn of an age of unprecedented freedom and happiness.

However, it was not long before it became clear that there are serious consequences to the lifestyles which lead to family breakdown. Divorce is not a trivial procedure, it can have far-reaching effects on children and the stability of society; abortion can affect a woman's physical and mental health; new generations of sexually transmitted infections can have serious, even fatal, outcomes; and the problems of lone parents are not all solved by social security payments.

No one could have foreseen the extent to which children would be affected by these changes in the social climate. The free availability of contraception and abortion to under-age children without parental consent combined with amoral and explicit school sex education has caused many young lives to be blighted.

The Family Education Trust, working under its operational title, Family and Youth Concern, is a national organisation with no political or religious affiliations. An Executive Committee which is elected annually at a national conference assists its Trustees. It is financed entirely by members' subscriptions and donations and administered by voluntary officers and salaried staff.

You may learn more about their work with families by contacting them at:

The Director
Family Education Trust
The Mezzanine, Elizabeth House
39 York Road, London, SE1 7NQ
www.famyouth.org.uk/about.html

For information about Delta Programmes contact:

Campaigner Ministries

Campaigner House
St Mark's Close, St Albans, Herts, AL4 0NQ
Tel: 01727 824065; Fax: 01727 825049
E-mail: info@campaigners.org.uk

Here are some other organisations that are here to help maintain family life:

Christian Family Network

Christian Family Network links together many of the UK Christian family and parenting ministries on the Net, and offers advice, resources, news, reviews, top websites to visit and more – all updated weekly. CFN also publish a free weekly e-mail newsletter which you can subscribe to by sending a blank message to join-cfn-newsletter@mail.cnet.org.

Marriage Resource

24 West Street, Wimborne, Dorset, BH21 1JS
Tel: 01202 849000; Fax: 01202 849934
E-mail: marriage@netcomuk.co.uk

Good News Family Care

Charis House
Hardwick Square East, Buxton, Derbyshire, SK17 6PT
Tel: 01298 24761
http://www.gnfc.org.uk/contact.html
This site contains many useful web page links.

In the USA contact:

Focus On the Family

http://www.family.org/

Christian Family Movement

http://www.cfm.org

Index of Family Sites

http://www.cgcic.com/family+individual.htm

And my God will supply every need of yours according to his riches in glory in Christ Jesus.
Philippians 4:19

CHAPTER 8

Living within a budget

A man rubbed the palms of his hands and gleefully announced to his friends at the pub, 'I have now borrowed enough money to pay off all of my debts! The drinks are on me!'

The sad thing about this fellow is he actually thought he had solved his problem. In fact, his problem is about to become worse. First of all, the loan he took out may well have paid off his many smaller debts, but what about the interest rate of the large new loan? Even if the rate is relatively low, his new debt is more than the combined cost of the other bills he tried to clear. Moreover, shortly the repayment bills for the loan will come, and unless this man puts aside enough money each month to make the payments, he will become buried deeper in debt. Sound familiar? It should. Journalist Lisa Bachelor reports that the average UK household debt has soared by 118 per cent over the last fourteen years.[1]

The problem of debt is equally serious in the USA. Americans carry on average $5,800 in credit card debt month to month. To clear such debt would take a family 30 years and $15,000 worth of interest, according to a leading debt expert.

1. *Guardian Unlimited,* 3 September 2002
   http://www.guardian.co.uk/0,6961,,00.html

Buy now pay later

Managing money is difficult, and it is set to become more so in this day and age of instant credit. Daily we are bombarded with a powerful message in the media, on the High Streets, and even in our once staid banks and building societies. The message is always the same: Borrow and buy today, and repay later. In reality, this is an idea that leads to a vicious cycle that could destroy a family. Certainly, it is a cycle that leads people to borrow and spend with no clear idea of how they will ever repay.

This chapter is designed to get people thinking about two things. First, to begin to think about ways to live simply in order to make the most of what you have (very unpopular idea that!). Secondly, it is designed to help people think about living within a budget as a normal part of the Christian lifestyle. What this chapter isn't – indeed, what it cannot be – is a comprehensive guide to managing your money and getting out of debt. For that you will need to consult one of the excellent resources provided at the end of this chapter.

Less is more

One of the great myths of today is the belief that more money will make us happy. If mere wealth could make us happy, Princess Diana should have been the happiest woman in Britain. To be sure, having money is better than not having it. For one thing, money allows us to buy the things we need. For many men and women, financial security relieves stress, gives a sense of wellbeing, and may even act as a temporary relief to depression. God knows that people have material needs, so there is nothing inherently evil about wanting wealth. The problem begins when people fail to manage the wealth they have by not living within their means. According to the *Guardian* newspaper, the Citizens' Advice Bureau deals with over a million debt cases a year.

Christians need a plan

Money management doesn't require a special gifting. It is a skill most of us may learn – or else suffer the consequences. The only way a person truly can live free of the misery of financial constraint is to set aside time to work out how much is earned in one year, and then deduct the total expenses for the same year and live within that framework.

All expenses may be divided into the following three categories:

1. *Necessities* (all liabilities such as rent/mortgage; insurance; credit arrangements; utility debts; taxes, etc.).
2. *Luxuries* (any spending over and above necessities).
3. *Emergencies* (money set aside for unexpected costs). Ideally, there should be more income than outflow. If, as is so often the case, outflow exceeds income, adjustments must be made to balance the equation. If Christians need help in working out their budget, they should ask their minister for advice.

But money is a private matter

Jim Wallis, editor of *Sojourners* magazine, has pointed out that the theme of money and wealth dominates the Old and New Testaments. So much so, he stated, that if you took a pair of scissors and cut out every text that dealt with wealth, its distribution or its creation, and indeed, its relationship to rich and poor, your Bible would be in tatters!

God certainly is aware of the importance of our finances. But the allure of money and spending is so great that St Paul warned us not to love money: 'For the love of money is a root of all kinds of evil. Some people, eager for money, have wandered from the faith and pierced themselves with many griefs' (1 Timothy: 6:10, NIV).

Moreover, Jesus said that there would be many Christians who will actually worship money. He warned that it is impossible to serve his Father in heaven and to serve the money god. 'No one can serve two masters. Either he will hate the one and love the other, or he will be devoted to the one and despise the other. You cannot serve both God and money' (Matthew 6:24, NIV).

Sackcloth and ashes?
Far from wanting us all to live doleful lives as paupers (as if this is somehow inherently Christian), Jesus wants us to be wise in money matters. In Matthew 25:14-30, he tells a story about a shrewd businessman who leaves for a long journey. Before going, however, he calls his staff together and gives them money (called in some translations 'talents'). This is a powerful passage, so let's consider it in full from the NIV:

> To one he gave five talents of money, to another two talents, and to another one talent, each according to his ability. Then he went on his journey. The man who had received the five talents went at once and put his money to work and gained five more. So also, the one with the two talents gained two more. But the man who had received the one talent went off, dug a hole in the ground and hid his master's money.
>
> After a long time the master of those servants returned and settled accounts with them. The man who had received the five talents brought the other five. 'Master,' he said, 'you entrusted me with five talents. See, I have gained five more.'
>
> His master replied, 'Well done, good and faithful servant! You have been faithful with a few things; I will put

you in charge of many things. Come and share your master's happiness!'

The man with the two talents also came. 'Master,' he said, 'you entrusted me with two talents; see, I have gained two more.'

His master replied, 'Well done, good and faithful servant! You have been faithful with a few things; I will put you in charge of many things. Come and share your master's happiness!'

Then the man who had received the one talent came. 'Master,' he said, 'I knew that you are a hard man, harvesting where you have not sown and gathering where you have not scattered seed. So I was afraid and went out and hid your talent in the ground. See, here is what belongs to you.'

His master replied, 'You wicked, lazy servant! So you knew that I harvest where I have not sown and gather where I have not scattered seed? Well then, you should have put my money on deposit with the bankers, so that when I returned I would have received it back with interest.

'Take the talent from him and give it to the one who has the ten talents. For everyone who has will be given more, and he will have an abundance. Whoever does not have, even what he has will be taken from him. And throw that worthless servant outside, into the darkness, where there will be weeping and gnashing of teeth.'

The message is clear. God wants a return for all that he invests in us. This includes wealth.

The pursuit of wealth – the crux of the Christian faith?

Jesus knew that wealth is an important part of the Christian faith, for with it, it becomes possible to invest in people's lives and help alleviate poverty. This theme dominates the Bible. See Psalm 31 and James 1:27.

On one hand, pursuing money exposes us to a dangerous temptation; yet, on the other hand, shunning money as if it is all a distasteful and ungodly commodity is equally wrongheaded. Like the Hegelian Synthesis, Jesus shows that out of the two extremes comes a way forward for Christians to think about the way they budget their money.

All work and no play?

Many financial advisers point out that when trying to trim expenses to make income exceed outflow, a mistake many people make is to cut out all luxuries such as holidays, family entertainment, or other leisure time activities. Unless a family is facing outright bankruptcy, no family budget should be so draconian that all pleasure spending is eliminated. Most experts agree that this is why many otherwise workable schemes fail. All work and no play makes Jack (or Jill) a dull person, indeed.

In recent years, there has been a movement based on the letters WWJD – What Would Jesus Do? For many people, when they think of Jesus, they think of a rather dour little man who enjoyed going about the land nagging people who were having fun. If we are honest, few of us think of Jesus as a jolly fellow, fun to be around, and attractive to others because of his sense of humour. Yet he was.

Think about it. Crowds constantly followed Jesus. While it is true many wanted to see his miracles, one segment of the crowd simply wanted to be near a happy person. I'm talking about children.

If Jesus was the sort of mean-spirited man centuries of bad stained-glass and, even worse, biblical exposition make him out to be, then children would never have flocked to him. Parents would have had to force their children to climb up on Jesus' lap. But if Jesus was a happy man who enjoyed the pleasures of this life as much as any man, then the opposite would be true. And of course that is exactly what we see in the Gospels. Mark records that the disciples tried to shoo the children away:

> When Jesus saw this, he was indignant. He said to them, 'Let the little children come to me, and do not hinder them, for the kingdom of God belongs to such as these. I tell you the truth, anyone who will not receive the kingdom of God like a little child will never enter it.' And he took the children in his arms, put his hands on them and blessed them (Mark 10:12-16, NIV).

Jesus wants us to be like children

What does it mean to be like children when it comes to budgeting money? It means that, like little children, we must become totally dependent on God for our needs – including our financial needs. Never forget that all wealth is God's wealth. Here's what he told the disciples: Don't be like the unbelievers who make work their god. You can't please my father and be a lover of money. Therefore, don't worry about your needs. Honour God, and he will give you what you require for this life (Matthew 6:24-33). I think Jesus meant that by trusting God to meet our needs, we can get on with the business of making a difference for good in this world. Being like a child is not the same as being a child! Adults may not abdicate responsibilities, including making sure that we are living within a budget. So neither become obsessive nor overly lax when it comes to putting pleasure into the equation. Above all, make Matthew 6:33 your motto. Jesus was chiding his disciples to be different from the unbelievers who thought they had to strive to provide food, shelter, clothing, and the other things God knows we need. Jesus said to put the Lord first, and then expect to receive all that we need. 'But seek first his kingdom and his righteousness, and all these things will be added unto you.'

Jesus and luxuries

Jesus didn't stint on luxuries. He liked parties, holidays, and large gatherings where people ate and drank. Indeed, his enemies criticised him for not fasting as they did (Matthew 9:14). Others called him a glutton and a wino (Matthew 11:18-19). Moreover, his first miracle was to turn water into wine at the wedding at Cana. Towards the end of his ministry, Mary of Bethany broke open an expensive alabaster flask of balm and poured it on Jesus, much to his delight. But not everyone was pleased with Jesus' supposed excesses:

> When the disciples saw this, they were indignant. 'Why this waste?' they asked. This perfume could have been sold at a high price and the money given to the poor.
>
> Aware of this, Jesus said to them, 'Why are you bothering this woman? She has done a beautiful thing to me. The poor you will always have with you, but you will not always have me. When she poured this perfume on my body, she did it to prepare me for burial. I tell you the truth, wherever this gospel is preached throughout the world, what she has done will also be told, in memory of her' (Matthew 26:8-13, NIV).

A budget that is tough on waste but generous on people

Two immediate impressions spring to mind when it comes to working out a budget. First, income must exceed outflow. Second, the budget must be people-centred. My own family budget has always included putting money aside to feed and entertain people in our home. Years ago, when my wife and I were students living in one room and cooking on a single electric burner, we welcomed scores of people who were alone, friendless, or simply at a loose end. Our combined income in those days was hardly more than enough to cover our rent and food. Nevertheless, we believed that when you put people first, God blesses the little and makes it go a long way, very much like the cruise of oil that refused to be spent, thereby keeping Elijah, the widow, and her son alive during drought at Zarephath (1 Kings 17:14-16).

I'm a fool

I can recall a time when I was underemployed and money was a serious problem. It was around the time the National Lottery had been introduced to the UK.

Although I never played the lottery, I recall thinking that it could be that God wanted me to play as a way to bless me. As I struggled with the temptation, I wrote the following essay. Perhaps if you are ambivalent about Christians playing the Lottery, it may help you.

On Monday, I thought I was losing my mind. It began when the man from the garage rang to say the clutch would cost two hundred pounds. Two hundred quid! I was still shaking when I put the kettle on. Then when I went to the cupboard, there was no coffee, so I had to settle for a cup of blackcurrant with my two-year old son, Michael.

Later on the radio, some guy was going on about the benefits of walking. He said a brisk walk's just the thing when you're stressed out. My mind went back to the car in the garage. I thought about my overdraft, plus the red letter I'd had from the gas board. *The foundation of my life is rotting*, I thought. Instead of worrying about money, I decided to take Michael for a walk.

In a shop window on Clarence Avenue, I noticed a handwritten sign: *It could be you! 30 million to be had. Buy a lottery ticket today.*

I rubbed the three-day-old stubble on my chin. Just last week I read about that cab driver up in Scunthorpe who won a million playing the lottery. I slipped my hand into my pocket and fingered a folded five-pound note.

Now the odds of me winning big in the lottery are – what, 25 million to one? But, I mean, *someone* has to win, right? And if I won, not only could I pay for the car repair, but I could visit my family in the States, pay off all my bills, stand my mates a pint at the local – and I'd still have hundreds of thousands left over. Boy, I could get used to that idea.

That's when my conscience pricked me. The fiver in my pocket was meant for food, not lottery tickets. 'Come on, Michael, my lad,' I said. 'Let's go to the swings.'

Michael was laughing and calling, 'Higher!' as I pushed him. But I couldn't get the lottery off my mind. You hear about people who win big cash prizes: they pack in their jobs; they buy expensive cars and move into fancy houses. Now me? If I won, I wouldn't change a thing about my life. Not significantly. Not really.

By the way, did you know that a percentage of the lottery takings goes to charity? And an article in the *Daily Mail* said that 3000 new jobs could be created through the Lottery. If you look at it that way, it's almost a sin not to buy a ticket or two, eh? Then I thought about the fiver in my pocket. I knew there was nothing in the house to eat and no more money would come until the end of the week.

Still, a lottery ticket's an investment, isn't it? I mean, compared to a loaf of bread or a can of beans – here today, gone tomorrow. A winning lottery ticket's something that keeps on giving.

My mind was made up. Ignoring Michael's wailing, I dragged him back up Clarence Avenue. But when I reached the shop, something odd happened. No sooner had I touched the door handle, the words of an old poem called 'Richard Corey' came floating back to me from my high school days. Do you know it? It's about a rich young chap who had everything he ever wanted – women, booze, cash – everything. He hadn't a care in the world. Then one day he went home and put a bullet through his head. Maybe winning big wouldn't solve all my problems after all. I shuddered and let go of the handle.

What's come over me? I wondered. Try as I might, I couldn't make myself go into that shop. Feeling like a chump, I turned on my heel and marched Michael back down Clarence Avenue.

Steady man, a little voice piped up in my head. *Let's be logical about this. Have you ever considered all the good you could do with that money when you win the lottery?*

I thought about that for a moment. If I won, why I could support Oxfam, Cancer Research – *That's right, purred the voice. You could even drop five thousand into the church collection next Sunday. Just imagine what the vicar would say!*

Next thing I know, I'm turned around walking back up Clarence Avenue with Michael in tow for the third time that morning. *Well done*, the voice crooned. *And won't your pals be green when they find out you won all that lovely cash!* Then the jig was up. I recognised that voice. 'Oh no you don't,' I said aloud. 'You're the voice who talked me into parking illegally on double yellow lines outside Michael's play group last month. That lark cost me fifty pounds!' Michael craned his neck to see who I was talking to. 'Now you want me to spend my last five pounds on gambling!'

Not a bit of it, the voice protested. *Anyway, life's a gamble. And if your number comes up, all your problems will be solved.* 'No!' I said. 'I won't do it.' *Here, look at your son there. He has a hole in his shoe. He could do with a new winter coat. Don't be a fool. Buy a ticket!*

Reluctantly, I fished the cash out of my pocket and went back to the shop. This time the door swung wide open and Michael and I walked inside. There was a queue of people waiting to buy lottery tickets. As I looked them over, I couldn't help but notice their eyes. There I could see expectancy, need, happiness; there was fear, anxiety, frustration – even confidence. For all that, something was missing. But what? Then it hit me: There was no faith in their eyes. I suppose there never is when you gamble.

By now some of the people in the queue were staring back at me. I wondered what they saw in *my* eyes. *Well, what're you waiting for?* The voice goaded. *Get into the line. It could be you!* Squirming a little, I took the money and stepped up to the counter. 'What'll it be?' asked the man. For a full second or two, our eyes met and I said nothing. Then I murmured, 'A tin of baked beans and a loaf of bread, please.'

Putting the change in my pocket, I took Michael's hand and tugged him out onto the street. As the door banged behind us, I distinctly heard someone whisper, *You're a fool!*

Time to act

This chapter is titled 'Living within a budget'. I have tried to show that God values the abundant lifestyle as much as

124

he values anything else – provided we are living within our means. Many of us have the need to live within a budget, but owing to pressures, including the subtle manipulation of the mass media, we fail to live within a proper budget. (Could this be why our debt rates are so high?)

Why not take time to think about your attitudes toward your money. After reading this chapter, do you agree that God wants us to enjoy life, yet live within our means? If yes, how may this be done?

Do you agree that our friends and neighbours will take notice as we seem to enjoy the good life, yet are not living beyond our means? If yes, what might this say to them about our Christian faith?

Real world application

If you are in debt and you want to be solvent once again, have a look at some of the material below, and see if any of it may be helpful to you. Remember, God wants you to live life fully and abundantly, but to honour God you must evaluate how you spend your money, and, if need be, make changes to live within your means.

Finally, every Christian alive today has been commissioned by Jesus to present the Gospel. People will be drawn to Jesus when they see you living the abundant Christian lifestyle. Remember: As a Christian, you are approved for blessings that a non-believer is not.

Financial helplines

National Debtline 0808 8084000
Debt Helpline 0800 138 1111
Scottish Debtline 0800 138 3328
Student Debtline 0800 328 1818.

Citizens' Advice Bureaux

There are nearly 800 Citizens' Advice Bureaux in England, Wales, Scotland and Northern Ireland where you can get advice on such subjects as:

- Consumer rights
- The law
- Family and personal problems
- Benefits/social security
- Employment
- Money
- Discrimination
- Immigration
- Housing
- Utilities
- Local Information

See your local telephone directory or Yellow Pages for your nearest bureau.

Additional reading

Escaping from Debt, Keith Tondeur
Published by: Sovereign World, 1999 (1852402350)

Financial Tips for the Family, Keith Tondeur
Published by: Hodder & Stoughton, 1997

In the USA

Log on to the Focus on the Family website at:
http://www.family.org/
and use the Focus on the Family search tool by keying in DEBT.

Greater love has no man than this,
that a man lay down his life for his friends.
John 15:13

CHAPTER 9

Choosing friends

Someone once said that chocolate is proof that God loves us and wants us to be happy. I agree. And the same may be said about friends. However, we must choose our friends carefully, or else suffer the consequences. Essayist Alexander Pope suggests that friends may be our guides, even our philosophers. Put another way, the people we pick to be our friends invariably will influence our lifestyle choices for better or worse.

Our children's friends

Many people will recall 20 April 1999: Two rampaging schoolmates armed with high-powered weapons killed 13 Columbine High School students in the USA. One student was 18-year-old Cassie Bernall. Seconds before her death Cassie was taunted about her Christian faith by one of the gunmen. Asking her if she believed in God, Cassie said simply, 'Yes.' That was the last word she spoke before she was executed. Her terrified classmates huddled beneath scattered desks and listened as the boy laughed and pulled the trigger. In her book *She Said Yes*, Misty Bernall writes about how her daughter Cassie's confession of faith changed many lives for the better. The national media picked up on Cassie's faith, too. The Baltimore *Sun* proclaimed that

Cassie Bernall confronted Christianity's ultimate question. And her decision to honour God has made her 'a powerful symbol of faith'.[1]

Cassie was brought up by her parents Misty and Brad to call Jesus her Lord and Saviour. What many people don't know is that because of intense peer pressure, Cassie didn't always live a Christian lifestyle. According to Misty, in her early teens, Cassie rejected the family's Christian values in favour of the opinions and attitudes of school friends. Cassie's friends were rebellious, secretive, and delinquent. The result was that almost overnight before her family's horrified eyes, Cassie changed from being a loving, open, vibrant person into a sullen stranger. Many parents face this situation every day. Some take steps to win their child back. Other let things stand as they are, hoping that their child will return to her former self one day.

Conventional wisdom suggests that for teens to reject their parents' values is normal, even healthy. But beware of conventional wisdom. The Bible offers this *unconventional* wisdom: 'Children, obey your parents in the Lord, for this is right. "Honour your father and mother" (this is the first commandment with a promise), "that it may be well with you and that you may live long on the earth"' (Ephesians 6:1-3). And 'Fathers, do not provoke your children to anger, but bring them up in the discipline and instruction of the Lord' (Ephesians 6:4). This counsel is at odds with the child-centred approach to parenting that may be paraphrased: *Parents, let your kids do their own thing. You won't be able to stop them anyway.*

---

1. From the foreword of *She Said Yes*, Misty Bernall (Pocket Books: London, 1999).

Of course, kids must have space to experiment with their peer group, and when they make new friends, parents must avoid making snap judgements. Spend time getting to know your children's friends. If they seem a little immature, imagine a sign over their head that reads: *Under Construction.*

Children ought to be free to choose their own friends. However, if the friends they choose turn out to be a bad influence, because they are experimenting with drugs, or alcohol, or premarital sex, then parents must separate their sons and daughters from those friends. To do otherwise is to abdicate our parental responsibility before God.

Keep in mind, when young people make friends, it is said they are trying to find out where they fit into the world. In fact, they are really seeking one thing – acceptance. Just as nature abhors a vacuum, teens abhor feeling left out. If parents are not modelling a Christian lifestyle, if they are putting careers first or are living selfish lives that treat children as second-class members of the family, moreover, if parents are not meeting their children's deep need to feel valued, then teens will naturally drift into any group that will accept them.

Some child psychologists argue that if children rebel, parents shouldn't automatically blame the children's peers. It is likely the problem is in the home itself. I have a lot of time for this point. When parents invest a great deal of time in their children, making them feel part of the family, and making family life structured, fun and interesting, then the children may be trusted to make the right decisions when the time comes.

Mary (not her real name), age seventeen, lives in a town in Suffolk with her two younger sisters and parents. Her mum and dad brought up the children to live a Christian lifestyle. From her infancy, they attended weekly church services as a family and held regular family devotions. Friday nights the family members eat pizza together, play games, read stories aloud, or watch videos. Mary's parents also keep regularly scheduled dates with each child, spending part of a weekend doing whatever the child wants to do.

At age sixteen, Mary began to branch out from her family. She joined a youth group that meets once a week across town. She has also gone alone on sailing holidays as well as retreats and camps. Mary told me this story.

'When I turned 13, I was allowed to spend an hour in the town centre with my school friends. I was excited about this as my younger sisters were not allowed to do this. One afternoon I was introduced to a new set of acquaintances – friends of my school friends – who I didn't know well.

'One of the new girls came up to me and said in front of all the others, "You look older than the rest of us. You can go into the shop and buy our cigarettes." I was stunned as I looked around at the other girls. I knew that if I said no, I would look pretty bad. But I also knew buying cigarettes wasn't something my father would like me to do. I replied, "No, I'm not going to do that." When I saw my friends were disappointed, I decided that I would rather be at home. So I left them standing there in the square.'

Mary's father takes up the story. 'I was working at home that day. When I saw Mary come home early, I didn't say anything to her. But I noticed she was quiet. The first opportunity I had, I invited her to come into my study and talk about what she had done in the town centre. I listened as she told me of the cigarette incident.

'When she was finished, I hugged her and said that

she had done the right thing. Because I myself hadn't been brought up in a Christian home, I admitted to her that if the same thing had happened to me when I was her age, I would have been flattered that someone thought I looked older.

'I added that I probably would have pushed the boundaries and gone into the shop to try to buy the cigarettes. And because I lived in a small town, I probably would have been recognised by the shopkeeper, who doubtless would have rung my home and told my parents what I had done. So I would have been in trouble – and for what? For some kids who didn't really care anything about me as a person. They just wanted to use me. Mary laughed when I said, "If I had been as sharp as you are at that age, I'd be awesome today."'

Our friends

Adults are no different when it comes to being influenced by friends. Only with adults, peer pressure is less obvious, though equally pernicious.

Over long years of association with our friends, their values gradually, almost imperceptibly, rub off on us. If we associate with godly people, their influence will be for our betterment. But if we keep company with ungodly people, we will be transformed for the worse. This is why the apostle Paul warns:

> Do not be yoked together with unbelievers. For what do righteousness and wickedness have in common? Or what fellowship can light have with darkness?
> (2 Corinthians 6:14).

Many have taken this to mean Christians must physically leave the world by entering monasteries or living as holy hermits. While this may be perfectly natural for certain personality types, or for people with a particular calling on their lives, for most of us, it is an impractical and even unwise thing to do. I think Paul is simply saying keep good company. The story of Christian apologist C. S. Lewis' conversion is a good illustration of the value of having good companions.

Belfast-born Lewis had been an atheist since his school days. His only Christian friend was Arthur Greeves, whom he left behind when he went to boarding school in England. Although they saw very little of each other, Lewis and Greeves carried on a life-long correspondence by post after Lewis went up to Oxford where Lewis wrote his first two books, *Dymer* and *Spirits* in *Bondage*. Both were profoundly depressing and atheistic works.

From the nature and tone of the letters, I'm certain Greeves exerted little influence over his gifted and talented friend, although he certainly prayed fervently for Lewis' conversion. Perhaps his prayers were answered. In the late 1920s, when Lewis had become a fellow at Magdalen College, he had befriended J. R. R. Tolkien, Hugo Dyson, and Nevill Coghill – three committed Christians.

Lewis' memoirs show that he found it hard to believe that his new friends could be both competent scholars as well as believers. Piqued by their faith, he first argued with them; later he read the books they suggested he read; and eventually, he found his atheism fading, until he became a deist – a believer in God. After many hours in lively discussions, especially with Tolkien and Dyson, Lewis gave his life to Christ in September 1931 while on his way to Whipsnade Zoo. He joyfully wrote to Arthur Greeves that he had passed from merely believing in God to definitely believing in Christ.[1]

---

1. Roger Lancelyn Green and Walter Hooper, *C. S. Lewis – A Biography* (Souvenir Press: London, 1988), p. 116.

Never one to do anything by halves, the very next book Lewis wrote was entitled, *The Pilgrim's Regress* (1933), an allegorical apology for Christianity in which his vast intellect establishes that Jesus Christ was, indeed, the living Son of God – a belief from which C. S. Lewis never wavered from the day of his conversion.[1]

Later in life, Lewis' faith was further moulded by a close group of Christian friends – writers and thinkers all – who went by the name of the Inklings. They not only built up Lewis' faith, but they also were there for him during his profound grief following the death of his American wife, Joy Davidman Gresham. Clearly, then, it could be argued that his friends greatly inspired and supported Lewis.

What would have happened, however, if up at Oxford, Lewis had chosen friends such as George Bernard Shaw, Aldous Huxley, D. H. Lawrence and Bertrand Russell – brilliant men like Tolkien and Dyson – but atheists to a man? Again, their influence would have rubbed off on him, and no doubt Lewis would have used his gifts to preach pessimism and despair as he had done in *Dymer* and *Spirits in Bondage*.

It's very likely he would have mocked Christianity, as did every atheist thinker in the twentieth century. Instead, C. S. Lewis was dubbed by *Time* magazine as the 'Apostle to the Sceptics' because of his gift for writing essays and books that converted agnostics and atheists. Lewis died quietly in his bedroom in suburban Oxford on 23 November 1963,

---

1. Regrettably, the film *Shadowlands* portrays Lewis as having lost his faith in God following the death of his American wife, Joy Davidman Gresham. Nothing could be further from the truth. One only has to read his final book, *Letters to Malcolm Chiefly on Prayer* to see that his faith was robust right up to his death.

just a few days short of his sixty-fourth birthday. But his books on Christian apologetics continue to influence millions all around the world.

As did C. S. Lewis, by feeding off the faith and depending on the support of a close circle of Christian friends, we can become agents of change in the lives of our other friends who don't happen to be Christians. We can be stretched and forced to grow in ways that we might not otherwise.

His letters and diaries show that Lewis befriended a wide variety of people – from believers to unbelievers – but his inner circle were committed Christians – Tolkien (Catholic), Dyson (Church of England), and Greeves (Nonconformist).

What a friend we have in Jesus

Jesus had friends – men and women whom he could influence, and who, undoubtedly, influenced him. I'll develop this latter thought a little later. First, though, I want to comment on the humanity of Jesus, for as the creeds state, he was true God, and he was also true man. This means Jesus had human emotions, needs and weaknesses just like you and me. Consider this passage: 'For we have not a high priest who is unable to sympathise with our weaknesses, but one who in *every respect* (italics mine) has been tempted as we are, yet without sin' (Hebrews 4:15).

If I'm reading this passage correctly, the same things that tempt us tempted Jesus. He had to overcome pride, greed, gluttony, anger, hatred, and selfishness. I imagine he may even have been tempted sexually by some of the women that he met in his earthly ministry. Many people may be offended by the thought of Jesus lusting over a woman.

But Jesus was a man. And this is what men are capable of doing.[1]

A few years ago religious groups criticised film director Martin Scorsese after he made *The Last Temptation of Christ*, a film that dealt with this very subject. From all accounts, it wasn't a terribly well-made film. Briefly, in it Jesus fantasises about making love to Mary Magdalene. In the end, Jesus rejects the idea. To say the least, Scorsese's highly subjective interpretation of Jesus' life was rife with historical inaccuracies, but the one point in the film that was correct is that while Jesus may have imagined having sexual intercourse with Mary, he never acted on the biological urge. In this, Scorsese was spot on – Jesus was tempted, but he never sinned (2 Corinthians 5:21; 1 Peter 2:22; Isaiah 53:9, etc.). So how did Jesus the man manage to resist temptation? Four ways: 1. Knowing scripture; 2. Making time for daily prayer; 3. Obeying his father in heaven; and 4. By keeping good company. I'll develop numbers one through three first.

1. *Knowing Scripture.* Early on in Jesus' ministry, he was prompted by the Holy Spirit to enter the punishing

---

1. The fact is, illicit sex probably wasn't as much of a temptation for Jesus as it is for us. For centuries, sex was considered to be a gift for one man and one woman to enjoy within the confines of marriage, chiefly for the procreation of offspring. In relatively recent years people like Sigmund Freud, Margaret Sanger, and Alfred Kinsey have 'liberated' sex from these narrow confines. One by one every sexual taboo has been eliminated. Today, you can't walk down a High Street in our nation without having to run the gamut of overt sexual images. One advertising executive summed it up succinctly: *Sex Sells*. Our culture may rightly be called sex crazed. For a fuller discussion of this matter, see 'Salvation Through Sex', Ch. 25, *How Now Shall We Live?*, Charles Colson and Nancy Pearcey (Marshall Pickering, 1999).

wastelands near Jerusalem. The story in Matthew 4:1-11 is well known. After Jesus endured forty days of wind, weather, wild animals, and intense hunger and thirst, Satan visits Jesus. Seeing that Jesus was at the lowest possible ebb humanly speaking, the devil, a master at exploiting human need, appealed to his physical and emotional necessities. Satan even quoted Psalms to tempt Jesus to sin. 'Then the devil took him to the holy city, and set him on the pinnacle of the temple, and said to him, "If you are the Son of God, throw yourself down; for it is written, 'He will give his angels charge of you,' and 'On their hands they will bear you up, lest you strike your foot against a stone'"' [Psalm 91:11-12] (Matthew 4:5-6).

In the end, Jesus proved he knew the Old Testament better than the devil, for he counters the satanic deception with an accurate reading of scripture: 'Then Jesus said to him, "Be gone, Satan! For it is written 'You shall worship the Lord your God and him only shall you serve'"' [Deuteronomy 6:13]. Then the devil left him, and behold, angels came and ministered to him' (Matthew 4:10-11).

Nowhere else in the Bible is it made more clear that Satan knows the scriptures inside out, and that he is not above using God's Word to fool Christians who don't know their Bibles. As Alexander Pope said, 'A little knowledge is a dangerous thing!' But if we know our Bibles, which is a part of living the Christian lifestyle, we, too, may be imitators of Christ, and thereby overcome the compelling temptation to sin. While none of us will ever be sinless as Jesus was, we have this promise in James: 'Resist the devil and he shall flee' (James 4:7).

2. *Making time for daily prayer*. Jesus managed to overcome temptation through intense prayer. 'In the days of

his flesh, Jesus offered up prayers and supplications, with loud cries and tears, to him who was able to save him from death, and he was heard for his godly fear' (Hebrews 5:7). And 'Very early in the morning, while it was still dark, Jesus got up, left the house and went off to a solitary place, where he prayed' (Mark 1:35, NIV). If Jesus, who was the very Son of God, needed to rise early to pray each day, how can we, who are sinners, justify not doing the same?

3. *Obeying his father in heaven.* Jesus overcame temptation through complete obedience to God. On the Thursday night that Jesus was betrayed by Judas Iscariot, he invited his friends to join him in prayer in the Garden of Gethsemane. When the apostles had fallen asleep, Jesus went to be alone and came under a monstrous spiritual attack. 'And taking with him Peter and the two sons of Zebedee [note he took friends with him!] he began to be sorrowful and troubled . . . he fell on his face and prayed, "My Father, if it be possible, let this cup pass from me [a very normal prayer spoken out of human frailty, for who in his right mind wants to suffer? But notice how Jesus submits his will to his father's]; nevertheless, *not as I will, but as thou wilt*"' (Matthew 26:37-40 – italics mine).
So these three elements – Knowing scripture; making time for daily prayer; and obeying his Father in heaven, kept Jesus from giving in to temptation. Having said that, I would suggest that the fourth element – keeping good company – greatly helped Jesus maintain consistency in his lifestyle.

Qualities our friends should possess

I believe it is important to have a wide circle of friends from many walks of life and Christian denominations.

Jesus certainly did. Ideally, you should be able to identify one or more of their characteristics in the people with whom you are most closely associated.[1]

It's worthwhile briefly to examine a few of Jesus' closest friends' characteristics for the sake of helping us to see that we need a broad spectrum of Christian to stretch us emotionally, intellectually, and philosophically. Although I am taking a good deal of artistic licence here, I think I give an accurate description of each friend, including their denominations. In any case, these are some of Jesus' closest friends. Note their personality types and churchmanship.

Peter: Older, bold, and passionate. On fire for God and capable of inspiring others to the same heights and higher. Assertive. *Pentecostal.*

John: Younger, impressible, and zealous to follow God. In need of input and guidance from older, wiser Christians. Affirming. *Baptist.*

Thomas: Intellectual, cautious, and unwilling to suffer fools lightly. Objective. *Anglican.*

Mary Magdalene: Experienced, vulnerable, needing to be loved. Yet able to offer advice to less experienced Christians about the dangers and pitfalls of life. *Catholic.*

Martha: Earthy, practical, and skilled in hospitality. A mentor. *Methodist.*

---

1. I long for the day when Catholics and Protestants will stop focusing on their differences and concentrate on our many similarities. As British evangelical J. I. Packer and American theologian and writer Fr Richard John Neuhaus said at the 11th annual Wheaton College Theology Conference in April 2002, it is time for Catholics and Evangelicals to stand on the same platform and proclaim Jesus Christ as Saviour. (Reported in *Wheaton*, Summer 2002, p. 43.)

Mary the sister of Martha: Intellectual, artistic, and full of the Holy Spirit. *Vineyard.*

Joseph of Arimathea: A member of the central Jewish council, the Sanhedrin. Urbane. Wealthy. Oxbridge type. Generous (Mark 15:43). His position in Jesus' close circle proves that relations between early Christians and Jews was not as strained as we may have thought.[1] *Messianic Jew.*

Notwithstanding my guessing about their denominational affiliation, it is worthwhile to take a Bible and look more closely at the lives of the other men and women who were part of Jesus' circle of friends. If our friends do not display the same characteristics, then perhaps we should take steps to widen our circle of friends.

From here to eternity

Let's go back to Misty Bernall. Misty and Brad decided that their daughter Cassie's acutely antisocial behaviour – which included an interest in the occult and dabbling in illegal drugs – was not a passing phase. Seeing there were few Christians at her current school, they moved Cassie to a new school where there were plenty of Christians her own age. Although this made things worse at first, eventually Cassie made friends with a girl called Jamie. Jamie came from a poor home, and in every way she was a typical teen, down to the dyed hair and outlandish clothing. But instead of being rebellious and angry, she exuded warmth and was full of Christian faith. In time, as Pope had said would happen, Jamie became Cassie's guide back to Jesus. Not

1. As suggested by Richard Coggins in *Who's Who in the Bible* (B. T. Batsford: London, 1981), p. 194.

long after, Cassie chose to die a martyr's death, showing that Jamie's good influence stretched from here to eternity.

Time to act

This chapter is titled 'Choosing friends'. I have tried to show that there is a correlation between whom we associate with and how well we maintain a Christian lifestyle. For most of this century, our society has been drip-fed secular values through the media, through the schools and universities, and even through an increasing number of churches. To counter that trend, why not dare to be radical about your Christian faith? The word *radical* comes from the Latin for roots. To root yourself more deeply in the Christian faith, choose friends who will challenge you, teach you, encourage you, and, most importantly, pray with you and for you.

Real world application

Far from being advice to cut yourself off from non-Christian friends, this could be the first step to helping us draw our unbelieving friends to Jesus.

Every Christian alive today has been commissioned by Jesus to present the Gospel (Matthew 28:18-20). Take time now to answer these questions:

1. If Christianity was outlawed tomorrow, how much circumstantial evidence would exist to convict you in a court of law?

2. How much time do you actually spend sharing your faith with unchurched friends?

3. How many of your closest friends are committed Christians?

4. How important do you think it is to have committed Christians as your closest friends?

5. How many of your friends come from denominations other than your own?

As Alexander Pope wrote – friends may be our guides, even our philosophers.

Try to make friends who share your Christian values. Spend as much time with these people as you can. You will begin to adapt their standards, and that can only enhance your Christian lifestyle. When a fire is burning, all the coals are cherry-coloured and radiating heat. But if one rolls away from the pyramid of blazing fuel, that coal soon cools and becomes an ash coloured lump. Like solid fuel you need the company of other coals to maximise your efficiency.

So God blessed the seventh day and hallowed it, because on it God rested from all his work which he had done in creation.
Genesis 2:3

CHAPTER 10

Enjoying a hobby

Most of us have at one time or other heard a joke that begins like this: 'God, Jesus and Moses (or St Peter) were playing golf one day . . .' The first time I heard a joke like this, I thought it was blasphemous to suggest that the creator of the universe might play golf. Now I've changed my mind.

Be still and know I am God (Psalm 46:10)

What about you? Do you think God approves of relaxation? Of course he does. He invented leisure, and as such, relaxation is a biblical principle. In Genesis God rested from his six days of labour (Genesis 2:3). While I am not saying that God went back to work after his rest, I can tell you this – he wants us to take time off from work, and he wants us to do something to refresh ourselves on a regular basis. That's why we are instructed to observe the Sabbath later in the Law of Moses.

Even though rest and recreation are biblical ideals, most people who have been on the church scene for a while begin to realise that we Christians are reluctant to take time for fun and relaxation. This is a tendency that frequently leads to excessive stress among Christians. Perhaps the most stressed out of all within the church is the leadership and their families who are on call twenty-four hours a day, seven days a week. Psychologists and medical doctors warn us that leisure is necessary for preventing excessive stress in our lives. Christians need to listen to God. *Be still and know I am God* is telling us simply to *relax.* Jesus understood this principle very well. The Messiah lived a very stressful life. He was busy as a teacher, a healer, a counsellor, a minister – and more. Yet he found time to get away from it all. Jesus had a daily quiet time, 'And in the morning, a great while before day, he rose and went out to a lonely place, and there he prayed' (Mark 1:35). Jesus frequently spent time alone in the desert. There Jesus found the time and space to do two important things. He was able to be alone with God, and, at the same time, he made time for rest and relaxation, which allowed him to recharge his spiritual batteries. As is often the case, good theology echoes good science.

Era of leisure

For generations of Christians, hobbies were few and far between, and relaxation was solely for the wealthy. This is not so today. Technology allows every class of people to have leisure, so much so that today, we have entire industries geared towards helping people find things to do with their spare time. Yet we do not make time for recreation in the Church.

We in Northern Europe and the USA are congenital over-achievers. Ministers, lay people, teachers, indeed the entire congregations are admonished to accomplish something great for God. The result is we are too busy for our own good. While I was preparing this chapter, I clicked on to the Internet search engine Google and typed in the word *leisure*. In less than a second, I had called up 8,290,000 possible websites dedicated to *leisure*, with literally hundreds of related websites. I did the same for the words *hobby* and *hobbies*, and another 13 million websites came up on screen. That means even allowing for false hits, there are roughly three leisure-pursuits web sites for every man, woman and child in the United Kingdom. To paraphrase Churchill, never have so many had so little time to do so much.

Plenty has been written in secular magazines about capitalising on our leisure time, but not much is taught about this subject within the church. Pity. I believe that being good stewards of leisure time has become a theological question for Christians, on a par with the need to be good stewards of our money, our land, and our resources.

Towards a theology of recreation

Most Christians know that work and play are essential to cultivating a wholesome attractive faith, but how many of us actually believe that playtime is an excellent way to reach people with the Gospel? Here are some Christian leisure pursuits to get you thinking of creative ways to combine fun and leisure with telling people about Jesus.

These boots are made for preaching

Avid walker the Rev Daniel Cozens is looking for Christians who enjoy rambling. The reason? To combine hiking across Britain with going into schools, pubs, police stations and even churches to tell people about the greatest man who ever walked on the face of the earth – Jesus Christ. 'The Walk of 1000 Men evolved about 1980,' said Cozens.

'It was the result of God giving me Hebrews 11:33-34,[1] a very powerful promise made to men of faith.'

In 1991 the first of four walks became reality. That first year 500 men tramped along the Pennine Way, fulfilling this unique vision. What goes on during these extended rambles? 'Our logo is a battered walking boot. And wearing our brightly coloured sweat shirts with the Walk logo emblazoned on them, we stride across the country, straying from the beaten path to nearby towns and villages to share our Christian faith with people we meet along the way.'

According to Daniel Cozens, 'British men are generally not known for outward expressions of emotion except at set-piece events such as football matches. But the focus of a walk makes it easier for men to talk about their faith. At the end of each day's walk, we preach in a different place. Pubs are one of our many venues, because Jesus made it a point to associate with men wherever they gather. With preparation, a pub can be better than a church for making converts.

'Of course pubs aren't the only places we frequent. Working closely with the local churches, we visit shopping precincts, clubs, schools and homes. We do door-to-door visitation, street evangelism, and sketch boards. Anything that reaches people where they live,' Cozens said.

As of January 2003, there have been seven walk missions overseen by Through Faith Missions. The starting vision was to take 1000 men down the Pennine Way in 1991. Since then similar walks have taken place in Cornwall

1. . . . who through faith conquered kingdoms, administered justice, and gained what was promised; who shut the mouths of lions, quenched the fury of the flames, and escaped the edge of the sword; whose weakness was turned to strength; and who became powerful in battle and routed foreign armies (NIV).

(1993), Ulster (1995), Offa's Dyke (1996), Kent (1999), the Isle of Man (2000) and the Isle of Wight (2001).

The walks are ecumenical, embracing a wide range of Christian denominations in a specific geographical area. Although there is a strong Church of England representation, groups include Roman Catholics, Methodists, Baptists, the United Reformed Church and the Salvation Army. Don't let the title, The Walk of 1000 *Men* fool you. The mission is not a bastion of male supremacy. Cozens stresses that women minister alongside the men. 'Women are involved in all of our mission. Basically the men do the walking, but men and women share in the evangelism. It seems to be a good combination as women are more outgoing than men when it comes to talking about their faith.'

Essentially, the walks combine outdoor recreation with the love of God. By all accounts, The Walk of 1000 Men has been a success.

Consider these statistics:

In **1991**, 500 men walked the Pennine Way. Working in conjunction with 174 local churches, the men visited 750 pubs where they were invited to preach the gospel. At the end of their three-week trek, 600 people accepted Jesus Christ as their Lord and Saviour.

In **1993**, 1000 walkers visited 1000 participating Cornish pubs over a six-week period. A total of 400 local churches joined the walkers in the outreach. More than 13,000 people asked for the tract, *Knowing God Personally*, a helpful booklet that explains how to find salvation through faith in Jesus Christ. In the end, 1100 individuals made public professions of faith as a result of the Cornwall walk.

In **1995**, 702 walkers called in at 600 Ulster pubs, working in conjunction with 350 Irish churches. This prompted Prime Minister John Major to send a personal letter in support of the walkers. According to Mr Major, '. . . the walk seeks to promote (peace) between man and God and I wish all of those concerned well in their endeavours. I understand that The Walk has generated a lot of interest in Northern Ireland and also further afield.'

In **1996**, 648 walkers tramped the length of Offa's Dyke. Along the way, 800 publicans invited the walkers to preach in their premises. More than 500 people responded with the help of 300 local churches.

In **1999** teams consisting of approximately 1028 walkers crossed Kent preaching, teaching, and laughing in towns, suburbs, and villages. Walk Kent teams led evangelistic missions in schools. They were booked by over 400 churches to conduct a total of 110 four-day or eight-day missions during the four-week walk. In one village alone, walkers visited 1500 homes

Daniel Cozens said of the **2001** Isle of Wight walk, 'It was a very sweet and successful mission.' I asked Cozens what happens after commitments are made. 'Follow-up occurs straightaway because we move in teams. As soon as the advance team move on in their walk, a back-up team come in to ensure that people who have made a decision to follow Christ receive proper aftercare.'

What sort of aftercare is laid on? 'We try to link new converts with existing nurture groups which are a part of the local churches' mission. Many first-time converts enter Alpha groups,[1] and we know that a high percentage have

1. For more information about Alpha groups see Chapter 11.

remained committed. In other cases, lapsed Christians go back to their fellowships or churches.'

Many sociologists have said that Britain is a post-Christian nation with little or no interest in the Church. Does your experience bear this out? 'To suggest that Britain is not interested in Christianity is just not true. We do surveys along the way. These surveys are designed to discover people's beliefs and attitudes towards the Christian faith. For instance, we ask, *would you like to know God personally?* The *yes* response is consistently high everywhere we go. This tells us that people want to know more about God, but they won't go into a church.'

So, if the people won't go into a church to meet Jesus, Christians must go to them and introduce them to the living God, right where they play. In case you think that the people who go on these walks are out for a cheap summer holiday, think again. I wanted to know how the men live while on the trail. 'The walkers live according to the generosity of host churches while on the move. They have pocket money, but they may only spend two pounds a day on buying a drink for another man while telling him about Jesus.'

What is the hardest part of the walk? Cozens said, 'When 1000 men go out in faith into Satan's territory, they are vulnerable. But this is good because it makes you pray as Jesus prayed. You know, Jesus preached in some very dark places. 'But the really hard part of the Walk comes *afterwards.* After the mountaintop experience follows the low valley experience. Many people experience a spiritual attack after the high ends. That is to be expected, of course.'

For more information about combining rambling with the Gospel contact:

Through Faith Missions
73 High Street, Coton, Cambridge, CB3 7PL
Tel: 01954 210239

Sail on!

Perhaps walking isn't your idea of a fun pastime. Then maybe a Venturers cruise is. What is the Venturers Cruise? The Venturers Cruise is an annual sailing holiday for young people. It was started over 50 years ago and is run by a Christian trust whose members are committed to the task of demonstrating the relevance of their faith to young people within the beautiful but physically challenging environment of the Norfolk Broads.

The Venturers explore about 60 miles of the northern rivers and broads of Norfolk, from the wild exposure of Horsey Mere and Barton Broad to the quiet and picturesque villages of Horning and Irstead. Each yacht is in the charge of an experienced and competent skipper who is assisted by a first mate.

The Venturers Cruise is licensed by the Adventure Activities Licensing Authority, and is a registered charity. Each yacht has four or five crew members who sleep and eat aboard and learn the skills of handling yachts and lugsail dinghies under the careful supervision of their skippers.

Each evening the flotilla of up to 11 30-foot yachts, three motor cruisers and thirteen dinghies moors for dinner (cooked on board) and then everyone goes off to enjoy the nightly live entertainment in a local village hall. The evening includes instruction on sailing basics and water safety. A live band and a relevant talk about Christianity are also included.

Many teens coming on the Venturers Cruise have felt

their lives greatly influenced by the experience. All have become more self-reliant and many have found a faith upon which to build their adult lives. To find out more about this holiday sailing scheme contact:

T. J. Smith
Venturers Cruise Bookings Secretary
5 Raymond Avenue, South Woodford, London, E18 2HF
http://www.venturers.org.uk/

Christian Camping International (CCI) may be your cup of tea

CCI is an association of Christian centres, organisations and individuals involved in camps, holidays, conference and outdoor activity ministries.

Formed in 1986, the association provides its members with fellowship and support, and a range of other services and benefits that enable them to accomplish their work more effectively.

Christian Camping International is a world-wide alliance of Christian camping, conference and outdoor centre leaders working through fourteen national associations to develop and promote effective Christ-centred camps and conferences. Members include over 140 Christian conference centres and outdoor activity centres, 38 Christian holidays and camps organisations, and about 100 individuals, for example, church youth group leaders, who use the Christian residential experience as a significant part of their year-round ministry. All CCI members subscribe to an *evangelical statement of faith*. CCI are now registered as an umbrella body for the Criminal Records Bureau (CRB). Members should contact the office to arrange for staff to be cleared. For more information on the CCI contact:

CCI
2 Leon House, Queensway, Bletchley
Milton Keynes, MK2 2SS
Tel and Fax: 01908 641641
E-mail: office@cciuk.org

Scripture Union Holidays

Scripture Union was founded in 1867 to work with children, young people and families, and to help Christians grow in faith and service. Since then, it has continued to share the Gospel in ways which are relevant to people's needs and which give them opportunities to respond to God's love. In partnership with supporters, churches and other Christian organisations, Scripture Union has brought the message of God's love to many people over the years, encouraging a personal relationship with God through prayer, volunteering and giving.

Each year, thousands of adults and children attend Scripture Union holidays throughout England and Wales. In a unique blend of activity and relationship building, and with a steady flow of prayer and love, they help people to open their hearts and minds to God leading to their lives being changed. This recipe for evangelism brings people back year after year, growing in faith, commitment and Christian character. Holidays and missions are based on friendships so that people can glimpse the Father's love through the love of others. SU always work with the Bible, relating it to the lives of those who attend. Every year their holidays and missions bring good news to thousands of people. For more details contact:

Scripture Union
207-209 Queensway, Bletchley, Milton Keynes, MK2 2EB
Switchboard: 01908 856000

Volunteer Hotline: 0500 856789
Fax: 01908 856111
E-mail: info@scriptureunion.org.uk

Christian retreat centres

Not all people are interested in outdoor leisure pursuits. Many prefer the quiet life found in a Christian retreat centre. There are scores of excellent such places in the United Kingdom and the USA and Canada, far more than may be adequately discussed here.

If this is something that interests you, I suggest that you use an Internet search engine such as Google or Yahoo. Print the words *Christian Retreat Centre UK/USA/Canada* and you will find many places from which to choose. Conversely, purchase a copy of *Retreats 2002 – Programme and events for over 200 retreat centres.* This review contains much more than the title implies. There are excellent articles by a wide variety of contributors, from experienced retreat leaders to those going on retreat for the first time. These will be of interest whether you are familiar with retreats or just finding out what they are all about. There are book reviews and help on choosing a retreat, followed by the details of what each retreat house is offering this year. Paperback – Publisher: The Retreat Association, ISBN: 13-69870-2.

Meantime, here is just a sample of what you may expect if you decide that you'd like to cultivate the retreat habit.

The Bishop Woodford House, the Ely Diocesan Retreat and Conference Centre

Readers of Elizabeth Goudge will know that her engaging novel *The Dean's Watch* is set in the thinly disguised Cambridgeshire city of Ely. No one knows for sure on whom

Goudge based the character of the Dean; perhaps it was none other than Bishop Woodford, a much-loved mid-Victorian figure who today lends his name to the Bishop Woodford House, the Ely Diocesan Retreat and Conference Centre.

Built in 1973, the conference centre is a curious mix of modern and ancient. The main building is a comfortable and attractive purpose-built conference and retreat centre, but a sturdy Victorian chapel forms the heart of the centre.

I asked Warden Mary Russell who comes on retreat here. 'We have mostly Anglican groups, but we also have United Reformed Church groups, Quakers, Catholics, and, of course, many organisations which have no religious affiliation at all. They are people who want a clean, friendly centre to offer a small venue and some audio/visual equipment for their needs. All are welcome.'

There is no escaping the fact that this is a faith centre, and that may be a key to its success. People are looking for spiritual meaning, even in this post-Christian day in which we live. Because of that fact, the centre is fully booked most of the time. 'We are busy,' admits Mary. 'I think part of the reason for it is we are on the edge of the Church. People who feel excluded from mainstream church, going to church on Sunday, and that sort of thing, often feel happy about coming to somewhere like our retreat house because it's not quite the same as church, and it's somewhere where they can feel safe and secure.

'Although we are a post-Christian society, people are still searching for something out there, and that is something they feel they can do in a retreat house setting.'

Many groups come with their own director and they have their own programmes, but Bishop Woodford House provides its own programmes, many of which have proven to be very popular. 'This year, for example, we have a painting and prayer retreat, organised in association with the Creative Arts Retreat Movement. People can come to that for a week and do a bit of painting, and there's also prayer. We include a morning Eucharist, morning and evening prayer. There is a full-time chaplain and a full-time tutor, so the chaplain will lead the worship side, and the tutor will give input on the painting side.'

In the main house there are 32 single bedrooms, one twin, and one three-bedded family room, most with washbasin, wardrobe, and desk. Shower, bath, and toilet facilities are all close at hand, as too are drink-making facilities. Mary pointed out that guests should bring their own towels and soap.

Although it is small, it can compete with any large, commercial conference centre, offering guests a spacious conference room, a comfortable and clean lounge, a board-room, a sitting room, a well-stocked library, a reading room, a small but interesting book and gift shop, and a drinks bar. Additionally, all conference and worship rooms are located on the ground floor, as are eight bedrooms and a disabled person's toilet.

The chapel, a clean, well-lighted place, is only a few steps away from the modern foyer. In fact, the chapel was originally sited elsewhere in the city and was dismantled and lovingly rebuilt at the heart of the centre.

Mary oversees the various types of activities that go on at the centre. She was drawn to this sort of work after try-ing many other jobs. 'I like the variety of the work I do here, welcoming people, setting up the chapel services, even the more mundane things, such as sorting out the leaky taps and changing light bulbs.'

Bishop Woodford has a reputation across East Anglia for its excellent meals. 'The food is traditional family cooking, but the meats and vegetables are bought locally and freshly cooked. We don't use any pre-packaged meals. We specialise in casseroles, roast beef, roast lamb and roast pork, and steak and kidney pie. And our puddings are also freshly made – apple crumble, a chocolate floating pudding – all very good and very traditional.'

Mary didn't hesitate when I asked her if the Bishop Woodford House was a business or a ministry. 'Both,' she replied. 'We have to be a business. People pay to come and stay here, and that money goes to cover all our costs – building costs, salaries, upkeep. Running a place for so many people involves substantial costs.

'On the other hand, we welcome pilgrims of every sort. We take their spiritual needs seriously. We offer hospitality with ministry.'

Elizabeth Goodge loved Ely and considered it to be one of Britain's great secrets, overshadowed as it is by Cambridge only twenty minutes south by car or train. The retreat centre is a five-minute walk away from the majestic cathedral, long referred to as the 'Ship of the Fens' because it looms over the surrounding Fenland like a mighty ocean-going liner. The attractive town centre is also five minutes away from the house.

For more information about Bishop Woodford House, contact:

The Warden
Bishop Woodford House
Barton Road, Ely, Cambs, CB7 4DX
Tel: 01353 663039

Time to act

This chapter is titled 'Enjoying a hobby'. I want to show that God values leisure time and hobbies as much as he values time spent earning a living. Many of us have a hobby, but owing to cultural pressures, we compartmentalise our spare time from our faith. Moreover, many Christians frown on leisure time, embracing God's call to be productive, but scorning his call to enjoy leisure. (Could this be why depression and mental illness rates are high among Christians?)

Why not take time to think about your attitudes towards leisure time, hobbies, and relaxation. Here are some questions to consider. After reading this chapter, do you agree that God wants Christians to make time for leisure in our lives? Have you ever used your spiritual gifts during your leisure time? If yes, what are the best ways to combine your favourite pastimes with giving away your faith? Do you stereotype Christians who enjoy sport? Do you have any prejudices against Christians who are drawn towards the contemplative lifestyle? Have you ever tried a pastime that is different from the ones you normally enjoy?

Remember, whether you enjoy outdoor activities, or you prefer indoor hobbies and pursuits, the Christian lifestyle is about giving glory to God – even while we relax.

Real world application

Every Christian alive today has been commissioned by Jesus to present the Gospel. If you are looking for a way to spend your free time that allows you to tell others about the love of God, you have ample opportunities. While I was researching this chapter, I came across Christian organisations for artists, joggers, bikers and a host of others. The lion's share of these organisations exist in North

America and elsewhere. I think it's a shame that there aren't more Christian organisations in Britain dedicated to combining faith with favourite pastimes. Why not think about organising a Christian organisation that does just this in your area? People will be drawn to Jesus when they see you enjoying yourself while living the Christian lifestyle. As a believer, you are called to draw non-believers to Christ during your weekends, holidays, and in between times, too!

Have you heard this one?

Moses, Jesus, and another chap were out playing golf one day. Moses stepped up to the tee and drove the ball down onto the fairway, but it rolled directly towards the water hazard. Quickly Moses raised his club and the water parted, causing the ball to roll safely to the other side.

Next, Jesus strolls up to the tee and drives the ball directly towards the same water hazard. It landed in the pond but fluttered over the water. Jesus strolled out onto the pond and chipped it up onto the green.

Finally, the third person casually swipes the ball over the fence and into a nearby street. It bounces off a truck and onto the roof of a nearby shack. Next it rolls into the gutter, clatters down the downspout, and rockets out onto the fairway, and plops into the pond. Suddenly, a hungry pike jumps out of the water with the ball in his mouth. Just then, a hawk swoops and grabs the fish and flies away. As they pass over the green, the fish drops the ball directly into the hole with a neat little plunk.

Moses turned to Jesus and said, 'I *hate* playing with your dad.'

In the USA

For a comprehensive guide to Christian recreation in North America, visit:

http://www.cgck.com/Recreation.htm

or log on to Dogpile search engine and key in CHRISTIAN VACATIONS, USA.

*Do not be deceived; God is not mocked, for whatever a man
sows, that he will also reap.*
Galatians 6:7

CHAPTER 11

Entertaining ourselves and others

Someone once said that the Gospel is like manure. You have
to spread it around your garden, or it does no good. If we
are serious about introducing others to Jesus, then we need
to spread our beliefs around, much like a keen gardener. To
do this, we need to stop talking about our faith and start
living it – openly – where people can see it in action and
judge for themselves if it's for them or not. Entertaining our
friends, relatives and acquaintances in our homes is one of
the best ways I know of to demonstrate to other people
what we believe. In the New Testament, we see that entertaining people in our homes is not an option: 'Practise hospitality ungrudgingly to one another' (1 Peter 4:9).

One thing is clear to me as I study the life of Christ,
Jesus' love of hospitality was a major part of his ministry
on earth. Many parables focused on the theme of hospitality – weddings, parties, and banquets. When the prodigal
son returned home to his father, a huge entertainment was
laid on for the returning son (Luke 15:22). This particular
parable is significant because heaven is going to be a place
of great joy with plenty of entertainment. Jesus calls
heaven a banquet (Luke 14:15) and a wedding feast
(Matthew 22:8). He of all people should know, for he had
come from heaven, and he longs for us to be there with

him and even now he is readying the great party that will be given in our honour when we arrive: 'In my father's house there are many rooms; if it were not so, would I have told you that I go to prepare a place for you?' (John 14:2). Some translations use the word *mansions* instead of *rooms* in this passage. It doesn't take much imagination to figure out what people do in mansions – they invite friends over and they enjoy each other's company. Jesus was always happy to entertain guests when he had the opportunity.

Again and again, we read of his being invited into the homes of his disciples, some whom he knew well (Mary, Martha, Lazarus) and some whom he knew less well (the Pharisees who invited him to dinner in Luke 11:37-54).

Without wishing to trivialise the Last Supper, that meal was essentially a dinner party laid on by Jesus for 12 of his closest friends. The details of the evening seen in Luke 22:7-30 support my belief. That Jesus was the host of the dinner is undeniable. The preparations should be familiar to anyone who has ever hosted a large sit-down meal. Luke shows Jesus as being concerned about the smallest detail. And so he should be. Passover was the highlight of the Jewish calendar, and Jesus gave his helpers very definite instructions about the meal. He wanted everything to be just so, even down to the venue: 'So Jesus sent Peter and John . . . He said to them, "Behold, when you have entered the city, a man carrying a jar of water will meet you; follow him into the house which he enters, and tell the house-holder, 'The teacher says to you, Where is the guest room, where I am to eat the passover with my disciples?' And he will show you a large upper room furnished; there make ready." And they went, and found it as he told them; and they prepared the passover' (Luke 22:8-13).

Notice there are several clues in this passage that show the importance of this event. Peter and John are named as helping with the arrangements. This is significant. Peter would soon become the undisputed leader of the fledgling church – the 'rock' on which the church was built (Matthew 16:18), and he was to be a prime witness to the reality of Jesus' resurrection (1 Corinthians 15:5). Although it is hard to know as much about John, for many claims have been made about him, it is known that Paul considered him to be a 'pillar' of the church in Jerusalem (Galatians 2:9).[1] Clearly this was an important errand to have enlisted such men.

Next, although it seems that the apostles met a man with a jar of water who appeared as if by magic to lead the apostles to the venue, it is not mysterious at all. Jesus would have gone in person earlier to make the preliminary arrangements, securing a place to meet, even ensuring that later in the day this man would be watching out for Peter and John. That the man is carrying water makes me wonder if, as he did at Cana, Jesus had turned it into the wine used for the first communion service – but that is mere speculation. What is not speculation is that Jesus was a generous and conscientious host.

We see Jesus practising hospitality again and again. For instance, Jesus supplied nourishing food for huge crowds of hungry people in Matthew 14:17 and again in Matthew 15:34. On another occasion, the disciples had spent a long, wearisome night on the sea fishing, but catching nothing. In the morning, not only did Jesus tell them where they could fish in order to catch entire shoals of fish, he took it

1. Richard Coggins, *Who's Who in the Bible* (B. T. Batsford: London, 1981), s.v. 'John', p. 192.

upon himself to lay on something everyone truly loves – a good old-fashioned barbecue: 'When they (the disciples) got out on land, they saw a charcoal fire there, with fish lying on it and bread . . . Jesus said to them, "Come and have breakfast"' (John 21:9-12). Can't you just see it? Jesus presiding over a sumptuous barbecue. He knew that the way to reach a person's heart is – literally – through the stomach.

It isn't stated in any of the above passages I have cited, but I know that Jesus enjoyed seeing needy people respond to his largess. In this, Jesus is modelling the way in which all Christians must approach evangelism: Meet people's physical needs before you try to meet their spiritual needs.

Alpha courses

Taking a clue from Jesus, the Alpha course, a sequence of talks addressing important issues associated with the Christian faith, begins with a supper. The meal is served at the beginning of each session, giving people a chance to get to know each other better. After each talk the partici-pants are divided into small groups to discuss a designated topic. Far from being a boring lecture, guests ask questions and express their own opinions. This stimulates further discussion and honest reflection on key issues.

Talk titles

- Christianity: Boring, Untrue and Irrelevant?
- Who is Jesus?
- Why did Jesus die?
- How can I be sure of my faith?
- Why and how should I read the Bible?

- Why and how should I pray?
- How does God guide us?
- Who is the Holy Spirit?
- What does the Holy Spirit do?
- How can I be filled with the Holy Spirit?
- How can I make the most of the rest of my life?
- How can I resist evil?
- Why and how should I tell others?
- Does God heal today?
- What about the Church?

A Mori poll stated that eight million people now know of the Alpha courses,[1] and as any marketing executive will tell you, product recognition is the first step to a successful exchanging of ideas.

For more information on the Alpha courses, contact:

Alpha registrar
Alpha International
Holy Trinity Brompton
Brompton Road
London, SW7 1JA
http://alphacourse.org/welcome/index.htm

The power of fine art

Fine art is a great way to open people's minds to God's plan for order and goodness in a seemingly disordered and evil world. A pet peeve of mine is the way modern-day Christians have relinquished fine art to the secularist. For

---

1. 'Eight million adults in UK know of Alpha', *Alpha News* (UK edition), November 2002-February 2003, No. 29, p. 1.

centuries Christians dominated the arts, setting trends, pushing the bounds, and doing all of this in a way that honoured God. I don't think Christians will ever dominate the art world again, but we can certainly contribute to it.

You don't need to join an Alpha group in order to entertain in your own home. Combining a tasty meal with home entertainment could be the best way to introduce your beliefs or some aspect of the Christian faith to unbelieving neighbours or friends. Let me say first of all, guests should be aware that discussing faith is to be part of the evening's entertainment.

Following a tasty meal, your time together could be invigorated with selections of your favourite music. Michael Card, Sheila Walsh, or Kevin Max (of DC Talk) express Christian ideas in exciting and accessible ways; moreover, Christians often overlook classical music as a wonderful means of expressing something meaningful to modern people about faith matters.

I have a Christian friend who paints. When he invites people into his home, his unique paintings often launch a discussion of what inspires him, namely Jesus. This often leads to talking about the work done by Christian artists today and in previous generations.[1]

---

1. The late Professor H. R. Rookmaaker of the Free University of Amsterdam argues in his book, *The Creative Gift – The Arts and the Christian Life* (IVP: Leicester, 1981), that the world is desperately short of believers who will use their creative gifts outside of the context of the church. He feels that Christians are morally obliged to be involved in the arts because of the power of art to communicate meaning and truth. I fully support this position. I wonder why British theological colleges do not include course work in art and humanities to better prepare tomorrow's ministers and priests for their vocations.

Imitation of Christ

Edith Schaeffer, co-founder of l'Abri Fellowship[1] and author of *Common Sense Christian Living*, adds another, and I think very Christ-like, dimension to hospitality evangelism. She sees entertaining guests as a way to serve – and by so doing, she is imitating Jesus. Each time she cooks and serves a meal (or prepares a cup of coffee or tea, makes up a bed, climbs up a ladder to the loft for extra blankets, etc.) for a guest, she silently thanks God for this privilege which she knows is good for her soul. Edith is a trim and attractive 70-something. How does she manage to stay that way? Edith admits that running up and down stairs, cutting vegetables, mixing dough and preparing large meals and serving them is a form of aerobic exercise, and that has helped to keep her fit.[2]

Entertainment is more than hospitality

We are what we eat, so says the philosopher. This means that we must be aware that what we take into our mind affects who and what we are. Jesus put it this way: 'The eye is the lamp of the body. So if your eye is sound, your whole body will be full of light, but if your eye is not sound, your whole body will be full of darkness. If then the light in you is darkness, how great is the darkness!' (Matthew 6:22-23).

1. L'Abri (The Shelter) is a Christian community that is set up to help people to learn how to combine their faith with their lifestyle. There are branches in Switzerland, the USA and in England. To contact English L'Abri, ring: 01420 538436. In North America contact L'Abri (Massachusetts) at: 49 Lynbrook Road, Southborough, MA, tel: 508 481 6490. L'Abri (Minnesota) at: 1465 12th Avenue NE, Rochester MN, tel: 507 282 3292.

2. Edith Schaeffer, *Common Sense Christian Living* (Thomas Nelson Publishers: New York, 1983), pp. 88-89.

Since this is so, he is warning us to shun immortality in every shape or form to the best of our ability.

Garbage in garbage out

Jesus warned: 'What comes out of a man is what defiles a man. For from within, out of the heart of man, come evil thoughts, fornication, theft, murder, adultery, coveting, wickedness, deceit, licentiousness, envy, slander, pride, foolishness. All of these things come from within, and they defile a man' (Mark 7:21-23). Jesus, a master at understanding the hearts and minds of men and women, knew what most modern psychologists know today – we are profoundly affected by our environment. To simplify this, I think of the old computer maxim: 'Garbage in; garbage out.' For this reason, Christians must be very careful about what they and their family read and view by way of entertainment. This is no easy task, for what passes as acceptable entertainment these days would have been unacceptable only a mere 30 years ago.

St Paul offers this proactive advice: 'Finally brethren, whatever is true, whatever is honourable, whatever is just, whatever is pure, whatever is lovely, whatever is gracious, if there is any excellence, if there is anything worthy of praise, think about these things' (Philippians 4:8). These words have no meaning unless we follow them even when we entertain our friends or ourselves. How did you entertain yourself last night? Does it match up to this high calling? If so – *good*. If not, why not?

We've been focusing on entertaining adults up to now. Let's consider how we may entertain children. Computer and video games are the fastest growing entertainment industries for children. Yet teachers, parents, and now a growing number of health experts, are worried about children's prolonged exposure to videos and computer games.

Before the advent of the microchip entertainment industry, children spent a great deal of time out of doors, running, playing, swimming and hiking. Today, most children prefer to sit in front of video games, watch DVDs, or simply sit and send text messages to one another via e-mail or mobile phones. The situation has got so bad that NHS and North American experts warn that today's children are developing previously unheard of levels of coronary disease and disease-related obesity.[1] Since this is so, keeping your kids entertained without an electronic gadget will take imagination, a sense of adventure, and willingness to drag the entire family out of doors into the fresh air! Fortunately, this can be quite a pleasant experience for the entire family.

To begin, we need to set some ground rules: Attitude will play a large part in how successful some ideas will be. Also, age is a key factor for how successful each activity will be. Most of my suggestions are aimed at children aged 14 and younger. Having said that, the more stimulating the activity, the more older teens will want to be included.

Let's go out today

Entertaining children over a holiday or on the weekend without a schedule is like taking a long car journey without a road atlas. A sure-fire way to court disaster is to allow your children to stay in bed until they feel like getting up. If everyone is up and washed and ready for breakfast at the same time, then you will be better able to organise your

---

1. 'NHS wakes up to child obesity crisis', Jo Revill, *The Observer*, Sunday, 3 November 2002.
   http://www.observer.co.uk/politics/story/0,6903,824976,00.html

day. Keep in mind that schedules are made to be broken, and so be flexible if it means trying a novel idea, such as allowing the children to make the breakfast and serve it to you in bed.

Another novelty is deciding to have a picnic breakfast in the garden – weather permitting! If you have no garden, have a picnic breakfast in a town park. The latter idea can include an hour feeding the ducks, the pigeons, or the birds with the crumbs, and then spending another couple of hours playing rounders, cricket, football, frisbee or softball.

Remember, the picnic breakfast and the games can be scheduled for the same day throughout the summer or weekend. This may seem regimented to you as an adult, but kids are quite used to their timetables at school. To make it more interesting for the children, why not suggest they invite their playmates to join in. The more the merrier!

Turn off the TV and turn on the imagination

Nearly all children are naturally attracted to computers, cameras and tape recorders. One summer, I was in charge of a group of 15 homeless boys. My job was to look after their recreational needs each afternoon. One Saturday, I announced that we would make a film. At first, they balked. But when they saw how much fun it was, they were won over.

Most parents would run a mile at the thought of making movies. But what I'm talking about is as old as childhood itself. Let me explain. Children have been making up their own plays for generations. So, have your children write their own plays and you film them as they act them out. All that's needed is a video camera – borrow one if you don't have one – and a bit of imagination. The films can be enhanced with computer software that allows you to edit, add graphics and music. Sophisticated home videos are as easy as point and click.

The world according to Grandpa

For low-tech fun, why not make a family tree? Kids love hearing about the old days. For this project, you don't need to be a genealogist. All you need is a tape recorder and a few older relatives, and hey presto, instant family history. How I wish I had thought of doing this as a boy. I realise now that my grandparents were Victorians, and they lived through every major event of the twentieth century. Now when I see their fading photos, I have to struggle even to recall their voices, let alone the stories they told about their lives.

If you have no elderly relatives, consider inviting neighbours or members of your church to be the subject of a talking history. Chances are they would be pleased to become the focus of your family's attention. A camera can enhance the activity by putting a face to the voice. No camera? Have the children paint portraits of your elderly subjects as part of the activity.

Make your home into a DIY youth club

Adults keen to have a home-based ministry have a great opportunity to reach out to the younger generation while providing something for their own children to do. Many Christians feel that youth outreach is best left up to the professional youth worker. Youth workers are highly dedicated people who do an admirable job, but they can't reach everyone.

We have friends who live in Suffolk with their three children. Wendy and Eddie Hepper felt someone ought to do something for the bored teens in their town. One day, the opportunity presented itself through their church, the West Suffolk Vineyard Fellowship.

Despite each having a hectic schedule and all the responsibilities of raising their own children, they open their home every two weeks for an informal evening of food, fun, discussion, and entertainment. During each session they address some topic from a Christian perspective. Some weeks Wendy and Eddie talk about prayer, school, films, or more serious topics. According to 15-year-old Lizzie, 'It's a comfortable atmosphere there. Wendy and Eddie are laid back. The balance between seriousness and having a laugh is perfect. It's just a cool place to be on a Friday night.'

I asked Wendy and Eddie why they open their home to the young people. Eddie pointed out, 'We open our home because young people are so rewarding and worth investing in. Once we'd got past our obstacles of "I'm not a youth leader" and "I'm not clued up on teenage stuff", we realised that our bunch just seem to want real and honest people who might be serious or mad in equal proportions. Whilst we have a programme and lead the way, the teenagers always have plenty to say.'

Keeping youngsters happy needn't be a strain. In fact, it can be quite a pleasant experience. I'm sure you can come up with more ideas of your own. Remember that keeping teens entertained over the year will take imagination, a sense of adventure, and a willingness to experiment with all aspects of the Christian faith. Moreover, when even one adult invests time in youngsters, the children will catch the Christian faith; and like a potent germ, they will infect countless other kids with the love of God. The result will pay dividends in this life and in the one to come.

Time to act

This chapter is titled 'Entertaining ourselves and others'. I have tried to show that there is a relationship between how we entertain ourselves and others and how we live out a Christian lifestyle. For most of this century, our society has been drip-fed secular values through the media, through the government, and through our educational system. To counter that trend, dare to root yourself more deeply in the Christian faith by choosing entertainment that will challenge you, teach you, encourage you, and most importantly, help you to focus on the glory of our God.

Far from being advice to cut yourself off from the world, why not invite unbelievers whom you know to share in an evening of wholesome fun? It could be the first step to helping introduce these friends to Jesus.

Real world application

Every Christian alive today has been commissioned by Jesus to present the Gospel (Matthew 28:18-20). Take time now to answer these questions. Do not spend time puzzling over your answers. Answer instinctively. When you finish, add up the points and match them against the key at the end. On a scale of 1-3, rate the following:

1= Nil; 2 = Minimum; 3 = Maximum

1. When it comes to your evening entertainment, how seriously do you take Paul's advice to focus on '. . . whatever is true, whatever is honourable, whatever is just, whatever is pure, whatever is lovely, whatever is gracious, if there is any excellence, if there is anything worthy of praise, think about these things (Philippians 4:8)?

2. If your minister or another Christian whom you respect walked into the room while you were reading, watching

television, or surfing the Internet, would you be able to invite that person to sit with you and join in the entertainment?

3. How much time do you actually spend entertaining non-Christian friends?

4. How many of your house guests are not close friends of yours?

5. How much time do you spend talking with, reading, and playing games with your family?

6. How often do you switch off a television or radio programme (or turn the page in the Sunday papers) because the content of the material is impure?

Scores

- If you scored 14 or higher, congratulations. You are in the same percentile as Jesus. You may expect God to use the way you entertain yourself to draw others to Christ.

- If you scored between 8 and 13, this is a bad state to be in, for Jesus warns us, 'I know your works: You are neither cold nor hot. Would that you were cold or hot! So because you are lukewarm, and neither cold nor hot, I will spew you out of my mouth' (Revelation 3:15-16). If this is the case, then perhaps you need to talk things over with your family or circle of friends to see how you may begin to Christianise the way you entertain yourself.

- If you scored lower than 8, look to make a major reassessment of your Christian values. Spend as much time with Christians you admire until you become like them, including the way in which they entertain themselves and others. As you adapt their practices, you may begin to use entertainment evangelism to reach your non-Christian friends and acquaintances.

In the USA

To find out more about Alpha groups near you, log on to:

http://www.alpha.org

or call this toll-free number: 1 800 00 Alpha,

or simply use a search engine by keying in ALPHA USA.

For we are the aroma of Christ to God among those who are being saved and among those who are perishing, to one a fragrance from death to death, to the other a fragrance from life to life.
2 Corinthians 2:14-16

CHAPTER 12

Creating beauty around us

What is beauty? Good question. Loveliness, comeliness, elegance, dignity – all this defines beauty. But no two people can always agree on what gives birth to beauty. For instance, John thinks J. S. Bach's 'Passion of St Matthew' is beautiful music, but Mary finds it impossible to listen to, preferring Stravinsky's 'Rite of Spring.' Hannah, on the other hand, thinks ballet is elegant, but Bob feels that way about morris dancing. Who's right and who's wrong?

Some people say that if you give your life to Christ, you will automatically be able to agree with other Christians on what is beautiful. But that isn't true; 31 years after my conversion, I know this – wherever two or more Christians are gathered, there, too, is – *disagreement*. Be that as it may, this much is sure: each of us is created by God to express beauty, however we define it. And when we do this, we say something to the world about the God in whose image we are made (Genesis 1:26). (See Appendix B for a discussion on art and the Christian message.)

God – the author of beauty
Some say God has no interest in beauty. But I disagree.

Look at his creation. Who hasn't delighted at the sight of a green and white snowdrop, a comet, a sunset, a stalagmite, or an autumn leaf? Have you ever gazed into the night sky? Consider the beauty the Lord has put there – planets, moons, stars, and nebulae. The sublime splendour of the red, green and sapphire pinpricks of light have always fascinated humans. Consider the patterns of the constellations. The ancient Greeks imagined they were deities. The Hebrews thought differently, though. Rather than seeing the wonders of the night sky as gods, the psalmist saw this light show as God's signature. King David expressed his response like this: 'The heavens are telling out the glory of God; and the firmament proclaims his handiwork' (Psalm 19:1). A composer and lyrical poet, and so one well acquainted with the interaction of design and rhythm, David is explaining the nature of God – that is, he is a God of order and beauty. God has a history of creating precision and beauty. Someone once said that God won a prize for Norway's fjords. I can believe it.

People are beautiful, too. Leonardo da Vinci, Michelangelo, and Rembrandt found sublime beauty in the faces of even the most plain folks; the evidence is seen in the care they took to reproduce them in their sketchbooks, on canvasses, and through sculpture. An apprentice once asked Michelangelo, 'Master, why do you put as much detail into the back of your statues as the fronts? When they are placed in a niche, no one will ever see the back.' Michelangelo is said to have retorted, 'But God sees the backs!'

Further evidence of God's love of beauty can be seen in the plans he gave Solomon for the first temple.[1] Here are

---

1. For a fuller discussion on the temple, see 'Temple', *New Bible Dictionary* (IVP: Leicester, 1982).

selections from 2 Chronicles 2-3 (NIV) which epitomise God's love of beauty:

2 Chronicles 2 *Solomon describes the temple to be built*

5 The temple I am going to build will be great, because our God is greater than all other gods.

6 But who is able to build a temple for him, since the heavens, even the highest heavens, cannot contain him? Who then am I to build a temple for him, except as a place to burn sacrifices before him?

7 Send me, therefore, a man skilled to work in gold and silver, bronze and iron, and in purple, crimson and blue yarn, and experienced in the art of engraving, to work in Judah and Jerusalem with my skilled craftsmen, whom my father David provided.

8 Send me also cedar, pine and algum logs from Lebanon, for I know that your men are skilled in cutting timber there. My men shall work with yours

9 to provide me with plenty of timber, because the temple I build must be large and magnificent.

Solomon wanted only the finest building materials. He collaborated on the temple project with Hiram, king of Tyre, a celebrated artist and an architect.[1] He wrote the following letter to Solomon:

13 I am sending you Huram-Abi, a man of great skill,

14 whose mother was from Dan and whose father was from Tyre. He is trained to work in gold and silver, bronze and iron, stone and wood, and with purple and blue and crimson yarn and fine linen. He is experienced in all kinds of engraving and can execute any design given to him. He will work with your craftsmen and with those of my lord, David your father.

1. See Kings 7:13-14.

2 Chronicles 3 *Solomon builds the temple*

5 He panelled the main hall with pine and covered it with fine gold and decorated it with palm tree and chain designs.

6 He adorned the temple with precious stones. And the gold he used was gold of Parvaim.

7 He overlaid the ceiling beams, door-frames, walls and doors of the temple with gold, and he carved cherubim on the walls.

8 He built the Most Holy Place, its length corresponding to the width of the temple – twenty cubits long and twenty cubits wide. He overlaid the inside with six hundred talents of fine gold.

Notice the attention to details here. This is not mere embellishment, nor is it meant to call attention to Solomon. This is an attempt by men to imitate what they see in God's creation. Author Francis Schaeffer points out that as such, whatever humans do in imitation of God is *artificial* (for only God's handiwork is real), hence the etymological meaning of the word *art* – a derivative of artificial – means to imitate God.

9 The gold nails weighed fifty shekels. He also overlaid the upper parts with gold.

10 In the Most Holy Place he made a pair of sculptured cherubim and overlaid them with gold.

11 The total wing-span of the cherubim was twenty cubits. One wing of the first cherub was five cubits long and touched the temple wall, while its other wing, also five cubits long, touched the wing of the other cherub.

12 Similarly one wing of the second cherub was five cubits long and touched the other temple wall, and its other wing, also five cubits long, touched the wing of the first cherub.

13 The wings of these cherubim extended twenty cubits. They stood on their feet, facing the main hall.

14 He made the curtain of blue, purple and crimson yarn and fine linen, with cherubim worked into it.

15 In the front of the temple he made two pillars, which together were thirty-five cubits long, each with a capital on top measuring five cubits.

16 He made interwoven chains and put them on top of the pillars. He also made a hundred pomegranates and attached them to the chains.

2 Chronicles 4 *The temple's furnishings*

19 Solomon also made all the furnishings that were in God's temple:

the golden altar; the tables on which was the bread of the Presence;

20 the lampstands of pure gold with their lamps, to burn in front of the inner sanctuary as prescribed;

21 the gold floral work and lamps and tongs (they were solid gold);

22 the pure gold wick trimmers, sprinkling bowls, dishes and censers; and the gold doors of the temple: the inner doors to the Most Holy Place and the doors of the main hall.

Why weren't the utensils of the temple merely functional? Why were they also attractive? It's because God's nature is to produce splendour, order and beauty, even in a pot meant to hold the charred bones of burnt offerings. And it is human nature to respond to what is beautiful.

Of course, the Hebrews were not the first ancient people to create splendid temples. Archaeological records show that Egyptian, Babylonian, and Mesopotamian temples were unsurpassed in terms of quality, ingenuity, and sublime beauty. Surely the Hebrews were inspired by the pagan places of worship they would have seen in other lands; however, I believe that the Jewish temple was superior in one main respect. This temple was designed to praise and worship God, and not the human builder. As did the ancient Hebrews, Christians may learn a good deal about beauty from other traditions.

Many eastern cultures believe in the importance of creating a balanced environment to help people live and work in comfortable and supportive environments. Out of this, it is said, a natural beauty is produced. Interior design experts agree. They point out that people are more comfortable when in an aesthetically pleasing environment. Simple lines, harmony, pastels and neutral colours lead to less stress and more productivity. But people subjected to garish, cluttered and ugly environments are less productive and prone to emotional outbursts.

In her remarkable book, *Hidden Art*,[1] Edith Schaeffer reminds us that Christians must produce beauty – just as God has created beauty – in all we do, for it is through beauty that non-believers can see something of the God whom we serve. Creating beauty flies in the face of modern ideas about what art is, or is supposed to be. But the late H. R. Rookmaaker, professor of art history at the Free University of Amsterdam, made the argument that by creating beauty we are using our creative gift to be salt and light in a dark and decaying world (Matthew 5:13).[2] Creating beauty, then, may not win you an invitation to show your artwork at the Tate Modern, but it will tell others about the beauty of our God.

1. Edith Schaeffer, *Hidden Art* (The Norfolk Press: London, 1971).
2. H. R. Rookmaaker, *The Creative Gift – Arts and the Christian Life* (IVP: Leicester, 1981), p. 44.

One person and his art

Dan Watts is an artist who lives in Pennsylvania. He once told me he is excited about the prospect of painting pictures that affect people emotionally. During a recent visit to his home, I looked at his work. A believer, Dan is adamant that his work says something about God. How is this achieved? According to Dan, 'I don't go in trying to express an idea about our Lord. I'm very aware of how prayerful the creative process is – full of listening, alertness, and receiving. I go in open to hear what the painting needs. Open to receive what it requires for its beauty, power, vitality – its *being*.'

He added, 'Jesus is my friend. When I come to understand something for the first time, he is there. When I experience physical or emotional pain, he is there. When I enter the stillness and joy of the present moment, he is there. As I walk with him, I feel his love, mystery and power! It is very satisfying to see new work come to be and to know there is more to be discovered.'

Earlier, I suggested that creating beauty should be a natural part of our Christian lifestyle. Dan understands this. Even though his paintings are abstract, they bless the onlooker, unlike the stinging rebuke of much modern art. We used one of Dan's paintings for the cover of this book. I asked Dan what he hopes will happen as the result of his painting. 'My prayer is that the work will be received and that it will feed those who are hungry for beauty.' Dan knows what Simone Weil knew. She said that the poor need poetry more than they need bread.[1]

Brimming with organic form and colour, one of Dan's paintings now hangs on the wall of my sitting room. I

---

1. As quoted by Fr John P. McNamee in *Diary of a City Priest* (Sheed & Ward: Kansas City, USA, 1993).

sometimes ask guests what they see when they look at the painting. What about your home? What kind of beauty do you have on display? Is there potential for using it as a means of telling other people about God?

Music evangelism

Music is one of God's greatest gifts to humanity. In 'God and Music,' a sermon given at All Souls Church, Langham Place, London, in 1972, the then rector, Michael A. Baughen, pointed out, 'Music reaches out to and reflects something beyond ourselves . . . (through it we may) magnify the Lord and spread his word.' His sermon set out the theology and vision that a few months later led to the establishment of the All Souls Orchestra (ASO).

Under the leadership of Director of Music Noel Tredinnick, a group of instrumentalists were gathered together to assist with the worship. From this inauspicious beginning ASO has grown into what's become the most distinctive Christian orchestra in the British Isles.

Few would have envisioned that the orchestra would one day perform regularly on BBC television and radio, much less appear at the Royal Albert Hall in London and other extraordinary venues around the country joined by Sir Cliff Richard, Graham Kendrick, Mary O'Hara and other performers. But the success story of the All Souls Orchestra consists of many ordinary stories, too.

For professional flautist Greg Mitchell, the ASO is more than just a chance to perform in public. 'Really, it's a chance to worship God using the gifts he's given to me. That's really important.' Greg became a Christian in 1989 through the influence of a former orchestra member. 'I grew up in the Anglican church, but I just drifted away as so many do in their teens. Later, I became a professional musician. You probably know that there aren't many Christians who play music professionally. My friend showed me by personal example the importance of knowing Jesus personally, something I hadn't been taught before. He also invited me to attend All Souls Church. There I learned more about what it really means to be a Christian.'

The ASO was well established by the time Greg began to attend All Souls regularly. Eventually he approached Noel and asked if he could join. 'I was struck by the way the entire orchestra and support team falls into place before a concert or a tour. It's really rather like the body of Christ as Paul explains it in the New Testament. Each person is important no matter what role he or she plays and God always seems to have right people in the right place!'

According to Greg, one of the purposes of the orchestra is to bring glory to God through music. 'I know that people are helped in their faith because of our commitment to Jesus. It's low-key evangelism, but people are affected in meaningful ways. And even though as musicians our abilities vary, I know that God is using us all to further his kingdom.'

How does making beauty (painting, acting, singing, etc.) communicate anything about God to non-believers? According to Greg, 'God is perfection and anything that can come close to that in a beautiful artistic way can point towards him.

'In so far as art can allow a person space to think or just transport their imaginations non-believers can be led towards the character of God. As God is a creator, so anything which is carefully and beautifully made can be a pointer to him. The very act of creation can identify a person with God.'

How does beauty in general and music in particular help

to build up the church? 'The church can benefit from seeing members give of their talents for the benefit of all,' said Greg. 'People can be brought to reflect on God through contemplation and it offers an opportunity to stop in busy lives. It can be used as an evangelistic tool too. Any art may be useful in bringing people together for a common purpose in service of others, especially perhaps music.'

If Greg is right, then there ought to be evidence that a Christian's music – be it classical or pop – should have a wide appeal. Well, it does. Think of John Rutter whose ecclesiastical music sets the standard for the world. At the other end of the spectrum, Graham Kendrick's worship music is sung in churches from San Francisco to Beijing. In the pop world, born-again Christian Sir Cliff Richard's lifetime achievements eclipse the career bests of George Michael, Madonna, Bruce Springsteen, Michael Jackson and Ice-T combined. Sir Cliff has used his success to prove that the devil really doesn't own all the best music.

The apostle Paul talks about having confidence to dare to serve God in radical ways. I say this includes our efforts to make our environment beautiful. Beauty points to God; therefore, art and beauty may suggest to people that there is reason to hope in the creed's promise of eternal life in a resurrected body (1 Corinthians 15:42).

Towards a theology of beauty

Few of us are called to be artists or musicians like Dan Watts and Greg Mitchell. But how about the décor of our homes? Can this be considered a work of art? Edith Schaeffer says yes. Everything from the way in which we lay the dinner table to the way we tend our garden gives us an opportunity to glorify God in our lives. If Christianity is garish, cluttered, and ugly, then who will be drawn to our God? That's why we should look for ways to beautify our homes and our churches, so that people will be drawn to them, feel relaxed and happy there, and perhaps even find Jesus in our midst.

Edith calls this 'hidden art'. She says that of all people on earth, Christians ought to live aesthetically and creatively because we are supposed to be imitating the Creator.[1] There is even a kind of beauty to be found in doing mundane tasks around the house.

All work is honourable, but few people realise that the most honourable work is often the most humble work. Think again of Jesus. In modern terms, he eclipses the gifting of C. S. Lewis, Pope John Paul II and Billy Graham rolled into one. Indeed, he was the Son of God. Yet '. . . though he was in the form of God, did not count equality with God a thing to be grasped, but emptied himself, taking the form of a servant [the Greek word is *slave*], being born in the likeness of men. And being found in human form he humbled himself and became obedient unto death, even death on a cross' (Philippians 2:6-8). But did Jesus create beauty? I think so.

Jesus and beauty

I have already said in an earlier chapter that Jesus produced a wine of such distinction that it prompted the guests at the wedding of Cana to exclaim that the steward had saved the best wine for last. Jesus was a skilled carpenter. The quality and the beauty of the clean lines and functional nature of his chairs, tables, cupboards and other furniture made him a much sought after carpenter in Galilee. Storytelling is a form of beauty. All children respond when a favourite uncle clears his throat and begins, 'Once upon a

1. Edith Schaeffer, *Hidden Art*, p. 32.

time.' Jesus seemed to have a gift for telling good stories. The great American writer Ernest Hemingway was once asked which is the greatest short story ever told? Without hesitation, he is reported to have said that the story of the 'Prodigal Son' was by far the greatest story – bar none.

Time to act

This chapter is titled 'Creating beauty around us'. I have tried to show that there is a relationship between creating beauty and maintaining a credible Christian lifestyle. When you prepare food and cook a meal and set the table, do you think about the way in which this task may reflect God's nature? When you decorate a room, do you wonder if the shade of paint or the arrangement of the furniture will bring glory to God? Have you ever thought that the way you arrange a vase of flowers has as much potential to express something of the living God as a hymn? A bit over the top you say? Not really. Go back and look again at the attention to detail that Solomon put into even the nails he chose to build a house of worship for the King of Kings.

Real world application

The writer of Ecclesiastes reminds men, women and children that God has 'made everything beautiful in its time . . .' (Ecclesiastes 3:11). Isaiah prophesied, 'In that day the branch of the Lord shall be beautiful and glorious, and the fruit of that land shall be the pride and glory of the survivors of Israel' (Isaiah 4:2). The *branch* is an Old Testament name for Christ.[1] From these two passages we see that God uses the beauty to bless us and the people around us. If we believe this, we may confidently view our attempts at creating beauty as a way to tell others about our faith.

1. *Harper Study Bible* (Zondervan: 1977); note to Isaiah 4.2.

As for the rich in this world . . . They are to do good, to be
rich in good deeds, liberal and generous.
1 Timothy 6:17-18

CHAPTER 13

Tithing

Many years ago, I was acquainted with an unemployed truck driver whose daughter sometimes played with mine. One day, it came into my head to give him my tithe. I'll never forget the cautious look on his face as I handed over the envelope while we awkwardly sat in the lounge of his flat. When I explained that I was a Christian, and that Christians do this, he looked incredulous. After a few minutes small talk, he pocketed the money and showed me to the door.

I have since learned that what I did wasn't tithing. It was giving alms – an offering, a gift. In other words, it was charity, which is why that poor fellow acted the way he did, but it wasn't tithing. So what is tithing? Contrary to popular belief, tithing, or giving a set portion of your wealth to God, did not originate with the ancient Hebrews.

Many ancient cultures practised this custom.[1] It's worth mentioning that the tithe was normally not a cash payment, but a payment of goods – the seed and fruit of the land (Leviticus 27:30-32).[2]

In Genesis 14:20 we see Abraham freely giving 10 per cent of his spoil to King Melchizedek of Salem – described

---

1. *New Bible Dictionary*, s.v. 'Tithes' (Inter-Varsity Press: Leicester, 1982).
2. Ibid.

in Genesis 14:18-20 as a 'priest of God most high'. In Leviticus 27:30-33, tithing is explained more fully, and here it becomes clear that tithes are given to God – or more specifically, to the people who represent God on earth, and not merely to the needy. In Numbers 18:21, it's clear that tithes were to be given to the tribe of Levi, and here we see something not done before – God orders the Levites to tithe on the tithe they received (Numbers 18:26).

The original intention of the tithe was to support the priests, who had not the means or the time to earn their own living. Significantly, tithing was a very enlightened form of sharing wealth. However, the laws on tithing became increasingly complicated over the years. The Jews of Jesus' day tithed, but little is recorded in the New Testament about the Jewish laws governing tithing. It seems to have been a form of legislation, meaning all men were obliged by law to practise this custom. From the sarcastic comments made by Jesus, it's clear that while he approved of tithing, he detested the hypocritical manner in which the scribes and Pharisees observed this custom: 'Woe to you scribes and Pharisees, hypocrites! For you tithe mint and dill and cumin, and have neglected the weightier matters of the law, justice and mercy and faith; these you ought to have done without neglecting the others' (Matthew 23:23; Luke 11:42).

Tithing died out in the New Testament, although people certainly gave money to church leaders and to the needy. This they did out of their relationship with God and in accordance with how he has blessed them. Sometime in the Middle Ages in Europe, tithing became a legal and somewhat oppressive obligation, and, to borrow a phrase from Winston Churchill, men handed over their tithe to the priest with a grunt. Today, tithing is done as a free will gesture, specifically given to one's church or to one's spiritual leaders.

If New Testament laws don't require it, why tithe?

The main reason for tithing is it's the best way to balance our greed and gratitude, so says author Donna Schapner.[1] This makes sense; especially if we consider that tithes given to the church we attend is in keeping with the original reason for tithing – to support our ministers.

Paul admonished Christians to give generously again and again. In 2 Corinthians 9:6-15 he reminds Christians that God rewards those who give liberally: '. . . he who sows sparingly will also reap sparingly, and he who sows bountifully will also reap bountifully' (6). Never one to use guilt as a motivator, Paul adds this caveat: 'Each one must do as he has made up his mind. Not reluctantly or under compulsion, for God loves a cheerful giver' (7). Paul teaches that by giving, you are, in essence, allowing God to bless you for having given in the proper spirit: 'And God is able to provide you with every blessing in abundance, so that you may always have enough of everything and may provide in abundance for every good work' (8). Paul was not talking about tithing here, but he was talking about the same principle. He concludes by quoting Psalm 112:9: 'He scatters abroad, he gives to the poor; his righteousness endures forever.' The rest of the passage invokes a sort of *quid pro quo* principle that has stood the test of time for all who have given away money out of genuine love for those in need.

1. Donna Schapner, *Why I Tithe* (Liguori Publications: Liguori, MO, USA), p. 4.

Support God's ministers

I have known many missionaries over the years. Most of them depend on the giving of other Christians to keep them in the field. This is as it should be, for missionary work is a full-time occupation, and few missionaries would have time to hold down a nine-to-five job and still have energy and time to preach, teach, evangelise, or translate (or whatever else their vocation is, including running hospitals, digging wells, or building houses!) Yet I have one missionary friend whom I will call Frank. Frank told me that when he felt God calling him into missions, he tried to go the traditional route. When a small mission board accepted him as a missionary, he was advised to apply for funding from his home church. 'Somehow this didn't feel right to me,' Frank admitted. Not long after, a series of things went wrong, and he was dropped from the mission board. To make a long story short, he returned the support money his church had given to him. 'After that,' he said, 'I still felt called to some sort of overseas Christian work, but I couldn't see joining a mission board again or asking people to support me. I knew it wasn't what God had intended.'

One day an opportunity came up that Frank couldn't refuse. He was invited to live and work abroad. Using his own money plus a gift from a close friend for air fare, he and his family moved to Europe to take the job. Since then, he has found ways to be involved in a variety of churches and Christian projects, all the while supporting himself though his work for a secular company.

Actions speak louder than words

A great believer in tithing, John Wimber once said that handling money has taught him everything he knows about the Christian life. If the Christian life is about loving, then at times, the best way to show we care about others is to dig deeply into our pockets and put our money where our hearts are. But whom should we love?

Love the poor

The poor will always be with us. Jesus made this clear in Mark 14:7 and John 12:8. Nevertheless, Jesus states that giving money to the poor is *the* major plank in this platform we call the Christian lifestyle. 'If you would be perfect, go, sell all you have and give it to the poor, and you will have treasures in heaven; and come follow me' (Matthew 19:21).

Many of the early followers of Jesus took Jesus at his word, selling possessions, giving away all but the clothes on their backs, abandoning family and friends in order to live as itinerant preachers of the Gospel. In some cases, the cost was great. For instance, Peter gave up his share in a lucrative fishing business. Luke gave up a successful medical practice. And Matthew turned his back on the easy money to be made in the Roman tax office. I have known of many people who felt God call them to live lives of complete dependence on him. I'm thinking of people such as Francis of Assisi, George Muller (of the Bristol orphanages) and Mother Teresa, whose lives show that they indeed were in God's will when they gave away all for the sake of the Gospel.

From each according to their ability; to each according to their need

On the other side of the ledger, however, there are Christians who are not called to make this kind of sacrifice. Consider Joseph of Arimathaea who provided a tomb for the crucified body of Christ, a thing he would not have been able to do if he had given away his considerable wealth (John 19:38). Lydia, a godly woman called a 'worshipper of God' (Acts 16:14), was a gifted businesswoman, selling expensive dyed goods in Thyatira. As the dye trade was mainly aimed at the upper classes, Lydia was probably quite well off – a sort of first-century Laura Ashley. Because she did not give away all her money, her wealth and open-handed hospitality made it possible for Paul and others to continue in their mission work in Asia Minor.

Paul refers to something called the law of expediency in 1 Corinthians 9:14: 'In the same way, the Lord commanded that those who proclaim the gospel should get their living by the gospel.'[1] From this we can see that people who make a living by preaching or caring for others in Christ's name are entitled to the support – financial as well as moral – of people who earn their living by other means.[2]

Clearly, Paul had the resources to support himself, but from time to time, he accepted gifts from people who, no doubt, felt it a privilege to support this passionate man of God. When we give a set amount to our church on a regular basis, then, we help pastors to live within a budget (see Chapter 8) as they earn their living preaching the gospel. Because of these reasons, I believe that all Christians ought to tithe.

1. See Deuteronomy 25:4 where the law says not to muzzle an ox while it treads out the grain. Many see the ox as a metaphor for a person who preaches the gospel.
2. Paul supported himself as a tent maker (Acts 18:3). Paul did accept gifts, but he made it a point not to ask for money from the people to whom he ministered: 'And when I was with you and was in want, I did not burden anyone, for my needs were supplied by the brethren who came from Macedonia. So I refrained and will refrain from burdening you in any way' (2 Corinthians 11:9).

How much should we give?

Most authorities agree that the tithe is 10 per cent of our gross income. Anything you give away over and above that amount is said to be an offering, hence one often hears reference to *tithes and offerings*. Had I known this all those years ago, I might have given my tithe to my pastor and then reached into my pocket and given a smaller gift to the unemployed truck driver, although I am sure that what I did was fine.

Few people know that C. S. Lewis gave away a great deal of his income each year. Lewis never kept records of his giving, hating arithmetic of any sort. He simply gave and gave, living frugally in his college rooms, and at the end of his life, in his humble Headington home, the Kilns, on the edge of Oxford. I don't think it ever occurred to Lewis to give away 10 per cent of his income, for by so doing, he would have given significantly less than what he already was willing to give.

Chris Parsons pastors a Vineyard Church in Bury St Edmunds. According to Chris, 'I have often thought that 10 per cent is the *minimum* a person ought to be willing to tithe, not the maximum – after all, it's all God's!' Chris added, 'Jesus commended the widow who gave her tithe – often translated as a penny or two – but it was all she owned, so he commended her for actually giving 100 per cent.'

Who should tithe?

Everyone, says Chris. 'However, I don't believe, personally, that people should tithe out of debt. Secured debt like loans or mortgages aren't the sort of debt I mean. I mean if you have a large unsecured debt, I am not sure you should be tithing. If I knew of someone doing that in my church,

I would tell him or her not to try to tithe until the debt was cleared.

'Tithing is not a matter of law – something we *must* do in all circumstances – but a gift from our heart to God. People with a large unsecured debt can give, of course, but I'm not sure that it's right in a structured way to tithe money that is actually not theirs to give, until their debts are cleared.'

I know of people who have no money to give away, but they compensate by giving their time to voluntary Christian work in the community, or other unpaid Christian work that requires time and effort to do. Others 'tithe' by setting an extra plate at the table, sharing what little food and drink they have with someone who has nothing, or who is a long way from home and in need of friendship and hospitality. This is pleasing and acceptable to God, and in keeping with Jesus' words in Matthew 23:23.

Beware legalism

Not everyone agrees with Chris. Some people teach that if you are in debt, or if you simply can't seem to make ends meet month after month, you still must tithe. They reason that by tithing, you will force God to bless you, citing any number of verses that back this belief. Moreover, they warn that by not tithing, you will lose God's favour (Malachi 3:8-12). I have some sympathy for this way of thinking, for I know from my research that those who give selflessly are indeed blessed, and selfish people often seem to be under some kind of a self-induced curse. But I don't believe that people who give in order to get impress God in the least. Tithing is not an insurance policy that guarantees you will be blessed as the result of legalistic tithing. Love must be the prime motive for tithing. (See Matthew 23:23!)

Why I tithe – Andrew's story

I am friends with a number of well-to-do Christians who use their wealth to reach out in love to the poor, and most do it by tithing. Suffolk entrepreneur Andrew Bird is a successful land agent. Far from succumbing to the temptation of making the pursuit of wealth and happiness his sole motivation in life, Andrew tithes 10 per cent of his company's profits, and makes giving a high priority for his company. 'As a young man, I was baptised in the Holy Ghost. Consequently, I didn't want to settle for what some call the good life. This was partly due to my childhood Christian faith, and partly due to a keen sense of adventure. So with little more than the shirt on my back, I left a good job and set off for Asia as part of Youth With A Mission (YWAM).'

Andrew worked in Hong Kong under Jackie Pullinger, ministering to drug addicts and prostitutes. 'My time abroad showed me that even though I was poor, there were thousands in far worse shape than I was. I'm referring to the down and outs, prostitutes, alcoholics, runaways and drug addicts I saw. I'll never forget the sheer scale of human degradation and misery that is the result of the so-called night market. After leaving Hong Kong, I returned to England and eventually married and opened my business.

'Although I now live in a comfortable home in a comfortable part of the world, my heart is still in evangelism.' So Andrew set up a fund to support missionary work. One of the most amazing results of his generosity is his donation to a charity in Hong Kong dedicated to rehabilitating drug addicts. In fact, the charity has been so successful that the pastor who runs it has come to visit Andrew in Sudbury to say thank you for the help. He is the Rev Samuel

Lai Chun Moon, himself an ex-heroin addict and now pastor of a large Hong Kong church with an outreach ministry to drug addicts. Andrew admits that he never could reach the street people that Samuel reaches. 'Samuel has had a very rough life,' confides Andrew. 'But I must say his background in the drug world gives him the street credibility someone like me can never have. That's why I am happy to support Samuel with my tithe.'

Time to act

This chapter is titled 'Tithing'. I have tried to show that there is a good case to be made for observing the Old Testament custom of giving away 10 per cent of your income as part of a credible Christian lifestyle.

Christians should make giving money (and time and food) to those in need one of their highest priorities. Since this is so, why not take time this week to pray about tithing on your income?

Tithing is one of the best ways to help the poor. Anyone who has ever spent any time in a city will know that today there are more beggars on the streets than at any time in recent history. How do you cope with the endless (at times hostile) demands for spare change?

You can always keep plenty of spare change on you when you go about your business, but this is hardly practical. Or you can select a fortunate few upon whom you may bestow your kindness. But this, too, hardly solves the problem of the vast majority of homeless and needy who sleep rough in our streets. Even the ones who manage to get a few handouts will be in need again the next day because they are caught in a seemingly endless cycle of poverty.

If you want the money that you give to help the maximum number of needy people, then I suggest that you give your money to a Christian charity, for big or small, Catholic or Protestant, there are many Christian charities that are committed to helping the poor. And where do the charities get most of their money? From Christians who tithe and give offerings. Of course, not all Christians tithe. If the estimated 6 million Christians of the United Kingdom tithed faithfully, as much money could be raised in a year by the churches as is raised by the National Lottery.

Real world application

One Christian organisation with which I have had contact is the Oasis Trust. Oasis has a broad range of projects across four so-called 'action' departments. Each one fulfils a key role as members demonstrate the Christian faith in action. They believe that the Christian lifestyle works wonders – in the sense that it has the solutions to people's needs – whether physical, mental, emotional or spiritual. As a result Oasis delivers practical solutions to meet needs wherever they arise. Oasis enables others who want their lives to make a difference for good to get involved in the projects they run.

So what does each department do?

Community Action expresses the love of God for vulnerable and socially excluded people through practical community projects. They run:

- The Oasis Health Centre which has about 12,000 visits from rough sleepers in London each year;
- Oasis Outreach and Oasis Collectors. Key volunteers make the work of the Health Centre more effective.

- Oasis Housing offers 14 young women accommodation, security and life skills training when otherwise they might have had none. In partnership with the local council, Oasis provides 18 young people in Croydon with accommodation and training to equip them for the world of work.

Youth Action demonstrates that Christian faith works for young people, too, and is an innovative provider and enabler of youth work and ministry. This is achieved through *Training*: a degree-level, youth-agency approved, Oasis Youth Work and Ministry Course. *Participation*: providing opportunities through Oasis Frontline Teams and Faithworks Community Weeks for young people to participate in community action projects. *Inclusion*: Oasis Youth Inclusion works in primary and secondary schools towards social inclusion for excluded young people.

Church.co.uk is an Internet site for those exploring the Christian faith. **Faithworks** communicates churches' potential to change their communities to national government and the media. It also resources churches to help them change those communities for the better.

Finally, **Global Action** exists to help some of the world's poorest people live life more as God intended. They achieve this through: *Projects:* the Oasis Wire the World initiative equips disadvantaged young people in developing countries to acquire computer skills to give them the opportunity of employment and economic advancement. *People:* they send Oasis Global Action Teams to 14 countries around the world throughout the year and provide opportunities for people to work in overseas mission situations on a longer-term basis. *Influence*: they work at influencing public, government and church opinion and practice in relation to the undeveloped nations of the world.

As you can see, Oasis has a very broad portfolio of activities. Oasis wants to show that people who live the Christian lifestyle have solutions people need. But no solution is possible unless there are supporters to put their money where their hearts are. I have selected only one Christian charity in this chapter. There are many, many others, too many to mention here.

Since this is so, why not log on to http://www.uk-christians.org.uk/cgi-bin/links/Charities/International/, a clearinghouse web site that will link you or your organisation to many excellent Christian charities aimed at overseas development. Or you may wish to try http://www.christiansites.co.uk/category.cgi?category_id=3, or log on to an Internet search engine and type in ChristianSites.co.uk. These will give you listings of Christian charities aimed at needs here in the United Kingdom.

In the USA

There are literally hundreds of charities from which to choose. Check the listings in your local telephone directory under Charities – Christian. You may also use a meta-search engine such as Dogpile. Key in CHRISTIAN CHARITIES, USA, and this will put you in touch with one that suits your interests.

Have no anxiety about anything, but in everything by prayer and supplication with thanksgiving let your requests be made known to God. And the peace of God, which passes all understanding, will keep your hearts and your minds in Christ Jesus.

Philippians 4:6-7

CHAPTER 14

Maintaining a devotional life

In 1979, Bob Dylan wrote 'You Gotta Serve Somebody', considered by many as one of the twentieth century's most theologically accurate pop songs.[1] Dylan pointed out that whether we are a king or a beggar, human nature forces us to worship someone – either the devil or God. In this, the folk-rock icon echoes scripture. Consider what Jesus said to the Pharisees who told the people that Beelzebub gave Jesus' powers to him. Jesus retorted, 'He who is not with me is against me, and he who does not gather with me scatters' (Matthew 12:30).

1. It is worth pointing out that the 1966 pop hit, 'Turn, Turn, Turn', based on the book of Ecclesiastes, and also theologically accurate, was written by Bob Dylan. Dylan made a public profession to the Christian faith in 1979, converting through the Vineyard Church. However, following a series of personal tragedies, including a drawn-out and acrimonious court case with his manager, the break-up of his marriage, and savage reviews of his Christian music in the international press, Dylan lapsed from his commitment to Jesus. I would encourage all who love folk rock music and who have appreciated Dylan's music to pray for him to turn back to Christ and use his awesome talent to bring many unreached people into the Kingdom.

Devotion unleashes God's power

Since Jesus was a human being, where did his amazing power come from?[1] I say it came as the result of his intense devotion to his father in heaven. Daily he rose before sunrise in order to praise God and pray. Frequently Jesus went out into the hills and prayed and fasted. Notice that his devotion was hardly what we modern Christians call a 'quiet time': 'In the days of his flesh, Jesus offered up prayers and supplications with loud cries and tears, to him who was able to save him from death, and he was heard for his godly fear' (Hebrews 5:7-8).

Jesus spent three years teaching his disciples by his example. When the disciples finally began to worship God as Jesus had taught them, he commissioned them to cast out demons and heal the sick (Luke 9:1-2). When the disciples returned, they proclaimed with astonishment, 'saying, "Lord, even the demons are subject to us in your name!"' (Luke 10:17).

It's clear that to enjoy the same powers that Jesus enjoyed, we must have a consistent devotional life. Jesus upped the ante by promising 'and greater works than these will [you] do' (John 14:12). However, this power is not automatic, as the disciples discovered in Mark 9. Following the Transfiguration (Mark 9:2-13), Jesus, Peter, John and James come down from the mountain and meet the disciples. The disciples, who had been trying unsuccessfully to deliver a boy from a demon (Mark 9:17-18), were embroiled in a heated discussion with some scribes. A large

1. Many people wrongly assume that Jesus' miracles were accomplished because he was God incarnate. This, of course, is incorrect. Jesus performed his miracles as a human being. The actual miracles were the product of his devotion to and his faith in God. This is why Jesus told his followers they will see and do greater things than the miracles done by Jesus (John 1:50; John 5:20; John 14:12).

crowd had gathered to watch. At this point, Jesus steps forward and performs deliverance ministry on the boy who is immediately healed. Abashed, the disciples 'asked him privately, "Why could we not cast it out?" And he said to them, "This kind cannot be driven out by anything but prayer"' (Mark 9:28). There is, therefore, a link between levels of devotion and the power to overcome satanic forces that is as true today as it was in the disciples' day.

Church attendance is devotion

Many people say they worship God, but they refuse to go to church. John points out the ancient scripture which stated of the Messiah, 'zeal for thy house will consume me' (John 2:17). True to form, Jesus attended the synagogue frequently and observed all the holy days. If Jesus, who was sinless, took seriously the need to go to church, how much more should we who are sinful? Moreover, in the eyes of a doubting world, a Christian who doesn't go to church is about as credible as a democrat who doesn't vote.

For Christians, devotion is expressed through equal measures of prayer, praise and worship, and the best place I can think of to do this is in church with like-thinking people. At any rate, whether we go to church or not, worship is something we are programmed to do daily without needing to be prompted. Bob Dylan's song warns that unless we are devoted to God, we are likely to become devoted to something else – football, hobbies, career, sex, drugs, creating wealth, our family, etc. – and thereby we forget to worship God.

Hard times breed devotion

From time to time God allows a calamity to make us realise that we need God 24/7. Is persecution good for the

Church? Perhaps. Persecution frequently leads to an outpouring of God's Holy Spirit. That's what happened in the days of the Roman emperor Nero. Back then, being a Christian cost you your life, but God was worshipped fervently, and miracles were a normal part of the Christian life. It's like that in parts of China today.

In 1966, Mao Tse-Tung led a Communist-inspired *coup d'état* in China known as the Cultural Revolution. Under Mao, Christianity was outlawed and hundreds of church leaders were martyred. This upheaval lasted until Mao's death in 1976. Beginning in 1977, China abandoned the Cultural Revolution's radical socio-economic polices. Today Chinese Christians may worship Jesus. Bibles are freely distributed in many provinces. Even a few government officials profess faith in Jesus Christ.

To be sure, Christianity enjoys acceptance mainly in the south-east part of the country. However, the further away from Macau, Hong Kong, Taiwan and Shanghai, the more Christians face persecution. Ironically, rather than preventing people from joining the churches, the injustice leads to mass conversions to the Christian faith.

Whereas a mere 30 years ago there were roughly one million Christians, today accurate estimates are impossible to establish due to rapid church growth in China. Pastor Kim (all names are changed) had seen the Holy Spirit at work among the unconverted when he preached in many south-eastern provinces. Kim made repeated trips into the north-west of China where there was known persecution in 1990. When his friends warned him away from that area he replied calmly, 'The Lord has said I had to be prepared to die for him. It would be a privilege if I could shed my blood or suffer in the most populous province of China.'

Although his co-workers wept at these words, he preached there many years with remarkable results.

Gui was ill the night he was to preach. He decided that he would speak for 15 minutes then sit down. When he stood at the front of a packed room, his sickness left him. He preached powerfully at great length while people wailed and cried out to be saved. Word came that police were outside rounding up Christians even as he was preaching. Instead of running away, Gui carried on preaching as more and more people pressed into the building and were being converted, some almost instantly.[1] Fortunately, persecution isn't the only way to enjoy church growth.

A lesson in Korean devotion

There is a cosmic principle at play when people openly devote their lives to God. It's summed up with this equation: $P + W = CG$ (Praise and Worship equals Church Growth). The Rev Ray Bellfield knows this. He is a pastor in Wigan. Ray says the record-breaking church growth in Korea is down to the unswerving devotion of the church in that part of the world. A few years ago, he attended a

1. Despite Government interference in church issues, westerners must take care not to focus exclusively on the repression in China. We must put what is happening there in its proper context. In the years since Tiananmen Square, Chinese authorities have made commendable efforts to improve the standard of living for most Chinese people. This includes making provision for the spiritual needs of the people. To that end, in July 1995 the Chinese Government granted permission for a United-States-based Christian organisation to purchase up to five million Bibles from the state-sanctioned Amity Press in Nanjing and distribute them to house-church Christians throughout China. Clearly, the Holy Spirit has not finished with his work in China. Meanwhile, we must pray for the persecuted Christians there, remembering that the prognosis is good for the future of the Church in China.

Korean prayer meeting that began at 10pm and finished at 5am: 'Approximately 14,000 people were at prayer. They shouted and rocked, which we call Asian-style prayer. Request after request was read out every 15 minutes, and everyone prayed together for that period of time.' Ray said that 30,000 converts had come to Christ in just three months as the result of such prayer. 'It was exciting stuff!'

Good health – the by-product of a devotional life?

Even though we don't see dramatic conversions in the West as a result of public acts of devotion, American research carried out in Kansas and San Francisco proves that people with an active devotional life are healthier than people who do not worship God. The *Observer* newspaper carried this news in early 2000. The first experiment took heart patients and had Christians pray for them over a month. The patients showed significant improvement in health, compared with a control group. In the second experiment, volunteers were given the first names of a group of patients and prayed for their recovery. A similar improvement was noted among them.

The Pioneer group of evangelical churches, led by Gerald Coates, is keen to test the beneficial effects of prayer on hospital patients here. Gerald Coates is cautiously optimistic about the results. He was quoted as saying that if it should prove to be beneficial as it has in the USA, it won't make British people suddenly believe in God, but it will make it hard for them to doubt his existence.

A lesson in British devotion

Key British organisations are dedicated to promoting the public devotion to Jesus Christ. One group is the Nottingham

Prayer Camps Network. According to a spokeswoman, their prayer network grew as the result of God's prompting. 'The prophetic calling came in 1967 and from 1967 to 1978 it was preparation time. In 1978 came the vision of Nottingham covered in black clouds with a war taking place underneath. The Lord said, 'I am going to call an army of prayers, and I will clear the way.' These prayers came from different churches and different denominations.

'We concentrated on Freemasonry for two years, and this particularly broke the hold in Anglican circles which began to accept that Freemasonry was incompatible with Christianity,' she added.

Through prayer, God seemed to be telling the prayer warriors that the four gates of the city were strategic prayer targets. 'God wanted to be "enthroned" in the gates. For a number of years we concentrated on establishing his rule on the four city gates, identifying the enemy and proclaiming the reign of Jesus over them.'

The results are encouraging: Nottingham City Council approached the Prayer Network to do a Prayer Walk to celebrate the year 2000. That developed into four prayer walks, north, south, east and west, culminating in a large celebration of churches together along with the Council. This event drew favourable media attention as well as citywide support and led to other events organised for Easter and Pentecost. The city Council asked Nottingham Prayer Camps Network to organise more activities. As a result, permission was given to meet together in the Castle grounds on Easter Sunday 2000 for a celebration in honour of Jesus, and a banner was raised on the flagpole which proclaimed, 'Jesus is Lord; this is his City'. Now that is what I call devotion!

I'm too busy!

Admittedly, many people are too busy to have a daily devotional time. Many live in families as children, brothers, sisters, fathers and mothers; others work in demanding careers such as doctors, nurses, and carers – roles that can be very time consuming to say the least. Yet people who long for more of God seem to make time in the midst of their hectic schedules for devotion to God. Again, it is through devotion that Christians manage to overcome their circumstances.

Consider Susanna Annesley Wesley, the mother of John and Charles Wesley, the founders of the Methodist movement in the eighteenth century. Susanna was endowed with a keen intellect and a thirst for knowledge. Her father's home was a hive of intellectual activity, and because of his enlightened attitude towards his daughter, he provided her with a classical education not afforded to many girls of that day. Having mastered several foreign languages, including Greek, she turned her inquiring mind to theological matters. In 1688 at age 19, she met and married the Rev Samuel Wesley. The romance was the stuff of fairytales, and, like a fairytale, they ought to have lived happily ever after. But it wasn't to be.

This vivacious young bride had no idea of the hard times that lay before her, including the staggering responsibility of bearing *19* children. Samuel turned out to be an emotionally crude man who refused to be involved in any form of childcare. To make matters worse, Samuel was an inept manager, and despite having a basic living as a Church of England minister, the family only managed to stay out of debtors' prison because of the charity of family and friends. At one point, following a minor disagreement,

Samuel abandoned Susanna and left her to fend for herself and the children for several months![1]

Instead of destroying her faith, her dreadful circumstances drove her closer to God. She prayed every day and often meditated on scripture. Favourite verses include: 'Cast all your anxieties on him, for he cares about you' and ' . . . after you have suffered a little while, the God of all grace, who has called you to his eternal glory in Christ, will himself restore, establish, and strengthen you' (1 Peter 5:7, 10). For Susanna, her daily devotion to God was like oxygen to her bloodstream.

It's said that to find space for her daily devotion in the tumult of her crowded home, she sat in a rocker in a corner with a shawl over her head for a bit of privacy! Significantly, each day beneath her shawl, she spent one hour studying the scriptures, praying and praising God. Knowing of the benefits of a daily devotional time, she shared her faith with her children. She started a school for them, which was for the purpose of teaching them their letters and 'the saving of their souls'.[2]

Today's devotions lead to tomorrow's blessings

Susanna's godly devotion affected our nation. All of her children grew up to be loving, kind and successful men and women, including John and Charles Wesley, two of the eighteenth century's most influential men, and the founders of a Christian movement that flourishes all around the world today.

1. 'Susanna Wesley – A Mother Who Made A Difference',
   In touch Ministries
   http://www.intouch.org/might portraits/susanna_wesley_213595.html
2. Ibid.

Few would have blamed Susanna Wesley had she divorced her husband and abandoned her faith, seeking instead self-fulfilment. Yet, because of Susanna's unflinching devotion to God and her consistent Christian lifestyle, her son John grew up to know the power of Christ. John's accomplishments are staggering. A social reformer, his revival sermons not only fought sin and ignorance, but they also went some way to elevate the status of Jews, Catholics, women and other oppressed groups. Consequently, whether or not they agree with his religious convictions, most historians say Wesley's preaching saved Britain from the ravages of an insurrection similar to the French Revolution (1789 to 1799).[1]

Towards the end of her long and hard life, Susanna confided in Charles that, although she lived with a broken heart and doubts, it was her *full* commitment to Jesus that empowered her to go forward in faith and hope.[2]

Time to act

God dwells in the praise and devotion of his people. This is the reason why God created us. To see more evidence of this claim, see Isaiah 43, especially verse 7. Take time to read the Psalm 24. Here, unwavering devotion to God by Israel in the Old Testament is a picture of the way we must

1. Every bit his mother's son, John Wesley was truly a man of many parts. A scientific man, he taught about the need for public health and sanitation. Indeed, he is the author of *Primitive Physic*, an early medical text which, quaint by today's standards, was in its day highly acclaimed. He also penned the *General Receipt Book*, a book of scientific recipes that included a section on making wine! He also advocated learning to read and the need for widespread education. The list of his accomplishments goes on and on.
2. 'Susanna Wesley – A Mother Who Made A Difference'.

be devoted to Jesus in the New Testament Church. Look, too, at Psalm 136, a beautiful poem that presents a myriad of reasons for having a daily time with God. If we are not openly devoted to God, we are like the people Paul describes in Romans 1: 'For although they knew God, they did not honour him as God or give thanks to him, but they became futile in their thinking and their senseless minds were darkened' (Romans 1:21).

Real world application

Every Christian alive today has been selected by Jesus to present the Gospel (Matthew 28:18-20). This call is seen throughout the New Testament. St Peter proclaims, 'But you are a chosen race, a royal priesthood, a holy nation, God's own people, that you may declare the wonderful deeds of him who called you out of darkness into his marvellous light' (1 Peter 2:9). A daily devotional time won't make us evangelists, but as we spend time worshipping God the way it is described in this chapter, we'll begin to experience the power of the Christian faith. The Rev Douglas Sullivan, an Air Force chaplain, reminds people, 'The shortest distance between a problem and a solution is the distance between your knees and the floor. The one who kneels to the Lord can stand up to anything.' I think he's right.

I believe it takes divine power to live a Christian lifestyle in the midst of an unbelieving culture. When it comes to devotion, the modern church has much to learn from ancient Israel. The Hebrews, after all, were well acquainted with God's divine power. Therefore, it's worth studying the way in which this people expressed their devotion.

One of the words they used to describe devotion is

related to the same word that means noise and bodily actions.[1] This implies that we must use the mouth and body during our devotional times.

Why would God want us to worship him so whole-heartedly? Well, for one thing, our bodies are gifts from God. Another reason is that gusto equals sincere joy. After all, when you worship God with your head, hands, feet, knees, and lips, it's awfully hard to fake sincerity.

The anatomy of biblical devotion

Take time this week to study the anatomy of devotion. You'll see that almost every part of our body may rightly be used to express our devotion to God.

The head

Genesis 24:2 – A servant of God bows his head and worships the Lord.

Exodus 4:31 – God frees Israel from slavery and the elders bowed heads.

The hands

Psalm 47:1 – Clapping is worship. People are admonished to clap with joy.

Psalm 63:4 – King David declares that his hands are lifted at the name of the Lord. This gesture is seen many times throughout the Bible.

Psalm 141:2 – King David's hands are a type of sacrifice of praise.

Psalm 143:6 – King David spreads out his hands . . . his soul longs for God. Open hands are a sign of dependence, of submission, of praise, or acknowledgement.

---

1. *New Bible Dictionary* (IVP: Leicester, 1982), s.v. 'Praise'.

The feet

2 Samuel 6:14 – King David's dance. Dancing is both humbling (no bad thing for coming before God) and liberating. Dance honours God, and anything that honours God throws satanic forces into a panic.

The knees

2 Chronicles 6:12-13 Kneeling makes God our sovereign. Bent knees are humbling. It is a genuine sign of worship. It is a sign of submission. Until we bow the knee physically, we do not truly acknowledge his authority in our lives. Yet one day all of creation will be forced to kneel **(Philippians 2:10; Isaiah 45:23)**.

Ephesians 3:14 – St Paul bows the knees. If it's good enough for Paul, it's good enough for us.

The lips (Shouting!)

Psalm 63:3 – Lips were made for praise.

Psalm 126: 2, 5 – The walls of Jericho came down after a mighty shout, not as the result of the trumpets! Up to half of the exhortations to praise are calls to shout about it.

Falling prostrate

Genesis 17:3 – Abram (Abraham) is one of the first of the great saints to show us the natural position to assume when coming before our mighty God. Make it a point to check and see how many great saints went on faces before God. A Christian lifestyle devoid of this form of devotion misses the opportunity of telling a society that worships material gods about the worth of our God.

Psalm 86:9 – All nations must bow before our God.

James 4:10; 1 Peter 5:6 and 2 Kings 22:19 – These scriptures (and others) admonish us to humble ourselves before God. Falling on our faces before God is the best way I know to express genuine humility. Moreover, we are rebels by nature. Falling prostate subdues our rebellion. It mortifies our pride. It leads to total dependence on God. *And that can't be bad!*

Finally, I imagine some people would never worship God in such an uncouth manner. I'm reminded of something Archbishop William Temple once said. He lamented, 'The Church is dying of good taste.' Since this is so, let's give up our modern ideas of good taste and demonstrate our devotion to God his way, not our way.

So I took the leading men of your tribes, wise and respected men, and appointed them to have authority over you — as commanders of thousands, of hundreds, of fifties and of tens and as tribal officials.
Deuteronomy 1:15, NIV

CHAPTER 15

Participating in a democracy

In June 2000, women in the developing nations routed radical feminists at the finale of a UN special session on women's rights. Through tactical voting, they forced Western powers to drop sex rights for children and the promotion of abortion from a new five-year UN agenda for women's advancement. The women based their objection on ethical reasons.

In spring 2000, when the Mothers' Union felt Prime Minister Tony Blair was using them for political purposes at their annual conference, they voted with their hands. The incensed ladies slow handclapped him at their conference. Leading political analysts said that one act alone has done more to force the Government to pay attention to particular voters than all the political lobbyists rolled into one.

The actions at UN Women's Conference and the Mothers' Union conference are only two examples of how the democratic process may bring about desired changes. But most Christians would rather run a mile than get involved in politics as evidenced by the low turnout for the recent national elections that included an equally low turnout by

Christians. For many in the church, politics is below them – or beyond them. In either case, this attitude must change.

Have I got good news for you!

I have met people who have told me they prefer to hide their faith when it comes to getting involved in the political process. That is a pity. For one thing, Paul wrote to the church in Rome, 'For I am not ashamed of the Gospel: it is the power of God for salvation to everyone who has faith, to the Jew first and also to the Greek. For in it the righteousness of God is revealed through faith for faith; as it is written, "He who through faith is righteous shall live"'(Romans 1:16-17). Here Paul means the Gospel has the power to change lives for the better – here and now, not only in the afterlife.

Our society is sick. Drug abuse is endemic. Sexually transmitted disease is the scourge of entire communities of people. Violent crime is at an all time high. We must be willing to step out of our comfort zone and into the political arena in order to heal our society. Christians must get involved in local, national and county politics. They should become school governors; they must become leaders in their communities; and they ought to join their PCCs. Their message must not be: 'We want to convert you'; rather, it should be 'We have answers to our community's problems.'

Perhaps God isn't calling you to head a campaign to end homelessness. Nevertheless, you are in a very good position to effect change in this shocked, depressed, apathetic nation. God is calling you to be an agent of change for the better for the spiritual and political life of our communities. You mustn't be afraid to take risks – 'For God has not given you a spirit of fear, but of power and a sound mind'. What can you do? You can vote.

Tactical voting

Perhaps you feel more suited to working behind the scenes in order to improve our national problems. If that's the case, never underestimate the power of tactical voting. Protestants, Catholics and other Bible-based religions must look beyond their differences, beyond party affiliations, in order to vote as one for candidates who uphold biblical values. Tactical voting fosters a political ecumenism that prevents party loyalty from splitting the Christian vote.

Tactical voting is impossible without an informed and involved constituency. In America, many parachurch organisations run training seminars to educate ordinary citizens about using the democratic process to support or to put forward their own candidates and to see them into office. Many churches publish a league table displaying the voting record of local, state and national politicians on issues of importance to people sharing the same values. Frequently American Jews and Christians (with a smattering of Muslims) will vote for the same candidates because, although they are miles apart on some issues, they have learned that it is better to focus on what they do agree upon and vote accordingly. This has created a proficient religious vote that all parties take seriously. I believe that the same can happen here, despite the differences between the American and British political systems.

First, we need to begin to talk to one another. For too many years, Christians have been afraid to enter into dialogue with non-Christians. Moreover, many Christian groups refuse to sit down at the same table with members of a different Christian denomination.

Stubborn and irrational entrenchment must end. We need to join forces and formulate a long-term plan with very clearly defined goals that we can all live with. Certain Christian organisations such as the Movement for Christian Democracy, the Christian Institute, and the Centre for Justice and Liberty, and Maranatha have already set up such coalitions, with the aim of influencing our Government. That's good. But perhaps the best way to influence our Government is to become a part of it.

Vote for me

We know there are many Christians in the American government, but did you know there are many Christians in Parliament? If that's so, how do they harmonise their faith with policies considered antithetical to Christianity? Conscience plays a large part for Conservative MP David Atkinson. 'I apply my own standards and values to whatever judgements I have to make as a Member of Parliament. My approach is the old mnemonic for the Soviet Union, CCCP: *Conscience, Country, Constituency and Party* in that order.

'As a Roman Catholic, I accept the doctrine that forbids divorce. I also recognise that this doctrine cannot apply universally. Other Christian churches approve divorce. So I agree with the current legislation which tries to take some of the sting and damage out of a divorce proceeding. What one cannot do is to legislate that families stay together. That is not the job of government. It is the job of the Church to take a lead in such matters.'

How would Lord David Alton like to see Christians engage their culture politically? 'I would like (all parties) to embrace the whole of the Christian gospel, not just a cafeteria Christianity where you take the bits you like and leave the awkward bits.'

Since many of his colleagues prefer to keep their faith private, how does he justify using his faith to formulate public policy? 'I do think Christians should speak about their faith publicly. You cannot privatise your faith and opt out of the world around you. Jesus is the best example to us. He was very open about his work. He went to the synagogue and proclaimed his mission to the world. Christians must not be any different. They must be brave and be willing to make a stand against the prevailing spirit of this age.'

It may be argued that the Labour Party grew out of the Methodist tradition, but how true has the party remained to its Christian antecedents? MP (Member of Parliament) Donald Anderson said, 'All parties reflect changes in society and the decline in Christian worship. So far as the Labour party is concerned, it is true that many in the early days learned their speaking skills and gained their confidence and world view from their Christian faith.'

Is it a good idea for candidates to uphold the Christian faith? 'Today, all parties contain Christians who prayerfully seek to apply their beliefs to the complex and often morally ambiguous issues they face. [However] There are clear dangers in wearing one's Christian beliefs on one's sleeve in politics. I think for example of the Christian Democrat parties on the Continent who often give a very bad name to Christ because the people who wear their label fall into corruption. Moreover, when politicians get into messy compromises as they inevitably do, there will be some Christians who will feel hurt. Finally, I think it can be wrong for candidates to say *vote for me because I'm a Christian*. I think faith should come across in the principles and actions – not merely the words – of the individual candidate.'

Over the centuries, politicians with faith in God have done much good. In his book *A Nation Under God*, David Holloway reminds readers that the Church has made countless positive contributions to society.[1] He's right, of course. What's more, history shows that Christians shaped our democracy, a fact frequently overlooked by today's historians and by many leading churchmen and women.

Christianity won't completely eradicate human sin, and hence, it never will totally transform our society into a utopia. But thanks to Christians getting involved in the political process over the centuries, cycles of social reforms occurred in western culture over the last two thousand years.

Two millennia of good being accomplished as a direct result of people taking seriously the Christian lifestyle – with its emphasis on love thy neighbour – is too vast a subject for a book this size. But here is a snapshot of the benefits which have come about when Christian faith intersected with the political processes. Note the obvious domino effect:[2]

AD 34 – The birth of the Church, thereby equalising of men and women in the eyes of God and later the law.

75 – Welfare for the sick, the infirm, the poor, and widows is instituted.

205 – Origen introduces Christian scholarship, which eventually led to the end of widespread ignorance.

300 – Middle Eastern and African universities, hospitals, and hospices are created.

432 – Despite the many legends that overshadow his life and work, Patrick brings Christianity to the British Isles, and beyond.

1. David Holloway, *A Nation Under God* (Kingsway: Eastbourne, 1987), p. 8.
2. All dates taken from *The 100 Most Important Events in Christian History* by A. Kenneth Curtis, J. Stephen Lang, and Randy Petersen (Revell: Grand Rapids, USA, 1991).

C 1100 – European universities, hospitals, and hospices are created.

1517 – Martin Luther reforms the corruption he saw in the Church.

1620 – British Pilgrims sign the Mayflower Compact, thereby ending the autocratic rule of kings and fostering the movement towards modern western democracy.

1738 – John Wesley's conversion and the beginning of abolition, the world's first anti-slavery movement.

1807 – British Parliament votes to abolish the slave trade.

1902 – The Welsh Revival affects key local and national politicians, and they in turn affect our laws.[1]

1. The days of the Welsh Revival are accepted as genuine times of revival. Certainly when revival hits, it is widespread in scope. There exists reliable documentation that crime rates plummeted, alcohol abuse diminished, and people generally cared more for their destitute neighbours at a time well before the universal welfare state was created.

Significantly, a record number of baptisms and confirmations were taking place in England and church growth during that period was an all time high for the twentieth century – giving lie to the belief that the Welsh revival had no effect on England. According to the late Professor Edwin Orr of Fuller Theological Seminary, during revival God creates an overflow reaching to people in close proximity to the ones directly affected – see Zechariah 8:23 and Acts 2:47.

Arguably, the Welsh Revival's effects even went beyond the British Isles. The revival spread overseas to the Continent, Africa, Asia and the United States. Citing evidence for a worldwide revival during the early part of the last century, Professor Orr asked the question, why did God cause this to happen then? 'I think it was God's preparation for a great trauma, WW1,' said Orr. 'During the Great War, the nations of the world suffered an unprecedented loss of life. But God in his mercy first sent a worldwide revival, beginning in small pockets in Wales, and ending up touching nearly every continent on the earth.' *(continued overleaf)*

1962 – The Second Vatican Council begins, inspiring countless Christians including many national and international leaders to allow their Christian faith to inform how they conduct their business.[1] I would argue that it was this revitalisation of the Catholic Church that inspired Polish Christians to throw off repressive Soviet Communism in the 1980s.

All of the above have clearly led to the improvement of society. Everyone would agree that it would be a crime if a person discovered a cure for cancer, but never bothered to make public this extraordinary good news. Likewise, when Christians refuse to participate fully in our democracy, they withhold the potential for the cure for many social ills.

Christian martyrs paved the way for today's freedoms

Sir Fred Catherwood has made the analogy that we are

(continued from previous page)

Many secular writers and historians are convinced we are on the brink of another great trauma. Whether it will be a war or an ecological disaster is a moot point. Meantime, God is stirring his Church today for another great revival to precede a national or global disaster. There are some compelling arguments that support this belief. Many people are becoming believers through Alpha Courses. Andy FitzGibbons says that the work at the Sunderland Christian Centre has convinced him that God is preparing for another revival, with great harvests as of yet not seen by this generation.

Whatever happens, revitalisation of society is key to understanding revival. I am convinced that if a particular move of God is a genuine revival, people's lives will be transformed for the better and sweeping social reforms will undo past injustices.

1. Although it must be said that many Catholics are critical of the Council, much may be written about the good that this movement has done to build bridges between Catholics and Protestants. Surely, the greatest good must be that Pope John XXIII placed the highest emphasis on pastoral care, the denunciation of atheistic materialism, and the need for the Church to 'rule with the medicine of mercy rather than severity'.

drawing from a Christian stock in a cupboard, but we are not replacing that stock. I am reminded of the Christian roots of democracy each time I look at a lone weather-beaten monument in front of Bury St Edmund's United Reformed Church. One day, I walked up to the monument to examine it. Upon closer inspection, I read: In memory of Elias Thacker and John Copping who were hanged in the town on the 4th and 5th of June respectively 1583 for disseminating the principles of independency [*sic*] – Erected August 1904.

Who were these two men and what have they to do with democracy? Thacker and Copping were two of Bury St Edmund's greatest proponents of freedom of speech. Their crime? Denying the authority of the Queen in religious matters by openly preaching the Gospel of salvation through belief in Jesus Christ outside of the established church.

History records that some government officials spoke out in their defence. Moreover, the man who spoke loudest had most to lose. Prominent in Suffolk as a justice of the peace, Sir Robert Jermin of Rushbrooke was annoyed that the Bishop of Norwich had imprisoned the men with neither charges nor trial, and he made sure the Crown was aware of his displeasure.

On a warm day in July 1582, Jermin was called before Queen Elizabeth. During this meeting, Elias Thacker and John Copping were described as troublesome fellows. When the queen asked Sir Robert for a defence of the men, he averred that Copping was a saintly man, called by some 'a shining light'. Nothing is recorded of Sir Robert's opinion of Thacker, except he too was arrested and imprisoned wrongly.

Sir Robert, while not sharing the men's religious convictions, defended their right to due process of law as

Englishmen. To her credit, Queen Elizabeth expressed dismay that the men were held without having charges properly lodged.

Jermin pointed out that not only were the men being held unlawfully, but they had been in jail since 1576 – six years. Stressing that freethinking was a serious matter, the queen nevertheless was persuaded to release the prisoners. So it was that Thacker and Copping were set free.

It's not known what Thacker and Copping said after their release, but clearly they didn't promise to stop preaching the Gospel, whether or not the Bishop considered it to be lawful.

Significantly, it wasn't civil authorities that wanted to suppress their religious expression. The ones who feared the non-conformists most were the professional clergy, who could lose their living if the Church were allowed to reform further than it had under King Henry VIII. It's worth noting that it was the same in Christ's day: Jesus' chief enemies weren't the Romans, but the Temple priests and lawyers who would lose their comfortable positions if people became persuaded that Jesus Christ was who he claimed to be – the Son of God who would deliver his people. At Jesus' trial, the priests incited the crowds to demand capital punishment for the rabbi when the judge, Pontius Pilate, offered to turn Jesus free: "'I did not find this man guilty of any of your charges against him; neither did Herod, for he sent him back to us. Behold, nothing deserving of death has been done by him . . ." But they all cried out together, "Away with this man" (and) they shouted, "Crucify, crucify him!"' (Luke 23).

Predictably, less than a year later, Thacker and Copping were in trouble again. In June 1583 during the Summer Assizes they, and one Thomas Gibson, a bookbinder, were brought before the Lord Chief Justice on a charge of sedition. Sedition in this case was having received books produced by another freethinking Christian called Robert Browne. The three were convicted and condemned to be hanged.

Prior to their execution, a court-appointed chaplain visited the prisoners. He told the men they would be set free if they admitted that they had been wrong. Thacker is said to have advised the chaplain to save his breath and leave them alone at once.

The chaplain began to play on their emotions, seeing that the promise of freedom didn't tempt the men. The chaplain begged the men to consider their wives and children who would be left behind, penniless and bereft of husbands and fathers. The chaplain turned the knife by pointing out that Browne had fled the country, leaving them defenceless and in prison.

Gibson was said to have recanted, and thereby was set free. 'There will be no further opportunity for you to gain public support for your case,' the chaplain warned Thacker and Copping. 'The justices who have favoured you are powerless against this charge of treason, and my Lord Archbishop will have no course but to have you hanged before these Assizes are over on the fifth of June, two days from now. Only if you will recant your errors will you leave this jail alive.'

Thacker is said to have retorted, 'Your face we fear not; for your threats we care not; and to come to read your [version of the Gospel] we dare not.' Copping is said to have added, 'To disobey [our] conscience may gain us years, but it will lose us eternity. All things work for the best to they that love God.'

On one hand, it's easy to dismiss this bit of Suffolk history as an unfortunate footnote with little or no bearing on people alive in the United States and Britain today. On the other, few realise that the sacrifice made by these two obscure men over 400 years ago has had a direct bearing on the liberties and rights we take for granted today – the right to trial by jury, the right to assemble and worship God, the right to freedom of speech, the right to practise any religion, or, indeed, the right to practise none.

Moreover, many assume that Christian martyrs no longer exist. The fact is, more Christians were killed for their faith in the twentieth century than have been martyred in the total history of Christianity.[1]

Today, thousands of Christians in Africa, South America and China are being singled out for campaigns of hate and terror by oppressive regimes, religious militants and terrorist groups. Thousands are imprisoned, beaten, tortured and executed because the Christian gospel presents a threat to totalitarianism. In so doing, they are no different from the nearly forgotten Suffolk martyrs, Elias Thacker and John Copping, who bravely laid down their lives in Bury St Edmunds over 400 years ago so we may enjoy civil and religious freedom today.

Years from now will our great-grandchildren benefit from our having replenished the Christian stock in our nation's cupboard, or will the cupboard be bare?

Time to act

God reminds Christians everywhere: 'I am the Lord your God . . . you shall have no God before me' (Exodus 20:2-3). This means that it is God not man-made political or economic

---

1. Reported by Baroness Carolyn Cox, Deputy speaker of the House of Lords; verified by numerous other sources, including Military Martyrs, http://www.ucc.ie.milmart/.

PARTICIPATING IN A DEMOCRA

systems that dictate events. God also says, 'Many are the plans in the mind of a man, but it is the purpose of the Lord that is established' (Proverbs 19:21). In practical terms, this means God expects us to express his will in the corridors of power in our nation. If we believe this, we may confidently view our County Hall, our Parliament, and indeed the European Parliament in Brussels as a medium for enacting fair and humane laws while sharing our faith with others.

Here is a specific example of what I mean. In West Suffolk, clergy have recognised the value of meeting with their local councillors and, indeed, their local MPs in order to find out their representatives' views on particular issues. During these regular meetings, the clergy let the politicians know what they and their congregations think about important issues of the day.

In 2001, the clergy approached local councillors to complain about a new sex shop that opened in Bury St Edmunds, despite the fact that the shop was too near a residential area and on the main route for scores of schoolchildren. In early spring 2003, a meeting was held with David Ruffley MP to discuss the question of war with Iraq and other matters.

This is an excellent example of what all churches should be doing. The principle of Christians making their voices heard in the halls of government works locally, and it works nationally and internationally as well.

Real world application
The 2001 British census startled many of the pundits when it transpired that upwards to 71 per cent of British

1. Statistics released in February 2003.

people considered themselves to be Christians.[1] Having said that, few people realise that most of the 374 million citizens in the European Union's 15 member states are associated with the church in some way or another – and many are churchgoers. The German evangelical news agency IDEA published the following statistics:

- 58.4 per cent are Roman Catholic
- 18.4 per cent are Protestant
- 11 per cent are Anglican
- 2.7 per cent are Orthodox
- Muslims account for 2 per cent
- 7.4 per cent have no religious affiliation

These figures prompted both Catholic and Protestant leaders in Germany to issue a joint statement proposing that references to God be included in a future European constitution. Because Christians have such a strong majority within the EU, they feel this should be taken into account when framing legislation.[1] But whether or not this will happen depends on the attitudes and beliefs of the few Members of the European Parliament (MEPs) who sit on unelected committees, and not the millions of Europeans and their church leaders. In other words a few individuals alone will determine what sort of constitution Europe will have (a case of the tail wagging the dog).

Secular and not Christian ethics have informed the current spate of laws that have come out of Brussels to date. In the light of this, can there be a more urgent reason for Christians to enter politics as a legitimate expression of their Christian faith?

1. As quoted in 'Euro Religion', *Compass*, Autumn 2002, p. 6.

Some may say this is trying to create an imbalance within the European Parliament so that Christians will have an unfair advantage over the other groups. On the contrary, it is a case of correcting the imbalance that now exists between a minority of powerful secularists and a majority of Christians.

The following groups are dedicated to giving Christians a fair voice in government. You may wish to contact one or more to find out how you and your church may begin to be salt and light in a dark and decaying political system.

The Christian Institute
26 Jesmond Road, Newcastle upon Tyne, NE2 4PQ
Tel: 0191 281 5664; Fax: 0191 281 4272
E-mail: info@christian.org.uk
http://www.christian.org.uk

The Centre for Justice and Liberty
The Quadrangle, Crewe Hall, Crewe, CW1 6UZ
Tel: 01270 259380; Fax: 01270 259381
E-mail: centre@justiceandliberty.co.uk
http://www.justiceandliberty.co.uk/
(Log on for eye-opening news)

Christian Solidarity Worldwide
PO Box 99, New Malden, Surrey, KT3 3YF
Tel: 020 8942 8810
www.csw.org.uk/

Maranatha Community
102 Irlam Road, Flixton, Manchester, M41 6JT
Tel: 0161 748 4858; Fax: 0161 747 7379

Movement for Christian Democracy
Mayflower Family Centre
Vincent Street, London, E16 1LZ
Tel: 020 7474 1142
http://www.mcdpolitics.org/

For the time is coming when people will not endure sound teaching, but having itching ears they will accumulate for themselves teachers to suit their own likings, and will turn away from listening to the truth and wander into myths. As for you, always be steady, endure suffering, do the work of an evangelist, fulfil your ministry.
2 Timothy 4:3-5

CHAPTER 16

Engaging the media: three approaches

Dizzy Gillespie (1917-1993), American jazz trumpeter, was one of the twentieth century's leading bebop and jazz trumpeters. He was a master of this unique American musical style.[1]

On the tenth anniversary of the death of Mr Gillespie, BBC TV broadcast 'All that Jazz – Debunking the Myth of Dizzy Gillespie', a programme about the roots of jazz. Dr D. W. Jerkins, the musicologist who presented the programme, proclaimed, 'I doubt that jazz originated with African Americans around 1915. In my opinion, jazz was a myth – a sort of coconut shy – created by greedy record company executives in the late 1950s to sell records to gullible white people.' Outrageously, he claimed that Dizzy Gillespie probably didn't really exist. 'And anyway,' he sniffed, 'if [Gillespie] did exist at all, he was probably a stooge that didn't even play the trumpet.' So where did billions of people get the idea that Gillespie was a master of his craft?

1. 'Gillespie, Dizzy', Microsoft® Encarta. Copyright © 1994 Microsoft Corporation. Copyright © 1994 Funk & Wagnall's Corporation.

Jerkins was ready with his reply. 'Over the years, people just made up stories about his ability to play the trumpet.'

I just made up this crock, of course. There was no programme like this, and anyway, a reputable broadcasting company wouldn't take such a musicologist seriously. So why is it when the media present programmes about Christianity they mostly feature agnostics as 'experts'? Case in point: Just before Easter and again at Christmas 2002, BBC television and radio programmes featured clergy who indicated that they didn't believe the Bible or the creeds.[1]

This, of course, is in keeping with a media tradition that began in the 1980s, when each Easter the then Bishop of Durham, Dr David Jenkins, was invited by national broadcasting companies to speak about the Christian faith. Jenkins is the bishop who publicly labelled the resurrection as a 'conjuring trick done with bones'.[2]

1. Clearly there are more Christian leaders who are certain of their faith than uncertain – people such as Archbishop Maurice Couve de Murville; author David Winter; *Everyday With Jesus* compiler, Selwyn Hughes; author and speaker, Nicky Gumbel; ethicists Dr David Cook and Dr Patrick Dixon; house church leaders, Terry Virgo and Gerald Coates; leader of London's largest Church (Kensington Temple), Colin Dye; authors and Bible scholars John Stott, David Pawson and Derek Prince; singer songwriter Graham Kendrick; composer Noel Tredinnick; novelists Lynda Rose and Davis Bunn; and publishers Hugh Kealy, Tony Collins, John Hunt and Joe Kelly to name but a few. Why does the media routinely ignore these Christian leaders? Surely this raises serious questions about the practices of our so-called free media. If you agree, let the BBC hear from you. Address supplied at the end of this chapter.

2. In 1984, Jenkins, a 60-year-old theology professor at the University of Leeds, was appointed Bishop of Durham. During the ceremony he called the resurrection of Jesus a 'conjuring trick with bones'. To present this man as an authority on the Christian faith at Easter several years running was deeply offensive to millions of Christians. Of course, the media would never insult other religions on one of their holy days precisely because people of other faiths wouldn't tolerate it – nor should they have to, as the BBC is a public utility.

Blatantly anti-Christian attitudes aren't the only problem. More and more, the media is the exclusive domain of talented but misguided people. Through ignorance or design, they seem bent on capturing large audiences with excessive doses of anti-social behaviour and violence rather than producing quality programmes. The effect is taking its toll on viewers.

Studies conclude viewing certain programs . . . can increase aggression in children, make them more fearful and less trusting, and desensitise them to violent behaviour by other people (National TV Violence Study).[1] According to an article in the June 1994 issue of *Psychology Digest*, a definite correlation has been established between the growing violence on television and in movies and the increase in aggressive behaviour of people in general, but especially in the young.[2]

In January 2003, the broadsheets reported a major review of Britain's censorship laws which was initiated by the Government's adviser on youth crime amid growing concerns about the influence of violent films, games and rap music on young people. Lord Warner, the chairman of the Youth Justice Board told reporters that there had been a coarsening of attitudes towards violence caused by screen images which have a negative impact on teenagers.[3]

Youngsters aren't the only ones at risk. Adult media programming trivialises complex world events by presenting

---

1. Source: North Carolina Coalition for Pulling the Plug on Media Violence via PR NEWSWIRE.

2. 'Computer Games, Violence and Children' by Bryan Leech. Reprinted from *PC Update*, October 1994, the *Journal of Melbourne PC User Group Inc.*

3. Telegraph.co.uk, 'Tougher censoring of screen violence examined', Rachel Sylvester *(Filed 14/01/2003)*.

them in disjointed and often biased 'sound bites'. This latter point is the basis of Neil Postman's *Amusing Ourselves to Death*.[1] Postman worries that by dumbing down people's ability to analyse world events in their proper context, over time, people lose their critical faculties and become passive and more apt to act on emotion rather than on reason.

Since the problem isn't going to go away on its own, there seems to be three viable options to deal with these problems.

Approach one: Time for a national turn-off?

A few years ago *The Universe* printed a letter by a reader who wrote to say maybe it was time Christians gave up watching television. He wrote, 'People who would never use swear words in public think nothing of using Our Lord's name in an offensive way and this has crept into the media.' The correspondent complained that in a particular programme on BBC 1, a swear word was bleeped out while three blasphemies remained. He argues it's 'just one example of how we are almost helpless to keep up standards on the BBC. If we disapprove of programmes we can switch off, but we still have to pay the licence fee.'

Here's where a TV moratorium becomes interesting. I wonder what would happen if Britain's six million Christians plus their sympathisers cancelled their television licences and turned off their TVs in protest of the shoddy state of the national airwaves? Some say that as the BBC is not a commercial entity, an economic boycott won't have any effect. I disagree. At £112 per licence,[2] the mind boggles at the colossal loss of revenue to the BBC. Moreover,

1. Neil Postman, *Amusing Ourselves to Death* (New York: Penguin, 1985).
2. Current fee at time of publication.

the loss in advertising earnings within the Independent network would be incalculable.

At first, the media pundits and politicians would ignore a Christian-led boycott or greet such a demonstration with derision, but as soon as the ratings plummet, the money dries up, and politicians become worried about elections, you may be sure that the protesters would get a bit of respect.

Personally, I don't think a boycott is a good idea. For one thing, it would end up drawing negative media attention, reflecting badly on the Church. Secondly, as Britain has no electronic Christian media on which to fall back, I think it would be a mistake for Christians to retreat from mainstream media. The problems I mentioned earlier would only get worse.

The second approach

Another idea is to allow Christians to set up exclusively Christian radio and television stations such as London's Premier Radio and the God Channel. But I see many problems associated with this idea. I fully applaud the men and women behind these ventures. Currently, these ventures receive little or no backing from the denominations of our land, yet they are doing an admirable job dragging the British churches into the twenty-first century by demonstrating the value of the mass media. The main denominations would have to dig deeply into their pockets to fund such broadcasting companies, which I doubt they would do unless they could also control the editorial polices. But there is another much more serious problem to overcome if Christians are to compete within the broadcasting world. At present, there are draconian laws that prevent religious groups from owning and operating their own national broadcasting companies. That is where the Centre for Justice and Liberty comes in.

The Centre for Justice and Liberty represents over 25 Independent Christian Broadcasting Media organisations. It is a not-for-profit company and is supported by donations. The Centre for Justice and Liberty is pleased that the Government has added a 'determination' under the disqualification to allow Christian Broadcasters to apply for local and national digital programme service licences. However, as disqualified from applying for multiplex licences, which these services sit on, the way forward is far from simple according to Gareth Littler who was the Director of United Christian Broadcasters (UCB), Britain's pioneer Christian radio station, during its first 14 years.

Today the Centre for Justice and Liberty, birthed by Littler and Patricia Hargreaves, is at the forefront of the battle for Britain's airwaves. Gareth says, 'Our request continues to be for the Government to remove the clause that disqualifies religious individuals or bodies, and instead allow the regulators (OFCOM) to use codes to prevent unfit persons or extreme groups from broadcasting. OFCOM also select the most suitable programming for each licence.

'[In early 2003] The Communications Bill [was] passing through Parliament and we have lobbied at every stage. Currently we have amendments in the Commons asking for the removal of the disqualification. If the vote looks like going against us, they will be moved to the Lords. The Government hopes the Bill will be law by July 2003. We believe this may be the last easily available opportunity to ask.

'We currently have case 110722/02 at the European Court of Human Rights, Littler and Hargreaves v UK, challenging this disqualification, which discriminates against us on the grounds of freedom of religion, freedom of speech and freedom from discrimination on the grounds of religion.'

The result of this case, and other media matters of importance to Christians, can be seen by logging on to the Centre for Justice and Liberty's web site: http://www.justiceandliberty.co.uk/.

Approach three: If you can't beat them, join them

As I have indicated, I am not in favour of a boycott, and in order to survive, Christian broadcasting companies, should they be allowed to broadcast freely, will be forced to compete fiercely for revenue from a limited number of sympathetic sponsors. But there is a third way forward. Imagine what British media fare would be like if committed Christians worked as the CEOs, producers, directors, presenters, and editors within the BBC and the Independent networks, as well as within print media? I have an idea things would be a lot better than they now are.

Unfortunately, few Christians are qualified for these demanding posts. Therefore, it ought to be the Church's responsibility to ensure that in the future qualified Christians work within the media. I'll come back to this point. Meantime, if people are unhappy with our media, but they remain silent about it, they have no right to complain. But what may be done? Here are four suggestions:

First – Political coalitions

In the short term, we may form a political voice consisting of Christians and anyone else interested in improving the output of the media. Collectively, we must tell Parliament of our views. This would encourage legislators to make more informed decisions about laws that govern media fare, particularly as it relates to the portrayal of sex and violence and other issues of importance to people of faith. We must also support groups such as Centre for Justice and Liberty, which are dedicated to changing the archaic laws that currently forbid religious groups from owning and operating national broadcasting companies.

Some argue that the Government won't respond to pressure groups. But political coalitions are an effective means of bringing about legislative change. Years ago Blacks and Asians were routinely stereotyped in the media until concerned people put pressure on legislators to enact laws that prevent negative racial stereotyping. That is the power of the democratic process. Christians have yet to invoke this power in the name of decency. That is the message of the Centre for Justice and Liberty, the Christian Institute and Family and Youth Concern.

Second – Strategic viewing

The media work on the basis of supply and demand. Programme makers and editors know who their audiences are, and they want to keep them. Many are unaware of the demand for programming which upholds traditional values. Therefore Christians must make their viewing habits known. By reading guides to media fare, families may begin planning their weekly viewing, listening or reading, thereby boosting the ratings of the features they most enjoy. Once it becomes clear that certain productions draw substantial audiences, then more of the same will follow.

Third – Media awareness

Get into the habit of noting the names of the people responsible for programming or publications and fire off a letter, fax, e-mail or phone call to make your opinion known. Gripe about what you hate; applaud what you like.

Producers and editors do respond to informed feedback. As a former BBC producer, I can say audience feedback is taken very seriously. Remember, let the programme organisers know your thoughts – positive or negative. Otherwise, we'll only get what we deserve from the BBC and ITV and Channel 4, as well as from our tabloids and broadsheets.

Fourth – Media participation

It's against BBC policy to proselytise – that is, to persuade listeners to adopt the tenets of any religious faith. Balance, objectivity and religious neutrality ensure that the BBC remains true to its public service charter. A good example of this policy occurred over a decade ago when Billy Graham's London Crusade was broadcast on national television. Although segments of Graham's sermons were presented live, when Billy Graham gave an altar call, the home viewers were presented with other aspects of Graham's work. And rightly so. In a pluralistic society, no religion has the right to use the airwaves to make converts.[1] Moreover, few, if any, western people are converted to the

1. However, one religious group is routinely allowed to seek converts via Britain's airwaves. I refer to *Secular Humanists*. The non-existence of God is the basic tenet of *Secular Humanism*. Indeed, *The Humanist Manifesto I & II* is to the humanist religion as the Bible and the Koran are to Christians, Jews and Muslims. *The Humanist Manifesto I & II* charges humanists everywhere to make converts by undermining all religion in general.

Christian faith by television programmes. Conversion comes out of nourishing, meaningful, and often lengthy relationships and that takes a real, live, church on the corner. Hence, there is no such thing as an electronic church. Nevertheless, the media may be seen as an important tool to be used by the churches to see people led to faith in our nation.

Once upon a time, Christians dominated the media, making no apology for their faith. They didn't have to. Their work was every bit as good as that of their non-believing colleagues. Lord Reith was no evangelist, but he was passionately committed to the principles of the Sermon on the Mount. He also knew the power of the media to change people's lives for good. During his tenure as director-general, the BBC set the world's standard for wholesome family programmes and unimpeachable journalism.

Dorothy L. Sayers turned the drama world on its head during the mid-1940s with her radio series entitled 'The Man Who Would be King.' Her decision to portray Jesus speaking in plain English instead of the stilted Elizabethan language of the King James Bible was considered so radical that the controller tried to censor the scripts. The plays went on to critical and popular acclaim and remain as fresh today as 60 years ago.

At the height of World War II, C. S. Lewis, best known for his polemical Christian works, took to the airwaves with a series of 15-minute talks at the invitation of the BBC. Lewis' biographer George Sayer recalls soldiers in pubs listening attentively throughout the entire broadcasts.[1]

1. These broadcasts were later printed into an out-of-print volume called *Broadcast Talks*. Later they were edited again and found their way into *Mere Christianity*, a book many leading Christians point to as instrumental in their conversion to Christ.

Born-again Christian J. Arthur Rank stood up to the Hollywood movie moguls and thereby saved this nation's film-making industry. Not only did he save it, but he is credited with ushering in the Golden Age of British film during the 40s and 50s.

Where are the Christian communicators today?

The fact is, communicators are not born, they are nurtured, and this process takes a long time, and help from others. The churches of this country need to reclaim radio, television, print, cinema, and drama as part of their mission. Would your church support a person trying to make a difference in the media?

I speak at many churches around the UK, and ministers often tell me about the number of missionaries they support in India, Africa, South America, etc. I am glad that churches are committed to overseas missionaries, but the time has come for us to see the media as a mission field. To that end, it's the Church's responsibility to ensure that qualified Christians work within the media helping to form the messages that affect the attitudes of this nation.

Theological colleges need to broaden their curriculum to include more than a nod at mass communications. Film and video making, journalism, radio production and other communication skills need entire departments. The end result not only would produce tomorrow's technicians, producers, and writers, but it would also teach tomorrow's vicars, priests, and pastors how to use mass media as part of their church's mission to the communities they serve. Such programmes have existed for years in the United States, and the time has come for them to be introduced here.

Parents ought to encourage their children to seek careers in the media, for the earlier a child catches a vision for a career in media, the more likely he or she will make the right decisions about GCSEs and A-levels, and indeed, colleges and universities, all of which are key factors in finding one's way into radio, television, and cinema.

Finally, when people think of BBC radio, they invariably think of Radio 1, 2, 3, and 4, presuming that these national stations pull in the lion's share of the listening audience on any given day. This isn't true. BBC Radio's largest audience comes from local radio stations, not the national stations. For that reason, Christians should listen to local radio with an eye to responding to invitations to share opinions and insights about topical issues. For example, on 20 January 2003, the media carried a story about motor neurone sufferer Reg Crewe, the first Briton to travel to Switzerland in order to commit suicide legally. Throughout the day, various BBC local radio stations asked listeners to comment on what they thought about this idea. I wonder how many local churches across the United Kingdom had planned to phone in these programmes to give a Bible-based response to the question of euthanasia.

How do I get started?

Each year the BBC sponsors projects geared to find new faces and voices for tomorrow's programmes. How many members from *your* congregation applied for these opportunities to work in the media? Pray that God would inspire godly youngsters to take the gospel to the nation through the media. The need is always there for new talent. Check out the BBC's own talent-seeking website: www.bbc.co.uk/talent.

Each week *The Guardian* newspaper's media section carries ads inviting young people to apply for places in BBC radio, TV and other media. Why not use that page to form a strategy for helping younger members of your congregation to break into a media career?

The Christian lifestyle is not merely personal; we are called to transform the culture around us as well. This means the media must be seen as a legitimate mission field for all Christians. Churches must establish boards to recruit those in their midst with the aptitude and the desire to work in the media. Please be aware that this is a long-term commitment, as it would require finding, screening, selecting, and nurturing candidates, seeing them into universities, and eventually into entry-level careers in media. Since this would be a minimum commitment of three to five years, the churches of this country need to view radio, television, print, cinema and drama as an integral part of their mission, making it a priority.

A few churches already do this. One of the best examples that I know of is called the Berkshire, Buckinghamshire and Oxfordshire Churches' Media Trust (CMT), a charitable trust that supports Christians working in the media.

The Rev Richard Thomas is the Communications Officer for the Diocese of Oxford. He heads CMT. According to Richard, 'I can't stress how important it is for local church leaders to be prepared to handle the media with skill. While there are very media-minded clergy . . . it's also true that many leaders – along with other thinking people – mistrust journalists and avoid contact whenever possible.

'They recognise the insidious nature of the sound-bite culture which can trivialise serious issues. Originally set up to encourage Christians in local broadcasting, CMT is fully ecumenical and seeks to promote excellence in media relations for churches and church leaders (by) raising the profile of print, broadcast and electronic media for churches and making the churches visible in the media.'

Since it was established in 1991, CMT has:

- Funded a religious production post for BBC Radio Oxford and another for BBC Radio Berkshire
- Helped fund Christian contributions to ILR stations in High Wycombe (1170) and Aylesbury (Mix 96)
- Provided funding for a 'Care Desk' at Fox FM in Oxford
- Provided equipment for a number of local church Restricted Service Licence (RSL) special event radio stations
- Made numerous small grants for media-related projects

A word of advice to writers

Although broadcasting is heavily regulated, print media is less so. Therefore, the Church has a powerful voice in mass media through the many fine Christian publishers here in the United Kingdom. Perhaps you have thought about writing.

Alison Hull is a commissioning editor for the Paternoster Press. She is an excellent communicator who has come up through the ranks as a freelancer. She offers this sober advice to all aspiring Christian writers. 'Anyone who wants to be a writer has to ask themselves some very stern questions. Firstly, are you sure this is what God is calling you to do? Why?

'Secondly, I think people need to find out whether they want to write or whether they want to communicate. This may sound tautologous, but it isn't. Many people love writing and find it enormously cathartic, but are less concerned with getting the thoughts and feelings inside them into others. Others want to communicate and will choose writing as one method of doing so. Or they may choose to use speech or a combination of the two. What sort of writer are you?

'To be a good writer, you have to study good writing. Read, read, read. Analyse – why does that book work while that one doesn't? Why could you not bear to put one book down when you couldn't bear to pick another one up? What is good writing?

'Can you bear criticism? No writer is infallible, producing sacrosanct script. If you cannot cope with editors changing your words and challenging you to do better, you don't have a future in writing.

'There is also the "So what?" question to be answered. It is unfortunately true that who you are matters in books and magazines, as well as what you write. It is of course true that a writer can come from nowhere and, on the merit of the book that they have written, become successful. But by and large, this happens to the writers of fiction. If you believe you have the key to solving the church's problems, or the economy's, or the problem of world poverty, politics or terrorism, you have to back that up.

'If you have worked in politics for twenty years, you have some credibility. Otherwise you don't and few reputable publishers will be interested in your thoughts. Similarly, don't write the definitive book to solve all the problems of church leadership if you are not a respected and established church leader.

'Don't go into writing if your main aim is to become rich. There are different kinds of writers – journalists, fiction writers, non-fiction writers, interviewers, feature writers, poets, dramatists – and you need to research what kind of writing you want to do and why. But then you need to get on with it and write. And write. And write.

'Be self-critical. Learn all you can about good grammar and spelling and punctuation, because if your work is poor in these areas it does mean that editors will have a more jaundiced eye. But work on developing your own style. Listen for the rhythm of words – not just in poetry but in everyday speech and even in newspaper articles.

'Don't fall so far in love with words that you cannot use them wisely. Remember, less is more when you are writing, particularly descriptions. Every adjective and adverb has to be there for a very good reason.'

Time to act

Churches must help Christians become properly trained for media work. Consider committing yourself to praying and supporting financially the organisations listed in this chapter.

Real world application

Is God calling *you* to a ministry in the media? Remember: if you can't beat the media, join it! Here are the names and addresses of the organisations mentioned in this chapter.

Centre for Justice and Liberty

Patricia Hargreaves
The Quadrangle, Crewe Hall, Crewe, CW1 6UZ
Tel: 01270 259380; Fax: 01270 259381
E-mail: centre@justiceandliberty.co.uk

Phone the BBC on 08700 100222; or write to:
BBC Information Office
PO Box 1922, Glasgow, G23 WT
E-mail the BBC feedback line at: info@bbc.co.uk

ITV/Ch 4

At the time this book went to press, Channel 4's Viewers' Enquiries/Complaints website was not functioning. However, you may contact them by post at:

Channel 4 News, ITN
200 Gray's Inn Road, London, WC1X 8XZ
Fax: 0207 430 4607
E-mail: news@channel4.com

The Churches' Media Trust
The Rev Richard Thomas
Diocesan Church House
North Hinksey, Oxford, OX2 ONR
Tel: 01865 208200
E-mail: thomasrp@thomasrp.demon.co.uk

Association of Christian Writers
73 Lodge Hill Road, Farnham, Surrey, GU10 3RB
Tel: 01252 715746
E-mail: admin@christianwriters.org.uk

He who oppresses a poor man insults his Maker, but he who
is kind to the needy honours him.
Proverbs 14:31

CHAPTER 17

Social action

In the room where I write, I have a large antique print based on a Hogarth painting. The original hangs in St Bartholomew's Hospital in London (or it did in 1772!). It depicts the parable of 'The Good Samaritan', the parable Jesus told a lawyer to teach him that Christianity is a lifestyle not a philosophy.

Philosophers are known by their words, not their actions. Since this is so, Jesus is telling us that Christians should be known by their actions as much as their piety.[1]

Hence Jesus said, 'go and do likewise' when we meet people in need (Luke 10:37). James, the brother of Jesus puts it like this:

> What good is it, my brothers, if a man claims to have faith but has no deeds? Can such faith save him? Suppose a brother or sister is without clothes and daily food. If one of you says to him, 'Go, I wish you well; keep warm and well fed', but does nothing about his physical needs, what good is it? In the same way, faith by itself, if it is not accompanied by action, is dead. But someone will say, 'You

1. This action should be seen as being motivated by a living faith in Jesus, not as a means of earning our salvation, for Jesus makes it clear elsewhere that salvation is a gift from God, not the reward of our merit (John 6:28, 29; Matthew 7;22, 23).

have faith; I have deeds.' Show me your faith without deeds, and I will show you my faith by what I do (James 2:14-18).

Martin Luther, one of the prime movers of the Protestant reformation, is said to have lobbied to have the book of James removed from the canon of scripture. He feared that the above passage might tempt people to think that they must try to earn their way to heaven. The book remained, but the opposite has happened.

Over the centuries, many Christians knowing they are saved by grace not by works have overlooked their responsibility to help the less fortunate. But not all Christians forgot. For instance, there came a massive social change as the result of John Wesley and other reformers.

Faith in action

A man of many parts, Wesley preached salvation by faith alone. However, a scientific man, he also taught about the need for public health and sanitation. A social reformer, his revival sermons not only fought sin and ignorance, but they also went some way to elevate the status of Jews, Catholics, women and other oppressed groups. Consequently, whether or not they agree with his religious convictions, most historians say Wesley's preaching saved Britain from the ravages of an insurrection similar to the French Revolution (1789 to 1799).

Later, Wesley's followers influenced the rise of unions, implemented humane labour laws, and proposed a host of other enlightened social legislation which today we take for granted. Largely due to the evangelistic zeal of one man, large numbers of influential people were converted to the Christian faith, birthing an era of humane laws and human rights.

Between 1800 and 1900, Christian legislators abolished the slave trade, Christian industrialists improved the lot of labourers, and the poor and children were placed on the government's agenda for the first time.

Charities and other welfare schemes for the sick, the infirm, and the needy grew out of Christian doctrines upheld by men like Lord Shaftesbury, William Wilberforce, and a number of MPs and community leaders who called themselves the Clapham Set after their church in Clapham in London.

The women's movement

Many feminists do not realise that the early advocates of women's rights were committed Christians. Elizabeth Cady Stanton, Lucretia C. Mott, Susan B. Anthony and Harriet Tubman based equality with men on the teachings of the Bible. In the twentieth century, Helen Keller linked the cause of women's rights with the rights of the handicapped, arguing that in Christ all are equal: 'There is neither Jew nor Greek, slave nor free, male nor female, for you are all one in Christ Jesus' (Galations 3:28).[1]

Change agents

Finally, John Newman, John Ruskin, Gerard Manley Hopkins, and, in the early twentieth century, G. K. Chesterton, Hilaire Belloc and others infused art, literature, architecture and journalism with the social conscience and the values of the Good Samaritan.

---

1. In the light of the Christian convictions held by this illustrious list of women's rights advocates, it is sad to see how humanists and atheists later hijacked the women's movement for their own purposes.

Truly, men and women committed to a Christian lifestyle exerted a great influence on society, both here and abroad, as you will see by the work done by Christians in India.

Christianity spreads democracy

Many historians have insisted that the British Empire corrupted Indian culture. Everything that was ever wrong in India – indeed, anything that is wrong with India today – is the fault of the British, or so the argument goes. But some Indians are grateful for Britain's past contributions to Indian culture.

In 1993 I wrote a four-part radio documentary on the life of William Carey, the man called the Father of the Modern Missionary Movement. He felt that God was calling him to work in India towards the last part of the eighteenth century. In addition to preaching the Gospel, Carey taught the people he met about sanitation, western medicine, as well as opening a college that has turned out countless Indian educators, politicians, and agriculturists over the last two centuries. For this Carey is greatly honoured in India. Even the Indian feminists admire William Carey, if for no other reason than that it was he who single-handedly caused the abolishment of *Suttee*, the ancient Hindu custom whereby a deceased man's widow was burned alive on her husband's funeral pyre. Carey championed other feminist causes by allowing women to learn to read and write.

'It is impossible to say just how much good the British did in India,' so says Vishal Mangalwadi, author of the book, *India: The Grand Experiment*.[1] 'Much of what is good in India today is the result of the work of key British Christians.'

1. All quotes appear with the permission of Mr Mangalwadi.

Winner of the Dr Bhimrao Ambedkar Distinguished National Service Award, Vishal Mangalwadi suggests that while history doesn't lie, historians often do – especially if they have a decidedly anti-Christian bias. In this carefully documented book, the author defends the work done by British evangelicals – all of whom were early advocates of Indian human rights.

Christian missionaries, he argues, were responsible for the rediscovery of Indian languages and literature, and for the introduction not only of schools and hospitals but, more importantly, for laying the entire foundation of Indian economics, agriculture, science and society – because they believed that the Empire was given to England by God as a sacred trust.

To be sure, *India: The Grand Experiment*, doesn't paint a picture of a happy, Golden Age in India presided over by the Raj. On the contrary, British colonisation of India was self-serving at best and criminal at worst. Nevertheless the work of key Christians – specifically William Wilberforce, Charles Grant and William Carey – stopped much of the exploitation by introducing the rule of law, human dignity, democracy, and a sense of moral certainty into a land rife with corruption long before the British arrived. 'We cannot underestimate the contributions made by the British when we look at India's history,' says Mangalwadi. 'The spiritual dynamics which democratised India were the same as those that made England and America politically free societies. When Baptist Missionary Society founder, William Carey, wrote the manifesto of modern Protestant missions in 1792, he was merely stating what seemed to him an integral part of the biblical worldview, i.e. that a Christian is responsible to teach people the laws of God as a means for free, responsible, civilised life. Carey knew that political liberty was God's desire for mankind.'

Of course, the directors of East India Company attempted to stop men like Carey. They feared the Gospel of Christ, viewing it as a form of liberation theology, and hence counterproductive to their desire to make profits by exploiting Indian workers. Sooner or later men who know they are made in God's image will want to be democratic and free.

Mangalwadi puts the cat in with the pigeons when he defends Victorian missionary activity in India. He argues, 'Contrary to modern condemnation of Christian missionaries, their influence brought higher education to the masses in India.

'The evangelical plan for higher education began to succeed in awakening the Indian mind for freedom, in "raising the subject to the pedestal of the ruler" . . . Although some of our historians do not always see the connection between higher education and political freedom, they at least acknowledge that the leaders of the Independence Movement were aware of the political significance of education.'

The author acknowledges that India has suffered from European influence. But they were influences such as secular humanism, Darwinism, unbridled capitalism, fascism, and communist Marxism – not Christianity.

According to Mangalwadi, 'God works through history to bless nations. India has received blessings through the Christian missionaries – few Indian historians will deny this. It could happen again – but not through mere human ideology.'

Action must be predicated by faith, not vice versa
As Vishal Mangalwadi points out, human effort alone will

never eradicate social ills. For genuine social change to take place, like the changes brought about through Wesley, Carey, Shaftesbury, and others, we must empty ourselves of human ambition and be totally submissive to the Holy Spirit – the genuine Christian lifestyle demands this.

This later point was driven home to me recently. Dennis Wrigley of Maranatha, an international prayer community dedicated to effecting social change through prayer, told an audience about a letter he had received from Mother Teresa when the Maranatha community was first founded. She said, 'If you pray without serving, your prayers are in vain, if you serve without praying, your service is in vain.' Wise words.

Faith in action

One organisation that fully appreciates the relationship between social action and total submission to God is the Nottingham Prayer Camps Network that I mentioned in chapter 14. The group is not a camp *per se*, but its members meet regularly to pray as led by the Spirit, or sometimes to pray according to a specific agenda. The network's name comes from Ezekiel 4:1-3, which commands God's people to set up camps – hence the name Prayer Camps Network. Their aim is to bring about radical social and spiritual change to the city of Nottingham.

Beginning back in the 1960s, this movement came about as the result of specific scriptures – Isaiah 55, Deuteronomy 1:8 and Isaiah 49:8-9. One woman – Ruth Bussell – set up the network. Not long after, 'Task Forces' were born. A Task Force is a group or groups of people from many denominations or none who concentrate on a particular geographic location and represent the Church in that area. Ruth points out that Task Forces are especially successful at forming good relationships, particularly with police and councils.

This led to the establishment of Neighbourhood Prayer Watches, similar to the scheme called Neighbourhood Watch, even including putting stickers on windows and setting up a telephone prayer chain. The aim is not to deter crime by reporting it. It is to deter crime and other vice by *praying*. More and more people became involved through monthly prayer breakfasts that included other towns in Nottinghamshire. The prayer leaders of these prayer breakfasts meet together once a month, and the telephone prayer chain is developing into a 24-hour Prayer Clock involving numerous churches in the county.

The Prayer Clock involves prayer co-ordinators from each church who watch over their particular area and ensure involvement. Administrators co-ordinate the 24-hour Prayer Clock and keep prayers informed of needs. 'Prayer co-ordinators currently meet together at regular intervals to pray and to share, continuing this theme of networking. Church leaders meet together regularly on a Thursday lunchtime with a particular emphasis once a month to include those unable to attend on a weekly basis,' said Ruth. This fixed prayer agenda keeps prayers focused on particular issues rather than becoming side-tracked by special needs.

The Lord Mayor has requested a clear Christian voice in Nottingham representing all Christian denominations. The prayer network has been accepted by Christian leaders, resulting in more corporate prayer and initiative – the vision called CTFN – Christians Together for Nottingham.

A Christian police inspector who believes in the power of prayer works more closely with local churches. The inspector feels the drop in the crime rate is due directly to the prayer network. This work is moving into two other inner city areas. What is happening is exciting, and Nottingham Prayer Camps Network realises that if they want this work to continue, they must train others to continue praying. According to Ruth, 'Training for Warfare courses are run regularly throughout the year to ensure that people are properly taught and prepared as they commit themselves to pray for the city.'

Nottingham isn't the only place where prayer networks effect social change for the better. Since January 2000 every home in the Shetland Islands has been prayed for every month. The vision behind the 'Every Shetland Home for Jesus' prayer team is to cover Shetland with a blanket of prayer with every home being prayed for every month.

According to spokeswoman Karen Drummond-Hunt, 'The vision came as a result of the longing in the hearts of many individual Christians in the Islands to see God move in power, and friends, relatives and neighbours come to know the Lord Jesus, and to breakthrough in prayer on their behalf.' Eventually, the many came together and the rest is, as they say, history.

The electoral register was used as a basis for the initiative and each area was divided up so that each person would be praying a few minutes for ten or so people a day, together with the relevant households. 'This meant that 74 separate areas were needed to cover the population of approximately 22,000. Significantly, we saw this target reached with every adult being prayed for by name every month together with their home,' said Karen.

'There have already been signs of answered prayer. On

one of the outer islands where there has been some friction between neighbours for many years over land disputes, the residents are now helping each other. In one situation, a family went to see another family with whom they had been feuding, and they apologised to each other for the fighting and hardness that had grown up between them.'

Karen points out that while the prayers are specifically directed at seeing people converted to Christianity, there have been remarkable side effects that demonstrate the power of prayer to break strongholds, including people being delivered from occult oppression and alcohol addiction. 'Prayer team members are bumping into people on their lists; previously unfriendly neighbours are smiling and even initiating contact with Christians. It is amazing to know that, as you walk around the towns and villages, the people you come across are all being prayed for.'

Karen told me that the initiative has also come to the attention of someone who is involved in the House of Lords who is now hoping to start a prayer team to cover all the MPs and Members of the House of Lords.

Time to act

God loves human beings (he created us to love him after all), and he loves social justice. To see evidence of this claim, take time to read the Old Testament book of Deuteronomy, a beautiful social manifesto that inextricably links the love of God with social action. As James reiterates in Chapter 2:14-17, faith is not subjective and inward looking. Faith calls for us to help the poor, and to fight injustice wherever we find it. In this the Old Testament and the New Testament agree. What about your church? What programmes are currently running that reflect the parable of the Good Samaritan? If there aren't any, *why not*?

Real world application

Every Christian alive today has been commissioned by Jesus to present the Gospel (Matthew 28:18-20). Being born again won't guarantee that we'll eradicate every social problem. But as we study the scriptures and try to live out the Christian lifestyle within the context of the story of the Good Samaritan, it's likely that we will find ample opportunities to share the love of Jesus with others in need. Here is a list of organisations you may wish to contact or support as a first step in putting your faith into action.

Christian Aid
Christian Aid, FREEPOST, London, SE1 7YY
http://www.christian-aid.org.uk/

Cafod
Romero Close, Stockwell Road, London, SW9 9TY
Tel: 020 7733 7900; Fax: 020 7274 9630
E-mail: hqcafod@cafod.org.uk

Oasis Trust
Oasis Trust, The Oasis Centre,
115 Southwark Bridge Road, London, SE1 0AX
Tel: 020 7450 9000; Fax: 020 7450 9001
E-mail: enquiries@oasistrust.org

Tearfund
100 Church Road, Teddington, TW11 8QE
Supporter Enquiries: 0845 355 8355 (local rate calls)
E-mail: enquiry@tearfund.org
Head Office: Tel: 020 8977 9144; Fax: 020 8943 3594

Scotland
Challenge House, 29 Canal Street, Glasgow, G4 0AD
Tel: 0141 332 3621; Fax: 0141 400 2980

Ireland
Rose House, 2 Derryvolgie Avenue, Belfast, BT9 6FL
Tel: 02890 682 828; Fax: 02890 682 829

Overseas House, 3 Belgrave Road, Rathmines, Dublin 6
Tel and Fax: 00 353 1 497 5285

Wales
Unit 6, Cefn Lla Science Park
Aberystwyth, Ceredigion, SY23 3AH
Tel and Fax: 01970 626006

The Salvation Army
The Salvation Army UK HQ
101 Newington Causeway, London, SE1 6BN
Tel: 0845 634 0101
E-mail: webmajor@salvationarmy.org.uk

Maranatha
102 Irlam Road, Fixton, Manchester, M41 6JT
Tel: 0161 748 4858; Fax: 0161 747 7379

To find out more about Vishal Mangalwadi, author of the
book, *India: The Grand Experiment*, contact:

South Asian Development Partnership
50 Grove Road, Sutton, Surrey, SM1 1BT
Or log on to: http://www.shouthasian.org.uk

In the USA

http://www.emmf.com/dompics.htm
Episcopal medical missions. Includes statistics for South America and the Caribbean.

http://www.medicalmissions.com/
Christian medical missions organisation.

http://www.globalmission.org/megamenu.htm
Megamenu of missions opportunities. Something for everyone.

How beautiful on the mountains are the feet of those who bring good news, who proclaim peace, who bring good tidings, who proclaim salvation, who say to Zion, 'Your God reigns!'
Isaiah 52:7, NIV

CHAPTER 18

Giving your faith away

Although it may be politically incorrect to say it, Christianity is not a private matter. The *raison d'être* of a Christian lifestyle is not merely about effecting social change or securing our own place in the afterlife. It is about evangelism – making converts.

Why should we try to convert people to our faith? For one thing, Jesus ordered us to: 'Go therefore and make disciples of all nations, baptising them in the name of the Father, and of the Son, and of the Holy Spirit, teaching them to observe all that I have commanded you' (Matthew 28:19-20). This passage, known as the Great Commission, sums up what it means to live the Christian lifestyle 24/7.

Essentially there are two categories of evangelism – local and global. When Jesus commissioned the apostles to go out and live the Christian lifestyle, he made this distinction clearly in Acts 1:8 which I quote in part: '. . .You shall be my witnesses in Jerusalem and in all Judea and Samaria [local] and to the end of the earth [global].' Of course, how we go about doing this varies according to our gifts and our calling. Here are examples of how two individuals have responded to the Great Commission – David Fanstone of

Open Air Campaigners (OAC) and George Verwer of Operation Mobilisation. See which of these two approaches appeals to you.

Local

'Presenting Christ by all means everywhere' is the motto of OAC. This involves one man or woman taking the Gospel to where people are.

According to UK founder and London Director of OAC, David Fanstone, street preaching is alive and well in the United Kingdom. While David was a student in 1965 at the Moody Bible Institute in Chicago, he came across the American OAC. 'I was drawn to it, as my call was evangelism. An evangelist must be outgoing in the sense of taking the church to people who don't come to church.' David returned to England and within three years, he had helped set up OAC here.

'OAC train and work with all ages using contemporary methods such as drama, puppets, and in some cases, Gospel magic – conjuring tricks, rope tricks and the like – to make a biblical application come alive. It's a visual aid with a message and people do react well to us, even if they know nothing about the Bible.'

Tony is a fruit vendor in London's Oxford Street. For many years he was unfriendly to a team of Open Air Campaigners who set up a sketchboard near him to explain the significance of the Gospel to shoppers. However, after hearing the many colourful Gospel messages, God came into Tony's life. Today, Tony directs his customers to stop and listen to the preachers near his stall. One never knows how far the work of a street evangelist goes to bring people to faith.

Bill agrees. Bill has spent his entire adult life telling people about Jesus through his work and his lifestyle. His life was impacted one evening in 1971 while he was returning home from a party with some friends. They had been drinking. When they came around a corner, they met an open-air evangelist. 'To make a long story short, I argued vehemently with this chap, and in the end, I laughed him off. But I had heard him say two important things before I walked away that night. The first was that I was a sinner. I already knew that, although I probably wouldn't have used that word at the time. I mean, I just knew my life was heading in the wrong direction somehow. The second important thing I heard that night was that there was hope for me, and that hope was Jesus.

'He had quoted a number of scriptures, including John 3:16, now a very familiar scripture to me, but at the time, I had never even heard it. Within 18 months, I heard the gospel again and again, and those times, I knew what it was about. In May of 1972, I gave my life to Christ and I've never looked back. Incidentally, a few years later, I happened to meet one other fellow who had been with me that night, and he told me he became a Christian, too. Sadly, he was killed in a motorcycle accident a few years later, but I know he is with the Lord now.

'When I give my testimony, I often say to my friends, I'm certain that that poor evangelist went home that night discouraged.' Bill laughed and added, 'I have told countless others about Jesus because that man preached the gospel in my city that night. Never underestimate the effectiveness of open-air preaching.'

Preaching isn't just words. It's artwork, too. OAC pioneered the use of the sketchboard for open-air preaching in Britain and thanks to OAC many towns and cities have open-air teams working on the streets of our nation.

According to Alice Fanstone, 'OAC evangelists are always in demand by local churches to speak at special events like Family Services and Youth Outreaches, and leading Holiday Clubs for children.' David adds, 'We're in demand because if you can get across the Gospel message on the street, you can communicate pretty well to anybody anywhere.

'We are low-cringe in our approach: clever visual aids, talking *to* rather than *at* people, and drawing them in using creative methods without compromising the message of the Bible – that's our style. The parables of Jesus were startling and relevant – even shocking – to his audiences, and we hope that our presentations will have the same effect on ours,' he said.

David points out that his vision is for every major population to have its own trained team of evangelists. 'We also share this vision for overseas ministry in Ireland, Albania, Greece and Romania.'

Open Air Campaigners has been working in Britain since 1968 when David preached at the first sketchboard open-air on the seafront in Brighton on the south coast. From the small beginnings, the British staff has grown. There are currently about 20 evangelists on the full-time staff scattered throughout the country. There is also one trainee, a General Secretary and a National Treasurer. The work is supported by a faithful council who meet regularly in London and work hard to keep the organisation on track with legal and other matters.

All evangelists are members of a local church and are often involved in preaching and teaching roles. The evangelists are trained to work within the church and are particularly effective in all-age evangelistic services. 'Many of our evangelists lead both adult, youth and children's missions within churches,' said David.

'This is a significant distinctive of OAC and all our evangelists are trained both to preach in the open air and to provide training in this area. The sketchboard or illusions/escapology would be most people's choice for this sphere of communication as a visual presentation is most likely to draw a crowd. Most of the evangelists operate an open-air ministry on a regular or semi-regular basis – as much as possible given the unpredictability of the British weather!'

In Britain it is a legal requirement that each child in school should attend a daily act of worship, and should also be taught Religious Education. OAC has the privilege of being able to go into state schools to take assemblies and also religion classes. Again the sketchboard is a useful tool for telling Bible stories, supplemented by illusions to illustrate gospel messages. OAC evangelists have one of the most extensive schools ministries in the country in terms of the number of children they reach with the Gospel on a regular basis. This has a direct effect in the open air when children and young people recognise the staff and the input can then be followed up.

Some of their staff in port cities are involved in co-operation with the Seamen's Mission in visiting ships. It is an effective way of sharing the Gospel with people from around the world.

In Britain many prisoners are coming to faith and some of the OAC staff regularly minister 'inside'.

A regular feature of British life are New Age festivals that take place mainly in the summer months and particularly down in the south-west of the country. OAC teams are frequently a feature of these events and are usually on the programme as 'Traditional Story Tellers'. David Fanstone adds, 'Our marquee is a good centre for people to come and relax and chat, watch children's presentations, get faces painted and many other things!'

OAC has always been a 'give away' organisation. Training and motivating individuals for evangelism is a central part of their ministry. In 2002 they ran one National Training Seminar in open-air evangelism in Glasgow, organised by Training Director Geoff Beckingham. In addition to this, many OAC staff are ready to provide training for individuals or groups, tailored to specific needs. There is also of course the national staff-training programme for those who want to work on the full-time staff.

OAC Ministries is a faith mission, and each evangelist is responsible for raising his/her own support. OAC is supported by a huge variety of people and churches who give, often sacrificially, so that the work can continue, and pray faithfully so that the work is effective.

Go global

Two thousand years after Pentecost, why are there still 2000 people groups representing hundreds of millions of men and women who have never heard the Gospel? 'Part of the reason is that many people assume someone else is doing the missionary work. They aren't,' says George Verwer, founder of Operation Mobilisation, and originator of Acts 13 – Breakthrough, a missionary scheme designed to ignite the church with a fresh vision for releasing missionaries into the so-called 10/40 window, a section of the globe covering parts of North Africa, Middle East and

India and the rest of Asia, and representing many of the world's least evangelised nations.

Acts 13 – Breakthrough is a strategy to help get 200,000 new missionaries from the whole body of Christ out into the mission fields that remain in every nation of the world. George Verwer explains where the idea came from: 'I was on a flight from Cordoba to Buenos Aires after taking part in Love Latin America in the mid-1990s. I have always had a burden for sending and mobilising missionaries but never expected a breakthrough like this. On that flight in Argentina, God gave me the vision of Acts 13 – Breakthrough.'

Verwer admits his idea is hardly original. 'It's nothing new as some churches have been doing it since the church in Antioch started things moving, as recorded in Acts 13. At present, however, across the globe, only a small percentage of churches are into Acts 13 sending, and our goal is to see this change. Only faith, prayer and action will do this.'

Supporters of Acts 13 – Breakthrough are praying for over 100,000 churches to be involved globally. 'Certainly there are many who doubt that the task may be done overnight. And they are correct,' Verwer said. ' I don't believe it is right to say we hope to accomplish this task by a specific time. But I sense that it is possible to mobilise 200,000 new missionaries in the next few years.'

Verwer anxiously points to Matthew 9:37-38: 'The harvest is plentiful, but the labourers are few; pray therefore the Lord of the harvest to send out labourers into the harvest.' Verwer added, 'If your church is too small to send one new missionary, consider partnership with another fellowship in your denomination or area. We have the resources. We have the money. We have the know-how. It will only take commitment and an openness to the prompting of the Holy Spirit. Much is already being done. Much more needs to be done.'

Who will go?

The plan is simple. Every church in the world needs to send at least one worker longer-term into the harvest field, even if it starts with a one- or two-year field-training programme. Tens of thousands are in various colleges and training institutions who need to be affirmed, supported and then sent out, especially among the unreached people.

Since there are already scores of sending missions doing just this, what makes this vision unique? 'Acts 13 – Breakthrough is a vision and concept in which we all become more focused and specific about sending out workers,' Verwer explained. 'We have a tape that presents how this can be done. We have as our goal the mobilisation of 200,000 workers, and we need about 100,000 churches around the globe to get involved in specific ways.

'There are many model sending churches around the globe and we can learn from them. Of course, God will lead different churches in different ways, and this is where I cry out that we would have a grace-awakened attitude towards each other.'

Chacko Thomas is Co-ordinator for the Missions Mobilisation Network, which supports Acts 13 – Breakthrough. He shares George Verwer's zeal for the strategy. 'This is a great plan which has enormous potential to help finish the task of world evangelism.' Thomas' associate, Cliff Newham, added, 'Acts 13 – Breakthrough is a vision, not a programme. It's a way that churches can get hold of and use for themselves the principles of Acts 13 to develop their own missions outreach in their own way.'

Some experts estimate that the world's unreached people groups contain as many as two billion people. These ethnic groups have very few believers and practically no churches. And while some of these people may have heard the name of Jesus, few have ever had any contact with Christian missionaries with a vision for their spiritual and physical well-being.

Missionaries are people who leave their culture to bring the gospel to the people of another culture. They may be so-called 'tent-makers' as the apostle Paul was in his day. Others may require support. In either case, George Verwer warns there is a danger in assuming that other people are doing the work – in the field or as supporters of full-time missionaries. 'We talk about it. We think about it. But by and large, the work isn't getting done. We need to work together using all our resources. People need to know of the need. Others will then respond. The local church with a vision for the global harvest is God's most potent means of bringing his good news.'

The Great Commission or the Great Commotion?

There are many who have become cynical. To them, the Great Commission seems more like the Great Commotion. But Verwer is certain that God is at work around the world. 'Let's not be discouraged. Today we are in one of the greatest harvest times ever. Church growth in parts of India, China, Africa, South America and other places is phenomenal. Let's learn from them as we move into the new millennium.

'Of course we must be prepared to suffer for our work. For if revival should ever come, you can be sure of a spiritual backlash from Satan. Problems will grow out of new converts. This has always been the case. We really have no excuse for not living our lives fully in the power and reality of the Holy Spirit in this great work of mobilisation of missionaries and this attempt to build up the church in obedience to the command of Jesus Christ in Matthew 28:19 to 'Go into all the world and make disciples . . .'

As individual churches and whole denominations take ownership of Verwer's vision in reality and action, then potentially, there will be tens of thousands of men and women who will get into the training and be headed to the harvest fields. Many churches only need to send one or two to enable Acts 13 – Breakthrough to reach its goal. 'Every church at their next business meeting should have an Acts 13 time of waiting upon God and then make the decision to actually send forth some workers,' says Verwer. 'It is the sensible, biblical act of love and faith that any church can engage in.'

Chacko Thomas points out, 'The most important thing is for pastors and church leaders and the whole congregation to work together to see the Acts 13 – Breakthrough vision embraced, and a clear plan needs to be adopted to see it happen. This can begin as leaders set a time of prayer and fasting, allowing the Holy Spirit to minister to them through the Acts 13 passage. Ask God to clarify your plans.'

According to George Verwer, 'The impact of Acts 13 is shown in Acts 17: 'These men who have turned the world upside down have now come here' (Acts 17:6). It is only when you and your local church are touched and ignited that the determination will begin to burn into an action plan which will help to reap the great harvest. No church is too small, too large, too rich or too poor to be involved.'

Ten steps to make Acts 13 – Breakthrough a reality in your church

1. Have someone share what missionary work is already being done and give thanks for all God has done.

2. Discuss a faith goal for future workers and perhaps make a list of all who come to mind.

3. Make the decision to do something specific.

4. Leaders share the vision with the congregation as soon as possible.

5. Prepare some information and literature for the whole congregation.

6. At the church meeting, try to have key material like 'Serving as Senders' available and, if agreed, then Acts 13 – Breakthrough information.

7. Urge those who are willing or open to pray and be interviewed by a church leader.

8. Start a programme to raise extra finance for this forward thrust. Workers must learn the way of faith and prayer. Individuals need to clearly understand the policy of the church.

9. Try to work out some kind of ongoing training, not only for those who go, but also for the whole church.

10. Have your next Missions Conference or Global Focus Conference feature the new vision as well as all that is being done.

For more information about Open Air Campaign Ministries

102 Dukes Avenue, Muswell Hill, London, N10 2QA
Tel and Fax: 020 8444 5254

If you are interested in more information about Acts 13 –
Breakthrough, contact

Missions Mobilisation Network at:

PO Box 660, Forest Hill, London, SE23 3ST
Tel: 020 8699 6077; Fax: 020 8699 7160
E-mail: info@missionsmobilisation.com
www.missionsmobilisation.com

In the USA

Open Air Campaigners
PO Box D, Nazareth, PA 18064
Tel: 610 746 0508; Fax: 610 746 0509
E-mail: info@oacl.org
http://www.oacl.org/

Take care to live in me, and let me live in you.
John 15:4, TLB

CHAPTER 19

Conclusion

The sun sets. A silent figure darts along the narrow back-streets of a large Middle-eastern city. He wears a heavy woollen cloak hitched high on his neck to obscure his familiar profile. In his fevered mind, every bump, every footstep means he's surely being followed.

At the shrill yowl of a cat, the man pivots down an alley, breaking into a canter until at last he reaches his secret destination at the top of a flight of narrow stairs. There he frantically taps on the door, then pauses. In the agonising seconds that pass, a curse springs to his lips. Growling, he pounds his fist on the door, grazing his hairy knuckles on the rough oak door.

At last, a timid voice from within calls, 'What do you want?'

'Open up, quickly. It's me!' he whispers through clenched teeth.

An iron bolt slams back and the door opens to reveal a gaunt man with a thick brown beard. The red rims and dark semicircles under his eyes show he hasn't slept in days, and his face is the colour of a flounder's belly. It's James, the brother of John.

'Peter, where have you –?'

Grabbing James by his bony shoulders, Peter cuts off the question. 'Are the others here?'

'Of course,' James replies, shoving Peter's hands away. 'Where else would they be?'

Peter peers into the street.

'What are you looking for?' James demands.

'I don't know. I just thought –'

James' bushy eyebrows shoot straight up and he laughs. 'What? You thought that Jesus was following you again?' The blood drains from Peter's face as he nods. Grabbing Peter by the arm, the younger man pulls him inside, scolding, 'Will you get inside, you old fool? Do you want the centurions to find us?' With that, the door slams shut and the bolt rasps back in place.

John records that following the resurrection the apostles were depressed, tense, and intimidated. That's why Peter was sneaking though back alleys, and the disciples were huddled behind locked doors in the Upper Room.

Christians aren't perfect

What's happening here? You might have expected the apostles to be happy. After all, the Lord was alive. First he appeared to Mary Magdalene outside his tomb (John 20:11-18). Later, he appeared to some disciples on the Emmaus road (Luke 24:13-15). He had also met with Peter (Luke 24:34).

Since the disciples knew that Jesus was alive and well, there should have been a celebration in the Upper Room. The men behind closed doors should have been toasting each other's health with wine and quoting Jesus who clearly said, 'I will be crucified, but in *three* days I'll be back in power and glory' (Mark 8:31; 9:31; 10:34). Perhaps John would have remembered that Psalm 22 had predicted the suffering Messiah hundreds of years before, quoting the words Jesus would speak on the cross as he was dying, and the fact that soldiers would cast lots for his clothing (Psalm 22:1; 22:18). Can't you just see it? John and James – the Sons of Thunder – joyfully singing Psalm 22? Soon all the men would link arms and join in a hardy Hebrew circle dance while they belted out Psalm 16, the psalm that predicted the resurrection:

> Heart, body and soul are filled with joy. For you will not leave me among the dead; you will not allow your beloved one to rot in the grave (Psalm 16:9-10, TLB).

Everything should have been wonderful! Jesus wasn't dead. Victory was at hand! All should have been full of confidence and joy!

But no. These men were demoralised. But there's more to this story. A little while after Peter arrived, Jesus came into the room to encourage them. He 'breathed on them, saying, "Peace be to you . . . Receive the Holy Spirit"' (John 20:21-22). This released the disciples from the cold grip of fear, and then the celebrations began. From that point on, the men were brave and full of power. Only Thomas was absent, but they would soon find him and tell him the good news.

In John 20:26, only eight days later, the men were petrified with fear and back in the locked room again. Again Jesus came and stood among them. Seeing the locked door and the pale and drawn faces of his friends, he knew they were afraid. Scowling at Thomas, the cynical doubter, Jesus blew up. He pointed at the men and said, 'You frankly disgust me.' He raised his hand in anger, and growled, 'What more can I do to convince you that the battle has been won? Now I am going to punish you for your pathetic lack of faith!' Did this really happen? Well, actually, no. Jesus' reaction to their disbelief was once again to say, 'Peace be with you'. He felt only compassion for these men. He even allowed Thomas to poke at the wounds in his wrists and feet and side to prove that he was really alive (John 20:27). When Thomas fell to his knees and said, 'My Lord and my God,' they were full of faith again, as they had been the week before.

A vicious cycle

Doubt, faith, doubt, *faith*. Do you recognise this pattern in your life, or am I the only Christian who goes through times of faith and times of doubt year in and year out as I try to live the Christian lifestyle? Far from being abnormal, this is typical for all Christians. And that's the most important point of this book. We simply can't live a perfect life. If we could, then Jesus wouldn't have had to die on the cross on our behalf. This pattern of getting it right one week and getting it wrong the next is proof that we need Jesus every day of our lives – 24/7.

You see, the Christian lifestyle consists of taking a step of faith forward, and maybe another, and then sin, the devil, or our weak flesh slams into us and sends us reeling backwards three steps. Our reaction to this is to lock ourselves into our own Upper Room and hide like the apostles. When that happens, Jesus is there saying to us, 'Peace be with you.' He breathes his Holy Spirit onto us, and he encourages us to go out of the room and back into the world in faith. He says, 'Yes, that's right. Take another step forward.' He knows that we are heading for another major fall, but still he says, 'I am with you. You can do this with my help.'

Of course the apostles did go forward in faith. They preached powerfully, cast out demons, healed the sick, raised the dead, and made countless converts. Yet they hadn't morphed into gods. Because they remained all too human, they continued to sin and make mistakes.

Many people disagree with my point. They say that the apostles' mistakes occurred prior to Pentecost (Acts 2). They argue that when they got the Baptism of the Holy Spirit and began speaking in tongues at Pentecost (Acts 2:3-4), the apostles were essentially perfect. Not true. In Acts 10:14, well after Pentecost, Peter demonstrates sinfulness that is hard to believe. He has a vision from the Lord in which he is ordered to eat non-kosher food. Although he is filled with the Holy Spirit, he replies impetuously, *No Lord! In all of my life, I have never eaten any foods that are unlawful!* This is rich, for here we see the former foul-mouthed fisherman telling God what the law requires of good Jews. Even using a gift of the Holy Spirit, a word of knowledge, God must drive home his point *three times* before Peter would accept that God was ordering him to eat pork, shellfish, and certain kinds of 'unclean' birds (Acts 10:15-16).

Peter also blows it in Antioch. It was there that he snubbed the gentile converts when certain Jewish friends of James came to visit. Because of his fear of the criticism of James' friends, Peter pretended that only Jews could be saved, not Gentiles.

Paul was incensed when he saw this. Yet he also makes a big mistake by the way he disciplined Peter. Instead of quietly taking Peter aside to correct him discreetly, he accused Peter of being a hypocrite in front of everyone and demanded that he repent (Galatians 2:11-21).

Paul frequently hurt the feelings of his fellow disciples. Trainee missionary John Mark was savagely criticised by the apostle Paul because the young man had badly let him down during an important mission outreach in Pamphylia. This led to a quarrel and a long-term rift between Paul and fellow missionary Barnabas. Can you imagine how upset all three Spirit-filled saints must have felt? (Acts 15:36-41). You see, being a Christian and having the Holy Spirit is not *insurance* against being human. Christians sin. And we will continue to sin until the resurrection. Speaking well after Pentecost, Paul makes this point very clear. He laments:

> When I want to do good, evil is right there with me. For in my inner being I delight in God's law; but I see another law at work in the members of my body, waging war against the law of my mind and making me a prisoner of the law of sin at work within my members. What a wretched man I am! Who will rescue me from this body of death? (Romans 7:21-24, NIV)

Why doesn't God simply make us perfect as soon as we become Christians? I have often asked myself that question. I don't know. And in 1 Corinthians 13:12 Paul admits he doesn't know, either. However, he advises us to be patient – with ourselves and with one another – until the resurrection when all will be made clear:

> For now we see in a mirror dimly, but then face to face. Now I know in part; then I shall understand fully, even as I have been fully understood.

This doesn't mean we should indulge our shortcomings, but it does mean we needn't feel guilty or scared when we get it wrong. This is the last thing a Christian needs. After all, the scriptures make it clear that it is by faith and not by human effort[1] that our debt is paid to God:

But now God has shown us a different way to heaven – not by being 'good enough' and trying to keep his laws, but by a new way (though not new, really, for the Scriptures told us about it long ago). Now God says he will accept – declare us 'Not Guilty' – if we trust Jesus Christ to take away our sins. And we all can be saved in this same way, by coming to Christ, no matter who we are or what we have been like. Yes, all have sinned and fall short of God's glorious ideal; yet God now declares us 'not guilty' of offending him if we trust in Jesus Christ, who in his kindness freely takes away our sins (Romans 3:21-24, TLB).

So let's forget racking up points on some imagined League Table. All we need do is allow the Holy Spirit to lead us, knowing that we'll have both good and bad experiences. It is our joy to thank God in the good times and our role to trust God in the bad. That is the way to live the Christian Lifestyle 24/7.

---

1. Being a Christian isn't about being perfect, for that eliminates the need for faith. Again and again you will see that it is by faith that we are saved. We must challenge the attitude that we may somehow attain salvation by ourselves, through discipline, ritual, or by a slavish adherence to things like diet, doctrine, or asceticism. Paul warns that these precepts and doctrines are an alluring heresy: 'These rules may seem good, for rules of this kind require strong devotion and are humiliating and hard on the body, but they have no effect when it comes to conquering a person's evil thoughts and desires. They only make him proud' (Colossians 2:23, TLB).

APPENDIX A

The Creeds
Know what you believe and why

When I was in graduate school, I had a professor who revelled in debating with Christians about what they said they believed. This man ended many an argument by asking, 'Is that in your creed? If it's not in your creed, then put it in!' This extinguished the discussion because over the centuries, creeds have been compiled as statements of orthodoxy to avoid heresy and to protect the church from the influence of other cultures. Understanding our creeds is an important step towards cultivating a credible Christian lifestyle. Yet most Christians don't actually know what's in the creeds.

What are the creeds?

First, the creeds are not a replacement for the scriptures. Nothing may replace the Bible as the ultimate authority concerning what we believe and how we ought to live our lives. However, it is important to point out that, in fact, some creeds predate the New Testament scriptures. You see, in the years immediately following the death and resurrection of Jesus, the good news of Christ's resurrection was passed on by word of mouth. It was the accepted mode at the time of preserving the historical facts as witnessed by the men and women who were alive at the time the events took place.

Not surprisingly, portions of these early creeds have found their way into scriptures. According to Professor Gary Habermas, author of *The Verdict of History*, the earliest creeds are a reliable source for the life and times of Jesus. They are the spoken eyewitness reports from a wide range of men and women who were there at the time. This means that belief in the death and resurrection of Jesus Christ is not based on faith, it is based on fact. However, because of the historical fact of the resurrection, we may have faith.

Creed comes from the Latin word *credo,* 'I believe.' Creeds started as a series of questions and answers that were a part of the early church's baptismal ceremony. This was to ensure that converts understood the basics of Christianity prior to making an outward profession of faith. Typically, the person doing the baptising would ask the baptismal candidate, 'Do you believe in the resurrection of the dead?'; 'Do you believe that Jesus died for your sins?', etc. The person would reply, 'I do.'

Secondly, the creeds are like a democratic constitution, setting the parameters of our belief system, while leaving room for particular denominational emphases. Here is an analogy. You may be a member of one political party and I may support another, but our differences do not prevent us both from being good democrats. Likewise, you may be a member of one denomination and I may belong to another, but as long as we can embrace the creeds, our differences do not prevent us both from being good Christians. To borrow a Latin phrase used on American coinage – *E Pluribus Unum* – Out of Many One.

Disunity sends out all the wrong messages to non-Christians who view our internal squabbles with bemused disinterest. As if anticipating the rise of Christian factions, Paul makes this point about the need for creeds: 'For just as the body is one and has many members, and all the members of the body, though many, are one body, so it is with Christ. For by one Spirit we have been baptised into one body – Jews or Greeks, slaves or free – and all were made to drink of one Spirit. For the body does not consist of one member but many' (1 Corinthians 12:12-14).

Paul drives home his point by showing how foolish it would be for the human foot and hand to criticise one another over their differences. Such criticism only serves to hurt the body! (1 Corinthians 12:26). Just so, a member of one denomination who accepts the creeds can't say to a member of another who also accepts the creeds, 'Because you don't attend *my* church, you aren't part of the body!'

Why is Paul so keen that Christians unite? For one thing, he knows it increases the church's credibility. More to the point, he's reminding us of what Jesus taught the apostles: 'My prayer for all of them is that they will be one, just as you and I are one, Father – that just as you are in me and I am in you, so they will be in us, and the world will believe you sent me' (John 17:20-21, NTL). In this light, our denominational differences fade into insignificance, and we may focus on our similarities!

Selling your Christianity

Evangelism is essentially a form of selling. Since all Christians are obliged to tell others about their faith (Matthew 28:16-20), think of the Gospel as a product we want to sell.

The best way to achieve success – whether peddling the Christian life or marketing pickles – is to know your product. People who don't understand the product, can't sell it. To better understand our faith, let's look closer at the creeds.

I believe

The creeds contain the fundamental articles of the Christian faith drawn from the Bible and Church history. But how did we get them? How many are there? Are some more reliable than others? What do the creeds say? These are important questions that merit entire volumes, not a mere chapter of a book this size. Having said that, on the next page, we'll examine the two most popular of the ancient creeds, the Nicene Creed and the Apostles' Creed.[1] These two creeds developed over several centuries from earlier creeds that affirmed the traditional teachings about God, creation, Jesus, the incarnation, the virgin birth, the resurrection, the Holy Spirit, the saints, the last judgement, and other articles of faith found in the scriptures. One reason why these two particular creeds took so long to develop is that many heresies[2] crept into some of the earlier creeds, and these took considerable time to put right.

The Nicene Creed was approved around AD 325 by a gathering of prominent church leaders and scholars known collectively as the Council of Constantinople. The creed is

1. During later periods of Church history, Protestant churches formulated new, longer creeds. And while these are, therefore, distinct from the Nicene and Apostles' creeds in certain theological and doctrinal points, they are still modelled on these two ancient creeds. For this reason, I want to focus on the two oldest and reliable creeds.

2. For a useful discussion of the major heresies see the *New Dictionary of Theology* (IVP), s.v. 'Heresy'.

said each Sunday in most liturgical churches (i.e. Anglican, Lutheran, and Roman Catholic).

Legend has it that the Apostles' Creed was written on the tenth day after Christ's ascension into heaven. Although this is unlikely, each of the doctrines found in the creed can be traced to statements current in the apostolic period. The earliest written version of the Apostles' creed is perhaps the *Interrogatory Creed of Hippolytus* (*c*. AD 215).[1] By the sixth or seventh century, the Apostles' Creed had come to be accepted as a part of the official liturgy of the Catholic Church. Significantly, the churches of the Reformation (the post-sixteenth-century Protestant churches) adopted the Apostles' Creed as part of their doctrinal collections and also used it in their worship.[2]

It must be admitted that the creeds have been divisive; indeed, disagreement over the creeds may be partly to blame for the schism between Rome and Constantinople in AD 1054. Despite this split, the Nicene Creed and the Apostles' Creed – taken separately or together – brilliantly unify the broad spectrum of Christian belief. Hence, the Christian creeds may justly be called an ecumenism of orthodoxy. See if you agree. I have set out each creed on the following two pages, numbering the paragraphs so you may compare and contrast the two doctrines line by line. At the end of the creeds, see the cross-references to passages from the Bible.[3] You will see that the creeds reflect – not replace – the scriptures.

1. http://www.creeds.net/reformed/creeds.htm

2. http://mb-soft.com/believe/txc/apostles.htm

3. *Harper Study Bible*, RSV Zondervan; *What Christians Believe*, Scripture Gift Mission, London (Bible references).

The Nicene Creed

1. We believe in one God, the Father, the Almighty, of all that is, seen and unseen.

2. We believe in one Lord, Jesus Christ, the only Son of God, eternally begotten of the Father, God from God, Light from Light, true God from true God, begotten, not made, of one Being with the Father. Through him all things were made.

3. For us and for our salvation he came down from heaven: by the power of the Holy Spirit he became incarnate from the Virgin Mary, and was made man.

4. For our sake he was crucified under Pontius Pilate; he suffered death and was buried.

5-6. On the third day he rose again in accordance with the Scriptures; he ascended into heaven and is seated at the right hand of the Father.

7. He will come again in glory to judge the living and the dead, and his kingdom will have no end.

8. We believe in the Holy Spirit, the Lord, the giver of life, who proceeds from the Father and the Son. With the Father and the Son he is worshipped and glorified. He has spoken through the Prophets.

9. We believe in one holy catholic and apostolic Church.

10. We acknowledge one baptism for the forgiveness of sins. We look for the resurrection of the dead, and the life of the world to come. Amen.

The Apostles' Creed

1. I believe in God, the Father Almighty, Creator of heaven and earth:

2. And in Jesus Christ, his only begotten Son, our Lord:

3. Who was conceived by the Holy Ghost, born of the Virgin Mary:

4. Suffered under Pontius Pilate; was crucified, dead and buried: He descended into hell:[1]

5. The third day he rose again from the dead:

6. He ascended into heaven, and sits at the right hand of God the Father Almighty:

7. From thence he shall come to judge the quick and the dead:

8. I believe in the Holy Ghost:

9. I believe in the holy catholic church: the communion of saints:

10. The forgiveness of sins:

11. The resurrection of the body:

12. And the life everlasting. Amen.

---

1. Various scholars have stated that here hell is better translated as Hades, a realm of the afterlife that contained the departed souls. Hell is more properly known in the New Testament as the ultimate destination of all who are rejected at the final judgement. For a fuller treatment of this point see *New Dictionary of Theology* (IVP), s.v. 'Eschatology'. Also see Ch. 4 of David Lawrence's *Heaven: it's not the end of the world* (Scripture Union, 1995) for an interesting overview of the Old and New Testament concepts of hell.

Cross-references

1. *We believe in one God, the Father almighty.* Note that the Apostles' creed refers to God in the singular, thus affirming, as does the Nicene Creed, that Christians are monotheistic. That is, we believe there is only *one* God who is the Father and creator of all human beings. Our God is all-powerful and therefore unequalled. In this we may superficially agree about the nature of God with any other monotheistic religion, including Muslims, Jews, and Sikhs. (Ephesians 4:6; 1 Corinthians 8:6; Psalm 86:10, Hebrews 11:13, etc.)

2. *Jesus is the Son of God* (2 Peter 1:16-18). In ancient times, sonship made the child equal with the father in the eyes of the law. This means Jesus is equal to the Father, and so is himself God. Jesus himself made it clear that he and his Father were one (John 10:30, 36-38.) Here we depart from all other monotheistic religions that deny Jesus is the Son of God or, indeed, that God has a Son.

3. *Jesus Christ was conceived by the power of the Holy Spirit and was born as the son of a virgin called Mary.* (Matthew 1:18-25; Luke 2:8-11). It's worth mentioning that some Bible scholars have expressed doubt about the historicity of the narratives found in Matthew and Luke, assuming these accounts contain embellishments of the facts surrounding a straightforward marriage and subsequent birth of a baby boy to a couple of otherwise typical Jewish peasants.

The reason for the scepticism is because these same accounts are not mentioned in Mark's Gospel, thought by some to be the earliest Gospel. Furthermore, Luke and Matthew differ in their accounts of the virgin birth.

Speaking as a journalist, I'm not troubled by this inconsistency. Few eyewitnesses report seeing exactly the same thing.

This is probably what happened with the Gospel narrators. Each reported on what they considered to be important given their own point of reference and cultural bias.[1] Indeed, if each agreed in every detail, I frankly would suspect collusion by well-meaning but unreliable chroniclers.

Another reason why I trust the Gospel accounts about the circumstances surrounding Jesus' birth is the way Joseph is portrayed in Matthew. We are told he was a man who knew his rights. Accordingly, he planned to divorce Mary after she admitted she was going to have a baby and Joseph wasn't the father (Matthew 1:19). Here we see that the potentially cuckold Joseph first had to come to terms with his scepticism and anger before he would honour his promise to marry her. Such unflattering details seem to me proof of objectivity.

4. *Jesus suffered under Pontius Pilate, was crucified, died, and was buried.* Significantly, until recent times, there was no evidence that Pilate ever existed, but now archaeologists have evidence that there was a Roman governor of Judaea called Pilate.[2] Moreover, there are reams of archaeological accounts of the Roman custom of crucifixion – a painful and degrading form of execution – including excavated graves that are occupied by crucified bodies. Therefore,

1. Speaking of cultural bias, it is also worth remembering that Matthew, a Jew, reported on what he thought other Jews might need to know. Luke, a gentile, picked out what might be of interest to other non-Jews. No wonder the details vary. Yet none of the four chronicles contradicts the others.

2. Jeffery Sheller, *Is the Bible True?* (HarperCollins: London, 1999); condensed in *US News and World Report* (25 October 1999); and *Readers' Digest*, 'Is the Bible True: Modern archaeology is making the sceptics think again' (March 2001), p. 118.

that Jesus suffered, died, and was buried after his crucifixion is in keeping with historical facts (Matthew 27:27-44).

His death was voluntary. Contrary to what so many people believe about the crucifixion, Jesus was no tragic hero, no victim of mob mentality and Roman law; he controlled his own destiny, declaring that no one could take away his life. He plainly said that he alone had the power to lay down his life and the power to take it up again – and he would demonstrate this fact (John 10:14-18). His death and resurrection demonstrate that he was the Son of God (Matthew 27:54).

Some people find Christianity repugnant because it teaches that blood was required to appease God's wrath. This attitude is understandable from our point of view, but it demonstrates our ignorance of the enormity of sin from God's point of view (Romans 6:23). Moreover, it shows our ignorance of the Old Testament's ways of putting sinful men and women in a right relationship with God. Blood sacrifices were offered to make atonement (Exodus 30:10; Leviticus 1:4; 4:20, etc.). Sin puts humanity in conflict with God and only animal sacrifice may appease God. Being a Jew, Jesus' sacrificial death epitomised the priestly sacrifices of animals found in Deuteronomy and Leviticus.

For centuries, Jews relied on the blood of animal sacrifices as payment for this debt. The New Testament writer of Hebrews explains fully how these blood sacrifices made by human priests were a foreshadowing of the ultimate payment which was made by Jesus, the one true sacrifice (Hebrews 9:1-28). Jesus' brutal death on our behalf was predicted centuries before the event in Isaiah 53:4-8.

At last, it was time to stamp 'paid in full' across an ancient bill that required the blood of a sinless man. Jesus was that man. This was his mission: 'He died for our sins, just as God our Father planned, in order to rescue us from this evil world in which we live' (Galatians 1:4, NLT).

He descended into hell. The Apostles' Creed adds that Jesus descended into hell after he died. Hell here actually refers to a place called Sheol or Hades, not to the hell of eternal damnation, called Ghenna.

Briefly, Sheol or Hades was a place understood to be the world of the dead. In fact, some modern translations of the creed state that he 'descended to the dead' which is a more accurate description of the event. Why would Jesus go there? For one thing, this visit broke Satan's power over human souls. As it is written in Colossians 2:15: '(His sacrifice) won the victory over powers and rulers. He showed that they had no power at all. He showed the world his victory through the cross' (World Wide English translation).

According to the *New Dictionary of Theology*, Christ is said to have gone to the world of the dead for the benefit of the faithful who had died prior to his sacrificial death on the cross, yet who had anticipated the coming of their Messiah (Matthew 27:52; Hebrews 12:23). For a fuller treatment of this point, see the new *Dictionary of Theology* (IVP), s.v. 'Descent into hell'.

5-6. *Jesus rose again on the third day.* The fact of Jesus' divinity was demonstrated by his power over death three days later at the resurrection (1 Corinthians 15:20; Romans 1:2-4; 1 Corinthians 15:12-14, 19-20). Christ's resurrection is the sure promise that all who follow him will also be raised from the dead. St Paul wrote, 'If Christ has not been raised, your faith is futile and you are still in your sins' (1 Corinthians 15:17). Clearly, that a dead man can be raised to life is a stumbling block to many people. Yet the fact of the resurrection is the lynchpin of the Christian faith.[1]

Jesus Christ ascended into heaven, and is seated at the right hand of the Father. Christianity is founded on the belief that Jesus, who once was dead and is now alive, rose from the dead and was reunited with his Father in heaven (John 20:17; Luke 24:49-51; Hebrews 1:1-3, 9:24, 10:12-13). Hebrews 12:2 says, '. . . he is seated at the right hand of the throne of God.' From there, he initiated the birth of the Church by sending his Holy Spirit to us at Pentecost (Acts 2).

7. *Jesus is to be our final judge* (Mark 8:38; Luke 12:8-10; John 5:22; 2 Timothy 2:12, etc.). Christians teach that our judgement is based on not how good we have been in this life; rather, it is based on putting our faith in Jesus Christ. St. Paul writes: 'For all have sinned; all fall short of God's glorious standard. Yet now God in his gracious kindness declares us not guilty. He has done this through Christ Jesus, who has freed us by taking away our sins (Romans 3:21-22, NLV). However, it is wrong to assume that Judge Jesus will not take into account our lifestyles (Matthew 8:38; Romans 2:6; Revelation 22:12, etc.). Having been saved by faith in Jesus, Christians are told throughout the New Testament that we are obliged to give evidence of our salvation by our charitable behaviour (see James 2:14-17).

Christians also believe that God will judge people of all religions and none (Romans 14:10-12), as well as the living

1. For a fuller treatment of this subject, see http://www.leaderu.com/. In the full search box, key in the word 'resurrection'. Or visit http://www.leaderu.com/offices/billcraig/docs/tomb2.html. Additionally, you may also wish to read *Jesus 2000* (Lion: Oxford, 1989) or read Carsten Thiede's *Jesus Life or Legend?* (Lion: Oxford, 1990), or Lee Strobel's *The Case for Christ* (HarperCollins: London, 1998), or Gary R. Habermas' *The Verdict of History* (Monarch: Eastbourne, 1988).

and the dead (Acts 10:42). At this point, the Nicene Creed adds that God's Kingdom will 'have no end'. This same point is made in the Apostles' Creed in line 12.

8. *We believe in the Holy Ghost or Spirit.* Christians believe that God is one God with three distinct persons, or *personas* – the Father, the Son, and the Holy Spirit. Hence, ours is therefore a triune God – a three-in-one God – equal and distinct. Some critics say that by this we believe in three distinct gods, which is not true. St Patrick is said to have explained the concept of a triune God by pointing to a clover which is *one* plant, yet having three unique components. Jesus (himself the second person in the trinity) refers to the Holy Spirit (the third person) and to the Father (the first person): 'Therefore go and make disciples of all nations, baptising them in the name of the Father and of the Son and of the Holy Spirit' (Matthew 28:19, NIV).

He also explained the role of the Spirit:

> And I pray the Father, and he will give you another Counsellor, to be with you forever, even the Spirit of Truth, whom the world cannot receive, because it neither sees him nor knows him; you know him, for he dwells with you, and will be in you (John 14:16-17).

Paul also refers to Holy Spirit in the context of the trinity: 'May the grace of the Lord Jesus Christ, and the love of God, and the fellowship of the Holy Spirit be with you all' (2 Corinthians 13:14, NIV). And: 'Because you are sons, God sent the Spirit of his Son into our hearts, the Spirit who calls out, "Abba, Father"' (Galatians 4:6, NIV). See also: John Chapters 14-16 for more on the nature of the Holy Spirit.

9. *The holy catholic/apostolic church.* This refers to the fact that God placed Jesus at the head of one universal Church

(Ephesians 1:22-23). The Church may be seen as a single spiritual body (Romans 12:5) with Jesus as its head (Colossians 1:18). Believers are baptised into this organism through the Holy Spirit (1 Corinthians 12:13). All believers, regardless of denominational affiliation, belong to this universal, i.e. catholic, Church of Christ.

The Bible calls *saints* all people who belong to God (1 Corinthians 1:2). The taking of communion epitomises the idea of the community of saints and the oneness of the body (1 Corinthians 10:16-17).

10-12. *The forgiveness of sins.* Because he loves us, God sent his Son Jesus to earth to live a sin-free life and die in our place for our sins.[1]

The resurrection of the body. Jesus promised that in the afterlife, we would have bodies in which to live. It is Jesus himself who will raise our dead bodies from the grave in order to give us new bodies like his own in which to live (John 6:39-40, 44; John 5:28-29; 1 Corinthians 15:23, 42-44, 50-54).

Life everlasting/life in the world to come. Jesus promised that all who followed him would have eternal life. For more about this promise, see John 3:14-16, 10:10, 11:25; Romans 6:23; Philippians 3:20-21; 1 Peter 1:3-5; 1 John 5:11-13; Revelation 21:1, 3-4.

1. When we were utterly helpless, Christ came at just the right time and died for us sinners. Now, no one is likely to die for a good person, though someone might be willing to die for a person who is especially good. But God showed his great love for us by sending Christ to die for us while we were still sinners. And since we have been made right in God's sight by the blood of Christ, he will certainly save us from God's judgement. For since we were restored to friendship with God by the death of his Son while we were still his enemies, we will certainly be delivered from eternal punishment by his life (Romans 5:6-10, NLV). (See also 1 John 1:9; 2:1-2.)

The Christian faith is supernatural

As you study these creeds in the light of the scriptures, notice the supernatural nature of our faith – the deity of Christ, the incarnation, the virgin birth, the resurrection from the dead, etc. Do you really believe what is being said here?

If you believe, then you are ready to think about ways to live the Christian lifestyle, which are addressed in the previous chapters. But beware. You are bound to meet Christians who say these things are nonsense. Oh, they allow that Jesus was a great human being, and a truly moral teacher,[1] but people aren't meant to take literally the wondrous events ascribed to his life.[2] Of course, when Christians tell you that the miracles never happened, just smile and repeat, 'Is that in your creed? If it's not in your creed, then put it in!'

Time to act

This appendix is titled 'The Creeds: Know what you believe and why'. I have tried to show that there is a correlation

---

1. C. S. Lewis debunks the image of Jesus as merely a moral teacher in his book *Mere Christianity*. Lewis points out that Jesus claimed to be God. A man who was merely human but made this claim cannot be a great moral teacher. Lewis, therefore, says Jesus is either who he says he is (God) or he is a madman or worse. From Chapter 3, *Mere Christianity*.

2. Although I am aware that many scriptures are open to cultural, personal, and idiosyncratic interpretation, I reject ministers who teach that the miraculous aspects of Jesus' life are not to be taken literally. St Paul warns us about such preachers. In Acts 20:29-31 Paul warns that preachers who change the Gospel to suit their own doctrines are like wild animals invading sheepfolds. 'I know that after my departure fierce wolves will come in among you, not sparing the flock; and from among your own selves will arise men speaking perverse things, to draw away the disciples after them' (Acts 20:29-32). His point is not lost 2000 years later. Be sure to know the doctrines of our faith, doctrines which are clearly stated in the creeds!

between knowing what you believe and maintaining a credible Christian lifestyle. For centuries, Christians have been encouraged to memorise these creeds. To that end, why not take time this week and memorise one or both?

Far from being a waste of time, memorising the prime tenets of our faith is the first step to helping us appreciate why our lifestyle must stand out from that of our culture's.

Real world application

Every Christian alive today has been commissioned by Jesus to present the Gospel (Matthew 28:18-20). Knowing the creeds won't guarantee that you will become a world-class evangelist. But it is likely that people will be drawn to Jesus when they see us consistently live the Christian lifestyle.

Actions speak louder than words. By living according to the creeds, we will show people our faith. Many well-known Christians were initially drawn to Christ when they saw Christians living in the light of the creeds. St Paul – then Saul of Tarsus – admits that the example of St Stephen, the first Christian martyr, left an indelible impression on him and prepared him for his conversion experience on the Damascus Road. Constantine saw the example of the early Christians who lived and died in the light of the creeds; likewise, his heart and mind were prepared for conversion to the Christian faith, even when it meant it pitted him against his family, his colleagues, and his nation.

Closer to our day, author and Cambridge don C. S. Lewis points to the lifestyles of a handful of believing scholars, including J. R. R. Tolkien, as a means to his first faltering steps towards confessing Christ as God. The elder statesman journalist turned Christian apologist Malcolm Muggeridge credits Mother Teresa's unselfish example of love for the unlovely for his baptism into the Church.

Finally, the historical creeds prove that there are no new Christian doctrines. Because the creeds have stood the test of time, they are a reliable authority to live by. Now go and preach the gospel by any means possible. Use words if necessary!

APPENDIX B

Art for art's sake – *Not*

Philosopher and author Francis Schaeffer recalls a discussion about art at Cambridge University.[1] It was clear that the Christians there could not define what constitutes a distinctly Christian style. Schaeffer concluded that while there is no such thing as a godly style *per se*, nevertheless, it is naïve to think that various styles have no effect on the message of the art form. Styles, he pointed out, are highly developed symbol systems (or vehicles) for certain lifestyle values. That is, even if not everyone gets the implicit message of the art form, someone will recognise the implicit message encoded in the style. He concedes this is a dilemma for modern Christian artists who may wish to use a contemporary style to say something, say, about redemption, a concept that seems to have no meaning to postmodern men and women. But it may be done. He gives the examples of how certain Biblical ideas do not easily translate into Japanese or Sanskrit. Nevertheless, Bible translators have devised ways of using these languages to convey the correct ideas.

This makes a great deal of sense, for the alternative would be to try to teach the Japanese or Sanskrit speakers how to

1. Taken from *Art and the Bible* (Hodder and Stoughton: London, 1973), pp. 49-53.

understand English (or Greek!) before we can hope to reach them in a meaningful way with the Christian message.

Just so, Christian artists would have to convert their audience before they could hope to teach them anything about the Christian faith. Since this is nonsense, we must employ contemporary styles to say something about our faith without allowing the lifestyle values of that mode of expression to dominate the message. Christian art has a unique message that must be presented to an audience without being watered down or altered. Happily, Schaeffer concedes that the biblical message – what we term *good news* – will be received if the message is presented in context.

Schaeffer gives the example of a Christian rock singer. (He speaks, too, of painters and poets as well, but this particular example will suffice.) If the artist sings the song in the rock style, he or she must then create an opportunity for the listeners to ask questions so that an explanation may follow the song. Sometimes the message will get through; sometimes not. Schaeffer was writing in the 1970s when people were more apt to engage the artist. However, that was then; this is now. It's my experience that today's listeners will not question the artist. The prevailing attitude is *Fine, if it works for you.* So it is up to Christian artists to combine the message with actions that show as well as tell people about Jesus. That, of course, is the point of this book.

What the media didn't tell us about the space shuttle *Columbia* disaster – Rick Husband's Christian testimony

The Columbia *disaster stunned all of us. However, this report is confirmation that some of the seven were committed Christians who were not afraid to talk about their faith at work. Here is an account of that faith which came to me from a reliable source during the last few days of my working on this book. I have edited to put it in the proper context for this book.*

I'm still numb from the horror of the loss of the *Columbia.* It's going to take a while for a lot of us to grieve and recover from that – and I can't fathom the depth of the shock and loss the families must feel. But this is a tremendous encouragement. It's the first time I've read the entire report. I had the privilege of attending a Steve Green concert on the night of 1 February, just 12 hours after the loss of *Columbia* and her crew of seven. What a surprise to learn that Steve Green (a Christian recording artist) was a close friend of Rick Husband's, the astronaut who was selected to be captain for this mission. Their friendship began a number of years ago when Rick and his wife stood in line to meet Steve after a concert in Houston. Rick told

Steve how much he enjoyed his music. (Consequently, a lasting friendship was begun that night.)

Steve was in attendance for . . . (Rick's last) launch. He sang both times at pre-launch receptions. He said the reception for the *Columbia* launch was very 'Christ-honouring', and that there were many unbelievers in attendance. Steve described Rick as a quiet, unassuming man who was, however, very vocal about his faith. He said Rick did not miss an opportunity to give glory to God and mentioned that when Mission Control said it was a beautiful day for a launch, Rick responded with, 'The Lord has given us a perfect day!'

A suit technician shared the following story with Steve. He said that after the astronauts suit up they walk down a hallway and then open a door to 'face the press!' Rick stopped the crew before they opened the door and said he wanted to pray for them. Later the technicians talked about this, and one said that in all his years he had never heard of a captain praying for and with his crew.

The spouses of the crew each get to pick a song for them to wake up to one of the mornings they're in space. Rick's wife selected 'God of Wonders' by Steve Green. Steve played a tape for us of Rick communicating with Mission Control after the song was played. The conversation went something like this:

Mission Control: 'Good morning. That song was for Rick. It was "God of Wonders" by Steve Green.'

Rick: 'Good morning. Thank you. We can really appreciate the lyrics of that song up here. We look out the window and see that God truly is a God of wonders!'

Steve also shared part of an e-mail he received from Rick, transmitted from outer space! Anyway, Rick wrote about how overwhelming it was to see God's vast creation from space. He said he had never cried while exercising before, but pedalling on the (exercise) bike and looking out the window at God's incredible creation brought tears to his eyes.

Steve also shared that he had been in Texas for a concert about a week before coming here. While there, Steve and his stage crew spent the day with Rick's wife, Evelyn, and their two children, and also Mike Anderson's family. Mike was also aboard *Columbia*. During the concert that evening, Steve had the two women stand and he asked the audience to pray with him for these women while their husbands were in space. It was encouraging to hear Steve say that there were at least three astronauts (including Rick and Mike) aboard the *Columbia* who were believers in Jesus.

It was a moving concert and a welcome surprise to learn all these astronauts loved Jesus! Steve did not name the third person or mention if there was a family left behind. But two of the families, at least, will be relying on God to carry them through this and will have opportunity to share God's love with families/friends of the other astronauts. Steve mentioned that before President Bush talked to the families, they had formed a circle and were praying.

Steve was even able to share with us pictures of Rick at different stages of his life, his career, and family. He and Rick's wife had put this together to be set to one of Steve's songs. They had done it a while back for some special event. Steve had it with him and shared it with us. He also gave us all a challenge from Rick's life. He said that astronauts lead extremely busy lives, and he (Steve Green) had been impressed with Rick's commitment to discipling his two children.

Steve asked us to think about if our lives were to end tomorrow and there would be no more opportunity for us to disciple our kids. Would we be happy with what we had done, or would we have regrets? I'm guessing from the pictures Steve showed that Rick's son was around five years old and his daughter ten. I may be off, but that gives you an idea. They certainly are not close to adulthood.

Rick made 34 devotionals by video before he left on the *Columbia*. There were 17 for his daughter and 17 for his son – one for each day he was to be gone. So each day his daughter and son had their own 'devotion with Dad' by video. What treasures they will be to his children! Thank you, God, for leading Rick to do that!

Well, I think I've given you every bit of information Steve gave us. It was certainly an encouragement and comfort to hear these things. I wanted to pass it on to bless others and to help you know how to pray for these families in the days ahead. God is at work in his world! To him belongs all glory!

By the same author

The Church's hidden asset
Empowering the older generation

The elderly can feel just as sidelined within the Church as outside it. Yet Bible history shows that God has work for his people in every season of their lives and nobody is 'over the hill' in his eyes. Michael Apichella's heartening – and timely – review of current culture and thinking is also a resource book: a thoroughly practical guide to building creative partnerships between people of all ages for the good of the Church.   MARK RUDALL

Mark Rudall is a writer and an Anglican Priest

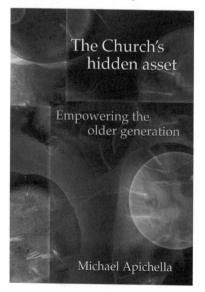

The Church's hidden asset

Empowering the older generation

Michael Apichella

ISBN: 1 84003 701 6
Catalogue no: 1500413

Also by the same author

Why me, Lord?
Advice from a successful failure

Easy to read but demanding to put into practice: it's the sort of book that could change your life.   DAVID WINTER

Who has never asked: 'Why me, Lord?' Being overlooked or rejected, loss of friendship, or sexual temptation can be wounds that run very deep and cripple us in so many ways. Mike Apichella not only tells of his own gaffes and failures but also helps us through Scripture and experience to confront failure – whoever is to blame – and become as whole as possible. This is an important book as God only collects failures.   GERALD COATS

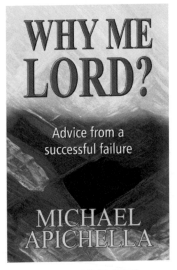

ISBN: 1 84003 902 7
Catalogue no: 1500501